Penguin Handbooks
The New Penguin Guide to Bargain Records

Edward Greenfield has been Record Critic of the *Guardian* since 1954 and from 1964 Music Critic as well. At the end of 1960 he joined the reviewing panel of *Gramophone*, specializing in operatic and orchestral issues. He is a regular broadcaster on music and records for the BBC, and in 1958 published a monograph on the operas of Puccini. More recently he has written studies on the recorded work of Joan Sutherland and André Previn.

Robert Layton studied at Oxford with Edmund Rubbra for composition and with the late Egon Wellesz for the history of music. He spent two years in Sweden at the universities of Uppsala and Stockholm. He joined the BBC Music Division in 1959, and as Music Talks Producer has been responsible for such programmes as *Interpretations on Record*. He has contributed 'A Quarterly Retrospect' to *Gramophone* for a number of years, and he has written books on Berwald and Sibelius and has specialized in Scandinavian music. His recent publications include a monograph on the Dvořák symphonies and concertos for the BBC Music Guides (of which he is series General Editor) and the first volume of his translation of Erik Tawaststjerna's definitive study of Sibelius.

Ivan March is an ex-professional musician. He studied at Trinity College of Music, London, and later at the Royal Manchester College. After service in the RAF Central Band, he played the horn professionally for the BBC and has also travelled with the Carl Rosa and D'Oyly Carte opera companies. Now director of the Long Playing Record Library, the largest commercial lending library for classical music on LP and cassette tapes in the British Isles, he is a well-known lecturer, journalist, and personality in the world of recorded music. He is a regular contributor (reviewing both cassettes and records) to *Gramophone*.

The authors also collaborated on the much-praised *Penguin Stereo Record Guide*, which has gone into its second edition, and more recently on *The Penguin Cassette Guide*.

Edited by Ivan March

The New Penguin Guide to Bargain Records (and Cassettes)

Edward Greenfield   Robert Layton   Ivan March

Penguin Books

Penguin Books Ltd, Harmondsworth,
Middlesex, England
Penguin Books, 625 Madison Avenue,
New York, New York 10022, U.S.A.
Penguin Books Australia Ltd, Ringwood,
Victoria, Australia
Penguin Books Canada Ltd, 2801 John Street,
Markham, Ontario, Canada L3R IB4
Penguin Books (N.Z.) Ltd, 182–190 Wairau Road,
Auckland 10, New Zealand

First published 1980

Filmset, printed and bound in Great Britain by
Hazell Watson & Viney Ltd,
Aylesbury, Bucks
Set in V.I.P. Times Roman

Contents

Preface – The Historical Background

When the first bargain records were issued at the beginning of the sixties, record prices had been stable for a decade. The cost of a premium-priced LP had hovered around £2 since its inception and was to remain at this level for another ten years, allowing for fluctuations in purchase tax. The introduction of a lower price-range for the reissue of older recordings was therefore as opportune as it was sensible. Decca's pioneering Ace of Clubs bargain LPs were launched costing 21s. (£1.05) each, and the catalogue was based on successful recorded repertoire from the fifties which in theory had already paid back its recording costs, artists being persuaded to accept reduced royalties. The Decca venture was a direct response to the lean time experienced by the whole record industry during the summer of 1958 after the first premature stereo issues. The British public, by nature suspicious of the new and untried, could not make up its mind whether stereo was really a step forward or just another gimmick. Until the situation clarified itself the dedicated record collector decided that it would be prudent to hold back from buying records altogether, and so,

at the height of the first great LP boom period, classical record dealers and equipment retailers suddenly found themselves almost overnight without customers.

The success of Decca's enterprise was proved when the other major manufacturers followed suit with their own bargain labels. Significantly, when EMI entered the field with its Concert Classics (which are still with us in the medium-price arena) a series of *new* recordings were featured, initially offered in mono, but later in stereo also. Eastern Europe, too, took the opportunity of the 'bargain revolution' to achieve a presence in the British market, and the Czech Supraphon label soon became familiar to British collectors, costing originally as little as 17s. 6d. (87½p). Smaller British companies now entered the scene to establish a 'super-bargain' range, retailing as low as 12s. 6d. (62½p) and even 10s. (50p). With the super-bargain issues came the pseudonyms. For the cheapest records the master tapes were sometimes 'seconds' – with musical and technical faults not edited out – and these were usually not credited with the names of the actual recording artists. Yet there were some genuine bargains, even among the seconds. It must also fairly be said that the smaller companies did not rely entirely upon imported tapes for their repertoire, but were responsible for producing a remarkable number of original first recordings of chamber music, instrumental music and songs by British composers. One of our finest singers, Janet Baker, made outstanding début recitals for Saga, and these records are still listed in today's catalogue; but their current cost takes them outside our present survey.

By the mid-sixties the profusion of cheap labels was making available a remarkably wide range of music within an increasingly expanding marketplace. Much of this music was unfamiliar, even unknown; indeed obscure baroque music seemed to become so popular that it vied with the standard classics in sales potential. With the coming of decimalization the 'magic' price of 99p achieved countless thousands of impulse purchases by music-lovers willing to explore when the cost seemed temptingly low. When we published our first *Penguin Guide to Bargain Records* in 1966, we set our upper price limit at 25s. (£1.25), yet there were already several thousand discs to consider, principally mono, but many with stereo alternatives.

The seventies saw a sudden and devastating rise in the cost of gramophone records, yet such an increase (rather more than 150 per cent) did no more than match inflation. It also reflected the huge rise in the cost of the oil-based polyvinyl raw material of which records are made. But, spoilt by twenty years of steady prices, record buyers have found it difficult to adjust to a premium LP costing well over £5, even though in *real* terms this is less expensive than the £2 record of the fifties. Of course heavy discounting helps. It was created by the abolition of resale price maintenance, and amplified by heavy competition in the marketplace, especially from chain stores like W. H. Smith and Boots, who can buy in bulk from the manufacturers (to the disadvantage of the smaller specialist record shop). Such discounting – sometimes as much as a pound off certain bestselling issues – also considerably reduces the difference in cost between full- and medium-priced records, which are less readily discounted except in special promotions. If the public is offered a brand-new recorded version reduced to £4.50 or £5, then a medium-priced older disc costing £3.50 or more may seem less obviously attractive.

So what is a bargain record today? We have taken the view that such a description can be applied only to an issue where an element of 'impulse purchase' still remains, and we suggest that ideally this means what it did in the days of Ace of Clubs: approximately half the cost of a premium issue, taking average discount into account. So for the purpose of this guide we have set our upper limit at about £2.50 – just twice the amount we chose in our first assessment of the bargain scene, made a decade and a half ago. At the time of going to press the average bargain issue costs around £2 on disc, with the equivalent cassette usually costing about 25p more. Cassettes assume a proportionately greater importance in the bargain area. With full-price recordings they often take only a small proportion of sales in relation to the equivalent disc, but in the medium and lower price-ranges cassettes are immensely successful, and their proportion of sales vis-à-vis LPs is increasing all the time.

Foreword –
The Current Bargain Scene

Members of the general public often voice the suspicion that cheap LPs are in some way manufactured with inferior material and that they will 'wear out' sooner than full-priced discs. That is, of course, not so. All LPs, in whatever price-range, are made in much the same way, and bargain issues are not even noticeably thinner. The key bargain labels are: Classics for Pleasure, DG Heliodor, the Pickwick-distributed RCA Camden series, and the RCA Victrola catalogue of classic mono recordings made by Horowitz and Toscanini. To these can be added the cream of the imported American Everest series, plus a few items from Murray Hill, an associated label; both are distributed in the UK by Cassion Records at a bargain basement price made possible by the favourable current dollar/sterling exchange rate. There are also a small number of twelve-inch HMV records playing at 45 r.p.m. (costing just under £2) and a much longer list of Decca's DPA 'Favourite composer' double albums (two LPs for less than the price of one). Almost all this material, except the historical records and the

American imports, is available in cassette form as well as on disc. Finally there are the boxed sets. Most boxed sets issued by the major companies come into the full or medium price-ranges, but a select few are offered at a cost per record that brings them within our survey, even if the actual outlay for the box may be £20 or more.

Both the Classics for Pleasure and the Heliodor catalogues offer discs of excellent technical quality, even though sometimes the recordings are far from new. Yet on making a count one is surprised to discover that while the C.f.P. list draws heavily on EMI back catalogue material, more than half the recordings are C.f.P. originals, often subsidized for prestige publicity purposes by companies such as Lambert and Butler. They offer the most brilliant modern sound. Moreover, in response to criticism in our *Penguin Cassette Guide*, virtually all C.f.P. cassettes have been remastered and now demonstrate the highest standards of cassette technology, with their dynamic range fully restored. Indeed many of them are almost indistinguishable from their disc equivalents.

Most Heliodor recordings come from Deutsche Grammophon's early stereo catalogue, but a few outstanding mono reissues from the fifties are also featured, displaying remarkably high standards of sound quality. One thinks of Fricsáy's splendid *Magic Flute* and his Verdi *Requiem*, or the first Leningrad Philharmonic recordings of the last three Tchaikovsky symphonies, conducted by Mravinsky or Sanderling. Similarly the Pickwick-distributed Camden catalogue relies on RCA's earlier stereo issues, featuring classic recordings by artists of the calibre of Gilels, Monteux, Munch, Reiner, Stokowski and the young Henryk Szeryng. There is also a single mono disc of the *Emperor concerto* with Artur Schnabel in partnership with the veteran maestro of the Chicago Symphony Orchestra, Frederick Stock. However, while the technical quality of these RCA recordings made in the late fifties and early sixties is impressive in its atmospheric and widely spread stereo effect, current British pressings are not always as clean as they might be and surfaces are less than immaculate. The equivalent cassettes, which in the past have suffered from an attenuated treble response, are all being remastered, and those sampled show a greatly improved frequency range and no noticeable compression of dynamics. A few are

transferred at too ambitious a level, with some consequent loss of refinement in fortissimo passages, and there is a tendency for the treble to become shrill at times; yet often the sound is cleaner than the equivalent discs, if having slightly less body. The only drawback to this cassette series is the absence of the excellent descriptive notes written by Peter Gammond for the LP sleeves.

The mono recordings made by Horowitz and Toscanini must inevitably be regarded as 'historical', but the performances can completely transcend the sometimes indifferent sound quality. In certain instances their power and virtuosity are so electrifying that the early provenance of the recording can be forgotten altogether. One or two of the Everest issues and the operatic Murray Hill series demand even greater sonic indulgence, yet these records can offer remarkable musical rewards, as in the unforgettable Furtwängler performance of Wagner's *Ring* cycle. The majority of the Everest discs offer the most vivid stereo, and the catalogue includes some indispensable performances by Aaron Copland conducting his own music and Stokowski in his brief recording period with the New York Stadium Orchestra. The only snag is that these American pressings are not reliably silent-surfaced.

The enterprising if limited HMV series of twelve-inch 'medium-playing' discs recorded at 45 r.p.m. must earn an accolade for originality, and one wonders if these records will catch on with the public. The idea of using this format for repertoire works that are too short to fill a 33 r.p.m. LP side, and at the same time taking advantage of the faster speed and wider groove-spacing to enhance the fidelity and dynamic range of the sound, is certainly admirable in principle. In practice the choice of repertoire has not always been apt. The recordings too are not especially recent. The end result can be that the brilliant remastering techniques act as a searchlight on a recorded texture that sometimes shows imperfectly focused inner detail, or sounds unnaturally fierce at the top.

Decca's DPA *Favourite composer*' series of double albums (with equivalent cassettes) is remarkably generous in the amount of music that is crammed on to four LP sides. There is no appreciable loss of quality: indeed the sound fairly consistently demonstrates the high standards for which this company is famous, on disc and tape alike. Although the retail price for each pair of LPs or cassettes is slightly above our £2.50 price limit, these recordings usually offer outstanding value, especially for those just beginning a collection.

In many ways the lower-priced boxed sets are the finest bargain investment of all. Each offers a substantial package of great music within which the listener can explore. Whether the chosen example be the Barenboim or Kempff boxes of Beethoven piano sonatas; the HMV Russian album of the Shostakovich symphonies; or Decca's admirable four-disc compilation of favourite dance music of the Strauss family (played by the VPO under Boskovsky), each is splendidly presented and very competitively priced.

Introduction

The object of this book is to give the collector of recorded classical music a guide to the currently available recordings (discs and cassettes) on bargain labels, retailing at approximately half the price of a standard full-priced issue. In a very few cases we have included an issue within the lower medium-price area, usually still costing less than £3; and where important repertoire is not covered at all in the bargain range we have sometimes suggested alternative medium-priced recommendations within the text. We have normally set our upper price limit at £2.50 per disc (or tape), although in the case of one or two boxed sets (and the Decca DPA/KDPC series) the cost is fractionally higher.

EVALUATION

As in *The Penguin Stereo Record Guide* and *Penguin Cassette Guide* we have adopted a starring system for the quick evaluation of recordings, and as usual we use from one to three stars. In our starring, price in inevitably taken into account, although there are a surprising number of bargain records and cassettes that would be worthy of three stars whatever their cost.

Bargain issues are usually, though not invariably, older recordings; some were made up to two decades ago. But this does not mean that the sound will necessarily be inferior: indeed some early stereo records, made with relatively simple microphone techniques, have a very convincing balance and an excellent atmospheric effect. Some of the earlier mono recordings, on the other hand, require considerable allowance to be made for their sound quality. With this in mind we have adopted the following standards of evaluation:

*** An outstanding performance in every way, well recorded on disc and successfully transferred to cassette (if available).
** A good performance and recording, satisfactory on disc, with a comparable cassette (if available).
* A fair performance, sounding acceptable.

Brackets round one or more of the stars indicate reservations about its inclusion and readers are advised to refer to the text. Brackets round two of the stars are often used for a recording which has great merit as a performance but which needs considerable tolerance for its sound quality; and brackets round all three of the stars may indicate that the actual sound leaves a very great deal to be desired.

In one or two instances a different starring is given to disc and cassette formats. Usually that difference is minimal, and the text will provide an assessment of the comparable quality of the two media.

Our evaluation is normally applied to the disc or cassette as a whole, unless there are two main works, or groups of works, on each side, and by different composers. In a few cases where short but major works are featured, this principle has been extended to give three separate entries in the appropriate places. Sometimes a short work which is of great interest may be found within a concert or recital (see below), and in certain instances we have discussed such a work within the composer index, giving a cross-reference to the review of the collection from which it comes.

ROSETTES

To a very few recordings we have awarded a rosette: ❀.

Unlike our general evaluation, where we have tried to be consistent, a rosette is a quite arbitrary compliment by a member of the reviewing team to a recorded performance which he finds shows exceptional illumination, a magic, or spiritual quality that places it in a very special class. The editor has in addition awarded a rosette to certain select issues which seem to offer quite outstanding value, combining a performance and recording which would receive an enthusiastic accolade whether or not the record or cassette was in the bargain basement. The rosette symbol is placed immediately before the normal evaluation and the catalogue number.

LAYOUT OF TEXT

We have aimed to make our style as simple as possible. Immediately before the disc catalogue number, the manufacturer and label are indicated. If the recording is mono this is shown thus: (m). Otherwise all recordings are stereo or stereo transcriptions of mono. The few HMV 12-inch 45 r.p.m. discs included are indicated with the term: 45 r.p.m. Otherwise all records are 12-inch LPs. If the recording is also available in cassette form, this is indicated immediately after the disc catalogue number by the cassette number in [square brackets]. Where the disc and cassette catalogue numbers are identical (as is usually the case) and the cassette format is indicated by an additional prefix, this alone is included in the square brackets: for example, 'C.f.P. 40076 [TC-CFP]' means that the cassette number is TC-CFP 40076.

In order to make our survey as concise as possible, where a work is listed several times its title is usually shortened; abbreviations are used for many orchestras and ensembles (see p. xvii); and we have given artists' surnames only, unless christian names are necessary to avoid confusion.

We have followed common practice in the use of the original language for titles where it seems sensible. In most cases English is used for orchestral and instrumental music and the original language for vocal music and opera. There are exceptions, however; for instance, the Johann Strauss listing uses the German language in the interests of consistency.

ORDER OF MUSIC

The order of music under each composer's name broadly follows that adopted by the *Gramophone Classical Catalogue*: orchestral music, including concertos and symphonies; chamber music; solo instrumental music; vocal and choral music; opera.

The *Gramophone Classical Catalogue* now usually elects to include stage works alongside opera; we have not generally followed this practice, preferring to list, for instance, ballet music and incidental music (where no vocal items are involved) in the general orchestral group. Within each group our listing follows an alphabetic sequence, and couplings within a single composer's output are *usually* discussed

together instead of separately with cross-references. Occasionally and inevitably because of this alphabetical approach, different recordings of a given work can become separated when a record is listed and discussed under the first work of its alphabetical sequence.

CONCERTS AND RECITALS

Most collections of music intended to be regarded as concerts or recitals involve several composers and it is quite impractical to deal with them all within the alphabetical composer index. They are grouped separately, at the end of the book, in three sections. In each section, recordings are usually arranged in alphabetical order of the performers' names: concerts of orchestral and concertante music (under the name of the orchestra, ensemble or, if more important, conductor or soloist); instrumental recitals (under the name of the instrumentalist); operatic and vocal recitals (under the principal singer or vocal group as seems appropriate). In certain cases where the compilation features many different performers it is listed alphabetically under its collective title, or the key word in that title (so 'Famous opera choruses' is listed under 'Opera choruses'). Sometimes for complicated collections only brief details of contents and performers are given.

RECORD AND CASSETTE NUMBERS

Enormous care has gone into the checking of catalogue numbers and contents to ensure that all details are correct, but the editor and publishers cannot be held responsible for any mistakes that may have crept in despite all our zealous checking. When ordering records or cassettes, readers are urged to provide their dealer with full details of the music and performers as well as the catalogue number.

DELETIONS

Inevitably a small number of the recordings reviewed here will prove to have been later withdrawn by their manufacturers, though this does not always mean that copies cannot still be found in the shops.

ACKNOWLEDGEMENTS

The editor and authors express herewith their gratitude to Mrs Judith Wardman for her help in the preparation of this volume, and also to E. T. Bryant, M.A., F.L.A., for his assistance with the task of proof-correcting.

Abbreviations

arr.	arranged by
ASMF	Academy of St Martin-in-the-Fields
Bav.	Bavarian
CO	Chamber Orchestra
cond.	conducted by, conducting
Cons.	Conservatoire, Conservatory
ECO	English Chamber Orchestra
ed.	edited by
Ens.	Ensemble
Fest.	Festival
LPO	London Philharmonic Orchestra
LSO	London Symphony Orchestra
m	mono
N	New
Nat.	National
NSO	New Symphony Orchestra
NY	New York
Orch.	Orchestra
PA	Pro Arte
PO	Philharmonic Orchestra
Qt	Quartet
RO	Radio Orchestra
ROHCGO	Royal Opera House, Covent Garden, Orchestra
RPO	Royal Philharmonic Orchestra
SO	Symphony Orchestra
Suisse Rom.	Suisse Romande
Virt.	Virtuosi

Distributors and Prices

This list is correct at the time of going to press, but the publishers cannot hold themselves responsible for any subsequent changes caused by alterations to manufacturers' prices or variations in VAT. Indeed the present inflationary trend seems bound to cause an upward movement during the lifetime of this book. For the convenience of overseas readers we have included the 'export' prices (i.e. without British VAT); these will also be useful to collectors at home, should the Chancellor decide to vary this tax. We have not included boxed sets, each of which has its own individual price. However, this information should be readily available from your record dealer.

	LPs			Cassettes	
	UK	Export		UK	Export
Classics for Pleasure (C.f.P.)					
CFP	£1.99	£1.73	[TC–CFP]	£2.25	£1.96
Contour (Pickwick)					
CN	£1.99	£1.73			
Decca					
DPA (set of 2 LPs)	£5.25	£4.57	[KDPC]	£5.25	£4.57
ECS; SPA	£2.99	£2.60	[KECC; KCSP]	£3.10	£2.70
JB (Jubilee)	£3.75	£3.26	[KJBC]	£3.99	£3.47
GOS; SDD	£3.99	£3.47	[KSDC]	£3.99	£3.47
DG					
Heliodor (2548)	£1.95	£1.70	[3348]	£2.25	£1.96
Accolade (2542)	£3.50	£3.04	[3342]	£3.75	£3.26
Everest					
All discs	£1.80	£1.57			
HMV (EMI)					
HMV (45 r.p.m.)	£1.99	£1.73			
SXDW (2 LPs)	£6.30	£5.48	[TC–SXDW]	£6.30	£5.48
SXLP	£3.45	£3.00	[TC–SXLP]	£3.65	£3.17

Lyrita
REAM   £2.94   £2.56

Murray Hill
All discs   £1.80   £1.57

Music for Pleasure (M.f.P.)
MFP (2 LPs)   £2.99   £2.60   [TC-MFP]   £3.25   £2.83

Philips
6747 041; 6747 199   £3.50   £3.04

Pickwick
SHM   £1.99   £1.73
PLA; PLD; 50DA (2 LPs)   £3.50   £3.04

Pye
GSGC   £1.99   £1.73   [ZCCCB]   £2.60   £2.26
GGCD   £3.15   £2.74

RCA Camden (distributed by Pickwick)
CCV   £1.99   £1.73   [C4]   £1.99   £1.73

RCA Victrola
AT 100 series   £1.99   £1.73
AT 200/300/400 (per disc)   £2.49   £2.17
VH   £2.49   £2.17

For Overseas Readers

The bargain record and tape scene is by no means internationally identical, and many bargain LPs and cassettes discussed in our pages are unlikely to be obtainable in some countries. Other recordings may appear in different price-ranges. However, where a required recording is not readily available locally it will probably be obtainable direct from England. Readers are invited to write to:

**Squires Gate Music Centre,
Squires Gate Station Approach,
Blackpool, Lancashire, England,
FY8 2SP**

Still available are two companion volumes by the authors of this book.

The Penguin Stereo Record Guide

The second edition, published in 1977, is still available in hardback only from Squires Gate Music Centre, Blackpool, Lancs.

'An invaluable guide to the merits of available versions . . . a model of accuracy . . . the book also happens to be ideal for dipping into at bedtime. For the serious collector it can only be money well spent.' – *Gramophone*

The Penguin Cassette Guide

This book is currently available from all good bookshops in paperback at £4.95, and in hardback at £5.95 from the above address.

'Those who know the equivalent *Penguin Stereo Record Guide* will know their way about this new volume. It goes with astonishing thoroughness into available cassette issues, discussing them at considerable length and with leisurely discourse on their artistic merits. It is a book to browse through and read, as well as an indispensable reference. We trust Messrs Greenfield, Layton and March simply because they always give ample reasons for their evaluations.' – *Peter Gammond*

A new volume, reviewing LPs and cassettes between 1977 and 1981, is planned for publication in 1981/2.

Composer Index

Albinoni, Tommaso (1671–1750)

Oboe concertos, Op. 7, Nos. 3 in B flat major; 6 in D major.
   *** Pye GSGC 15011. Rothwell, PA Orch., Barbirolli – CIMA-ROSA and MARCELLO: *Concertos.****
   ** C.f.P. CFP 163. Sutcliffe, Virt. of England, Davison – VIVALDI: *Concertos.***

There are two outstanding collections of oboe concertos recorded by Evelyn Rothwell with her husband conducting, and while both are equally desirable they are also quite different in character. This is partly caused by the recording, which here balances Miss Rothwell fairly well forward, gives her a more ample tone than on the companion disc (Haydn; Corelli; Pergolesi) and reproduces the orchestra with a pithy athleticism. This suits Sir John's strong classical style and gives these two fine concertos greater stature than usual. Miss Rothwell's line in the two slow movements is ravishing without being too romantic, and the *spiccato* playing in the opening movement of Op. 7/6 and the crispness in the same work's finale are a joy.

Nicely stylish performances from Sidney Sutcliffe, with a beautifully sprung, crisp accompaniment from Arthur Davison. The recording is clean and clear to match the music-making, and, with a fetching sleeve, this disc will give pleasure if not taken all at one sitting.

Allegri, Gregorio (1582–1652)

Miserere.
   *** C.f.P. CFP 40339 [TC-CFP]. Tallis Scholars, Phillips – MUNDY: *Vox Patris caelestis****; PALESTRINA: *Missa Papae Marcelli.***(*)

The famous Argo recording of Allegri's *Miserere*, with its arresting treble solo from Roy Goodman, is available within a splendid '*Festival of King's*' collection (see under 'King's College' in the Vocal Recitals and Choral Collections section below); but this new version from the Tallis Scholars is no less impressive, and it too features an outstanding treble contribution, from Alison Stamp. Peter Phillips emphasizes his use of a double choir by placing the solo group in the echoing distance of Merton College Chapel, Oxford, and the main choir directly in front of the listener. The contrasts are dramatic and hugely effective, the ethereal quality of the distanced singers clearly focused by the soaring treble line. Yet the solo treble voice does not dominate the texture in quite the same way as in the King's version. The recording itself is superb, as is the singing. Allegri's ravishing piece made such an impression on Mozart when he heard it in the Sistine Chapel that he wrote it out afterwards from memory, so that it could be performed elsewhere. This imaginative new recording must be strongly recommended.

Bacarisse, Salvador
(1898–1963)

Concertino in A minor for guitar and orchestra, Op. 72.
* Pye GSGC 15030 [ZCCCB]. Cubedo, Barcelona SO, Ferrer – RODRIGO: *Concierto.**

Bacarisse was director of music of Spanish Radio in Republican days. His *Concertino* is an unpretentious piece in four movements. The quality of its invention is moderately engaging in the first movement and in the ingenuous *Romanza*, but then falters, and the finale is banal. Cubedo provides a pleasant, homely performance and is acceptably recorded, although given a larger-than-life forward balance. The cassette transfer suffers from distortion and is not recommended.

Bach, Johann Sebastian
(1685–1750)

Brandenburg concertos Nos. 1–6, BWV 1046/51.
**(*) Decca DPA 577/8. Philomusica, Dart.
** C.f.P. CFP 40010/11 [TC-CFP]. Virt. of England, Davison.
* RCA Camden CCV 5007 and 5033 [c4]. Boston SO, Munch.

Dating from the early days of stereo, Thurston Dart's set offers fresh and electrifying performances marked by brisk tempi and clear textures. All the performances are enhanced by Dart's own harpsichord continuo, often provocatively elaborate but always rhythmically exhilarating. Dart interpolates a movement from a Bach violin sonata between the two regular movements of No. 3, which works well, but controversially he opts for trumpets instead of horns in No. 1. The result will not please everyone, but the extra brightness of trumpets playing an octave higher than usual is certainly refreshing. The recording is a little wiry by today's standards but very acceptable.

Davison directs a distinguished group of London musicians – one to a part, which, with excellent recording, makes for admirable clarity – in brisk, unfussy performances. Outer movements tend to sound relentless through Davison's squareness of rhythm, and this effect is exaggerated by the close microphones, which produce a comparatively limited dynamic range. But, except perhaps for No. 6, all the concertos come over strongly and convincingly. No. 3 is given a curious cadenza for viola and continuo between the two movements, but is striking for its vigour in both those movements. The cassettes have recently been remastered and offer outstanding, demonstration quality. TC-CFP 40010 is indistinguishable from the equivalent disc; TC-CFP 40011 has marginally less emphasis on the upper range than the disc, and many will prefer its slightly smoother and richer sound, especially in No. 4.

Munch's set dates from 1958 and for most listeners will sound unacceptably old-fashioned. Although Munch uses a reduced number of players the reverberant Boston acoustic produces a fairly beefy texture in the tuttis, and the projection of the soloists has been achieved by close microphones. The solo trumpet in No. 2 sounds piercingly brilliant in consequence, although the balance in No. 4 is attractively fresh, with lightened textures. No. 5 uses a piano continuo and often creates some engaging if hardly authentic colouristic effects. But the solo playing in the first-movement cadenza is rather lumpy. Munch often chooses slow tempi, and the first movement of No. 3 is flabby. However, the performances undoubtedly have attractive moments, and current pressings produce warmly agreeable string sound, even if the focus is not always absolutely clean. Excellent sleeve-notes from Peter Gammond are an attractive feature of this and many other Camden reissues. We have been able to listen to the remastered cassette containing Nos. 4, 5 and 6. The sound is brighter and fresher than the disc, but there is some fuzzy distortion in the upper string frequencies which is emphasized by the cleaner focus generally. The tape transfer itself is well managed. •

Violin concerto No. 1 in A minor, BWV 1041.
   *(*) RCA Camden CCV 5041 [c4]. Laredo, Boston SO, Munch – MOZART: *Violin concerto No. 3.***(*)

Violin concertos Nos. 1; 2 in E major, BWV 1041/2; Double violin concerto in D minor, BWV 1043.
   *** C.f.P. CFP 40244. Sillito, Bean, Virt. of England, Davison.

Violin concerto No. 2; (i) Double violin concerto.
   * Everest (m) 3410. D. Oistrakh, Moscow CO, Barshai, (i) with I. Oistrakh.

Kenneth Sillito and Hugh Bean, both of them distinguished orchestral leaders as well as fine virtuosi, are outstandingly successful as soloists in the *Double concerto*. Theirs is one of the most beautiful accounts of the lovely slow movement of that masterpiece on record, deeply felt but pure and restrained. Though Davison's accompaniments are not always ideally resilient, the scale is right, and the performances can be warmly recommended. The solo concertos are shared; Sillito plays the *A minor* and Bean the *E major*. The recording is modern and well balanced. A very real bargain.

Jaime Laredo also plays the *A minor Concerto* eloquently, but the slightly flabby quality of the opening orchestral tutti demonstrates that the Boston acoustic was not an ideal venue for recording Bach. Nevertheless Munch accompanies attentively in his somewhat old-fashioned manner. The slow movement is sensitively done, and there is a very attractive Mozart coupling. The remastered cassette version offers lively sound which is fully acceptable and matches the disc fairly closely. However, the excellent musical notes provided with the LP are not included with the cassette, although there is plenty of blank space for them on the liner leaflet.

The Everest recordings date from the 1950s and are mono. No complaints need be made about the performances, which have warmth and vitality to commend them. The sound, however, is distinctly thick and wanting in transparency. Climaxes tend to be a little rough. If you are prepared to accept inferior sound quality, there is no doubting the excellence of the players, but generally speaking it is well worth paying the little extra for cleaner and more up-to-date sound.

Orchestral suites Nos. 1 in C major; 2 in B minor (for flute and strings); *3 in D major; 4 in D major, BWV 1066/9.*
   ** Decca DPA 589/90. Stuttgart CO, Münchinger.

Chamber performances of Bach have now become the rule rather than the exception, and Münchinger's 1962 recordings of the *Orchestral suites* are rather solid German performances, lacking in charm if far more reliable on discipline. Münchinger does not take the repeats of the slow introductions but he captures the formal grandeur, and in movements like the overtures of Nos. 3 and 4 the allegros are all the more exhilarating for the crispness of discipline and bite of attack. The famous *Air* in No. 3 is played with reserve but does not lack eloquence of line. Rampal's playing in the *Second Suite* is very fine indeed, while Münchinger's comparatively stiff beat is mitigated by the alertness of the playing. Recording brilliant in the Decca manner and not sounding too dated.

Organ music

Concerto (for solo organ) *No. 2 in A minor, B W V 593* (after VIVALDI); *Fantasia and fugue in G minor, B W V 542; Fugue à la gigue, B W V 577; Prelude and fugue in B minor, B W V 544; Toccata and fugue in F major, B W V 540.*
** C.f.P. CFP 40241. Kynaston.

The organ of Clifton Cathedral is quite beautifully recorded, with clean, sparkling sound and a clear yet ample bass response. The recital opens splendidly with a buoyant account of the *Fantasia and fugue in G minor*, bringing out all its spontaneity. Then follows a gay account of the delightful *Fugue à la gigue*. However, with the *Prelude and fugue in B minor* the playing appropriately adopts a more serious mood, and here tension is lacking as the fugue moves towards its culminating climax. Similarly on side two the *Toccata and fugue in F major* is very relaxed, and in the Vivaldi-derived *Concerto* (which is drawn from No. 8 of *L'Estro armonico*), although the registration is attractively

bright-eyed, the central *Adagio* is surely too reserved in manner.

Those wanting a first-class account of the famous *Toccata and fugue in D minor* can turn to Janet Parker-Smith's excellent disc, reviewed below in the Instrumental Recitals section.

Beethoven, Ludwig van (1770–1827)

Piano concertos Nos. 1–5.
Ⓢ*** D G Heliodor 2701 014 (3 discs). Kempff, Berlin PO, Van
· Kempen.
*** C.f.P. CFP 78253 (4 discs). Lill, Scottish Nat. Orch., Gibson.

The earlier of Wilhelm Kempff's two Beethoven concerto cycles shows this prince of Beethovenians at his most sparklingly individual. In places – as at the opening of the finale of No. 4 – one might object that in his pointing of phrase he becomes idiosyncratic; but through everything there is the unmistakable stamp of the inspiration of the moment. Highly sensitive as he is, Kempff might have been expected to become inhibited (as Schnabel was, for example) in the recording studio. Instead, as he has said himself, he is always so happy recording he hardly notices when the red light goes on. This set from beginning to end gives evidence of that, and his clean, sharply articulated style and magical phrasing place all these performances among the freshest ever put on disc. The 1953 mono recording, obviously dated, has been freshened very acceptably, and with the concertos complete on three discs this set is a bargain in every sense of the word.

John Lill has never been more impressive on record than in his set of the

Beethoven concertos, for in each of the works he conveys a sense of spontaneity and a vein of poetry that in the studio have too often eluded him. Gibson and the Scottish National Orchestra provide strong, direct support, helped by good modern recording, and though there have been more strikingly individual readings than these, as a set they make a very impressive cycle. The records are issued in their original sleeves but within an attractively robust box, and the value for money is remarkable.

Piano concerto No. 1 in C major, Op. 15; (i) *Choral fantasia, Op. 80.*
**(*) C.f.P. CFP 40232. Lill, Scottish Nat. Orch., Gibson, (i) with Scottish Nat. Chorus.

John Lill's performance of the *First Concerto* is refreshingly direct, with a thoughtful, measured account of the first movement and concentrated readings of the slow movement and finale. The recording is modern, full and clear, with the piano a little too forward. In the *Choral fantasia* Lill gives a formidable account of the opening cadenza, and the vocal contributions are effective and well balanced. With good modern recording this coupling can be warmly recommended.

At medium price, but with no coupling, the Bishop-Kovacevich version with the BBC Symphony Orchestra under Colin Davis is also a very serious contender. This performance, which combines clarity of articulation and deep thoughtfulness, is among the very finest of this concerto at any price, with recording quality beautifully refined in the Philips manner and an excellent cassette alternative: Philips Festivo 6570 134 [7310 134]. In the same price-range on Decca, Backhaus couples the *First* and *Second Concertos*. Some might feel that the brisk manner he adopts in No. 1 suggests superficiality, but this is by no

means the case, and repeated listening yields increasing pleasure: the almost brusque way the pianist treats the slow movement falls into place within the reading as a whole. The *Second Concerto* is even finer. Here Backhaus is more generous in his variations of touch, and the flowing spontaneity and vigour of the music-making bring a feeling of youthful freshness. The disc is excellent value, and so is the crisply transferred cassette: Decca SPA 401 [KCSP].

Piano concertos Nos. (i) *1 in C major, Op. 15;* (ii) *4 in G major, Op. 58.*
*(*) RCA Victrola (m) AT 106. NBC SO, Toscanini, with (i) Dorfmann, (ii) Serkin.

This issue is worth investigating for the fascinating artistic interchange between Toscanini and Serkin in the *Fourth Concerto*. With the dry acoustic of Studio 8H in Radio City hardening subtleties of expression, much allowance has to be made, but it is still clear that the unrelenting Toscanini was being persuaded to soften his style with a partner he respected. In the *First Concerto* with Ania Dorfmann he presses on savagely, and though the soloist manages more than capably, she is never allowed to relax. The finale is prickly with tension. The recording, made in Carnegie Hall in 1945, is marginally better than on the reverse.

Piano concertos Nos. 2 in B flat major, Op. 19; 4 in G major, Op. 58.
**(*) C.f.P. CFP 40271. Lill, Scottish Nat. Orch., Gibson.

If Lill can sometimes seem too uncompromising a pianist, the *Fourth Concerto* reveals that in this most poetic of Beethoven works he can relax with individual touches of imagination and a fine range of tone-colour. There is fire too in the first movement, though in all three Gibson is somewhat square in his accompaniment. He is more at home in the *Second Concerto*, where Lill again plays with ease and imagination. With good modern recording the generous coupling makes a first-rate bargain.

One must also remember Gilels's outstanding medium-priced version of the *G major Concerto*, a strong, poetic reading of striking authority and eloquence. The recording is remarkably good, and the coupling, Mozart's *G major Violin concerto, K. 216*, played by David Oistrakh, is equally fine: HMV SXLP 30086 [TC-EXE 156].

Piano concerto No. 3 in C minor, Op. 37.
    *** DG Heliodor 2548 238. Fischer, Bav. State Orch., Fricsay – MOZART: *Concert rondos.****
    *** C.f.P. CFP 40259 [TC-CFP]. Lill, Scottish Nat. Orch., Gibson.

Annie Fischer gives a sparkling reading, highly personal and spontaneous, one which charms the listener into accepting speed-changes and rubato that with some other pianists might seem mannered. Her contrasts of tone-colour are often magical. With the two Mozart *Rondos* for fill-up and recording of excellent quality – the acoustic is open and fresh and the piano image bold and realistic – it makes an outstanding bargain, as fine a version of this concerto as is available at any price.

Lill is at his most imaginative in the *Third Concerto*, a work for which in the concert hall too he has shown a special affinity. He is crisp and direct and rather fast in the first movement, spacious and concentrated in the central *Largo*, sparkling in the finale. The sound is first-rate, making this competitive with

other versions of whatever price, and the tape transfer is vivid and well detailed.

At medium price the Bishop-Kovacevich version with Colin Davis must also be mentioned. It is among the most satisfying available, intense and concentrated in the first two movements, relatively relaxed in the finale but with extraordinarily clean fingerwork. The sound is clear and refined on both disc and tape: Philips Festivo 6570 135 [7310 135].

Piano concerto No. 5 in E flat major (Emperor), Op. 73.
    *** C.f.P. CFP 40087 [TC-CFP]. Lill, Scottish Nat. Orch., Gibson.
    ** RCA Camden (m) CCV 5028 [c4]. Schnabel, Chicago SO, Stock.
    *(*) RCA Victrola (m) VH 009. Horowitz, RCA Victor SO, Reiner.

In the *Emperor*, the first of his Beethoven concerto cycle to be recorded, John Lill's combination of power and poetry is captured with striking spontaneity. With first-rate modern recording, marred only by some lack of edge on the violin tone, this is an excellent record, even making no allowance for price. The cassette version originally suffered from a lack of refinement in the orchestral sound, but it has been remastered and now sounds admirably clear and clean.

This concerto is also exceptionally well represented on both disc and tape in the medium price-range. Bishop-Kovacevich's version with Colin Davis is one of his most deeply satisfying performances (Philips Festivo 6570 013 [7310 013]), while in the splendid Gilels version, strength is matched with poetry in a most commanding reading, Szell displaying a tremendous grip on the accompanying Cleveland Orchestra (HMV SXLP 30223). Both Backhaus (Decca SPA 452 [KCSP]) and Curzon (Decca SPA 334 [KCSP]) offer impressive versions at a slightly lower price, although the Curzon issue does not belie its early recording date (1958).

Schnabel's 1942 Chicago *Emperor* is surprisingly well recorded. There is some rawness in the orchestral sound (the acoustic is clear-cut rather than atmospheric) and a transatlantic ping to the piano, familiar in American recordings of the war years. The performance is strongly assertive, with Schnabel's aristocratic poise suddenly letting up in the first movement for the bravura octave passage, which is furiously played. The slow movement opens warmly in the orchestra (Frederick Stock's contribution very much part of the overall interpretation), and Schnabel's restraint produces a patrician control of the melodic contour without any suggestion of emotional coolness. The opening of the finale is superbly prepared, and the extrovert mood makes an excellent foil for what has gone before.

Horowitz made his classic account of the concerto in 1952, and although the quality of the sound leaves much to be desired (the piano is wanting in timbre and colour, particularly in the bass), the RCA transfer offers a more cleanly focused image than the original. The first movement is very brisk indeed: the design is tautly held together – so tautly, indeed, that some listeners may feel it a shade hard-driven. The slow movement, on the other hand, finds both soloist and conductor at their most searching: there is genuine repose and sensitivity here, and no want of poetic feeling and aristocratic poise from Horowitz himself. It goes without saying that with artists of this integrity there is no trace of idle display and virtuosity. But in the outer movements some readers will feel that too tight a rein is kept on the proceedings, even if there is no lack of rewards.

Ultimately this lacks the humanity and vision of Schnabel and Gilels, and the work is perhaps better represented in this vintage by Edwin Fischer and Furtwängler, who recorded it the previous year (HMV HLM 7027).

Violin concerto in D major, Op. 61.
⊛*** D G Heliodor (m) 2548 299 [3348 299]. Schneiderhan, Berlin PO, Van Kempen.
*(*) C.f.P. CFP 40299. Campoli, RPO, Pritchard.

Schneiderhan's 1953 mono recording stands alongside Kreisler's 1926 version as one of the greatest performances of this work ever recorded. The first movement has more lyrical thrust than in Schneiderhan's stereo remake with Jochum, fine though that is. The soloist's tone is richer, and his phrasing admirably combines classical feeling with lyrical ardour, against an orchestral backcloth which displays splendid life and power. The slow movement is glorious, the intensity of the reprise of the secondary theme overwhelmingly beautiful and utterly spontaneous in feeling. The finale has a genial, dancing sparkle which is irresistible. The mono recording is remarkably full and lively, and the transfer to tape, at a high level, is expertly managed.

Campoli first recorded the concerto in the early 1950s with Krips and the LSO. The present version comes from 1962 and has the advantage of good though not distinguished recorded sound. Responding, perhaps, to criticism of his earlier account, Campoli takes a somewhat brisk view of the first movement (his tempo is close to that of Heifetz and Toscanini here) and relaxes more in the second, which makes a strong impression. Here his playing is lyrical and expressive, and has at times a seraphic elegance that is most moving. There are many musicianly touches in the outer movements, though his very first entry in the opening movement could be more beautiful. John Pritchard and the RPO give good support and the performance as a whole gives pleasure. All the same, in terms of sheer musical personality it does not compete with such outstanding medium-priced versions as those by David Oistrakh with Cluytens (HMV SXLP 30168 [TC-EXE 197]) or Grumiaux with Galliera (Philips Festivo 6570 051 [7310 051], especially competitive in including also the two *Romances* for violin and orchestra), nor indeed with the superb Schneiderhan version, albeit in mono.

'Favourite composer': (i; ii) *Piano concerto No. 5 in E flat major (Emperor), Op. 85;* Overtures: (ii) *Egmont, Op. 84;* (iii) *Leonora No. 3, Op. 72b;* (iv) *Symphony No. 6 in F major (Pastoral), Op. 68;* (v) *Piano sonata No. 14 in C sharp minor (Moonlight), Op. 27/2.*
  *(*) Decca DPA 529/30 [KDPC].
  (i) Katchen; (ii) LSO, Gamba; (iii) Israel PO, Maazel; (iv) Suisse Rom. Orch., Ansermet; (v) Gulda.

These two discs are generously filled, but are let down by Ansermet's *Pastoral symphony*, which suffers from poor wind intonation, and Maazel's hard-driven account of *Leonora No. 3*. Taken as a whole this is a disappointing collection, in spite of the excellence of Katchen's *Emperor*, which is full of characteristic animal energy and superbly recorded. The first and last movements are taken at a spanking pace, but not so fast that Katchen sounds at all rushed. Plainly he enjoyed himself all through, and it is good too that this pianist, who sometimes seemed too rigid in his recorded playing, here seemed to be coaxing the orchestra to match his own delicacy. The slow movement is very relaxed, but, with

the tension admirably sustained, it contrasts well with the extreme bravura of the finale. The cassettes are well transferred. The quality in the symphony is exceptionally good – bright and very lively. The concerto is not quite so open in acoustic, but the overtures have plenty of life and the piano tone is natural, if seeming a little confined in range.

Overtures: *Coriolan, Op. 62; The Creatures of Prometheus, Op. 43; Fidelio, Op. 72c; Leonora Nos. 1–3, Opp. 138; 72a; 72b.*
  **(*) RCA Camden CCV 5009 [c4]. Boston SO, Munch.

A first-rate collection of Beethoven overtures in electrifying performances. A generous selection too, and though the recording has some American hardness which may not sound well on all machines, the bargain is obvious. Often the four overtures to Beethoven's opera make a whole LP on their own, and here *Prometheus* and *Coriolan* provide a splendid makeweight. Munch's manner with Beethoven is brisk and brilliant, and particularly in the two non-*Fidelio* overtures the results are strongly sympathetic. The recording is of mid-fifties vintage but is still very acceptable. The newly remastered tape transfer is also most successful, and the tape is every bit the equal of the disc, with brilliant sound, somewhat light in the bass, especially telling in the last two *Leonora* overtures (on the second side).

Symphonies Nos. 1–9. Overtures: *The Consecration of the House, Op. 124; Coriolan, Op. 62; The Creatures of Prometheus, Op. 43; Egmont* (with incidental music), *Op. 84; Fidelio, Op. 72c; King Stephen, Op. 177; Leonora Nos. 1–3, Opp. 138, 72a, 72b.*
  **(*) HMV SLS 788 (9 discs)

[TC-SLS]. Philharmonia Orch., Klemperer (with soloists and chorus).

Symphonies Nos. 1–9. Overtures: The Consecration of the House; Coriolan; The Creatures of Prometheus; Egmont; Fidelio; King Stephen; Leonora Nos. 1–3; Namensfeier, Op. 115.
 **(*) Philips 6747 135 (9 discs). Leipzig Gewandhaus Orch., Masur (with soloists and Berlin Radio Chorus).

Symphonies Nos. 1–9. Overtures: Coriolan; The Creatures of Prometheus; Egmont; Fidelio; Leonora No. 3; The Ruins of Athens, Op. 113.
 **(*) C.f.P. CFP 78251 (8 discs). Berlin PO, Cluytens (with soloists and chorus).

Symphonies Nos. 1–9. Overtures: Coriolan; Egmont; Leonora No. 3.
 *** HMV SLS 5053 (7 discs). Philharmonia Orch., Karajan (with soloists and Vienna Singverein).

Klemperer's set at well under £2.50 a disc provides outstanding value for money in showing this conductor's commanding achievement in Beethoven's orchestral music. To have virtually all the overtures included, and even some of the incidental music from *Egmont*, is especially welcome. Even the comparatively slight *King Stephen* is given strength, and *The Consecration of the House* has seldom sounded so magnificent on record. In the four overtures written for *Fidelio* the approach, as one expects with Klemperer, uses measured tempi to bring out the architectural strength – even *Fidelio* is more serious than usual – but such is the conductor's control over tension that no unbiased listener could find the result dull and

heavy. In the symphonies there are some disappointments, notably in Nos. 1, 5, 7, 8 and 9 (in varying degrees), but Klemperer is never less than interesting. The performances of Nos. 2, 3, 4 and 6 are among the very finest ever recorded (the *Pastoral* was awarded a rosette in the *Penguin Stereo Record Guide*), and as a whole the set provides consistently fascinating insights from one of the great Beethoven interpreters of our time. The recordings have been freshened and generally sound well, if inevitably sometimes dated. The cassette box brings considerable reservations about layout. Not all the music is readily accessible, and the appearance of the *Prometheus overture* at the end of the *Choral symphony* makes an incongruous anti-climax. Originally the dynamic range of the sound was compressed in the tape mastering, but this is likely to have been corrected by now, as the separate reissues of these recordings on HMV Concert Classics have been technically successful.

Kurt Masur's set on Philips costs approximately the same as Klemperer's and includes much the same amount of music, with *Namensfeier* in the place of the excerpts from the *Egmont* incidental music. As such it is remarkably competitive. Individually none of the performances storms the heavens, yet the cycle as a whole adds up to an impressive experience, and many will prefer the unforced expressiveness and the naturalness of these performances to the more highly characterized readings of either Karajan or Klemperer. At times, as in No. 8, there is a want of tautness and concentration, yet there are many touches of distinction. The *Eroica* is uncommonly fine, particularly the nobly paced slow movement, which is totally free from excessive expressive emphasis. In the *Fourth Symphony*, Masur brings great imagination and poetic feeling to the slow movement and, as throughout the set, the Gewandhaus Orchestra responds with wonderfully alert playing. The woodwind are marvellously blended and their intonation true, while the strings produce a refined, rich quality. This is a cultured orchestral sound by the side of which many orchestras sound garish and overbright. The Philips recording has great smoothness, a natural perspective, a warm acoustic ambience and a genuine sense of realism. Only the timpani could sound more integrated and clearly defined. Not least of the attractions of the set are the commanding accounts of the overtures. *Egmont* is particularly fine and shows the rich sonority of the Gewandhaus strings and the lifelike recording to great advantage.

Cluytens's cycle is admirably consistent. Most successful of all is the glowing performance of the *Pastoral symphony*, and the success of that is symptomatic of Cluytens's approach to the other symphonies too, fresh and warm-hearted rather than toweringly dramatic. Neither the *Eroica* nor the *Ninth* lacks weight, only the last degree of intensity; the account of, the *Fifth* is admirably strong and unaffected, while the *Seventh* reveals its pastoral leanings in an unusually relaxed account of the first-movement allegro. The recordings – on the reverberant side – add a warm atmosphere to the Berlin Philharmonic's superb playing, hardly betraying their early sixties vintage.

In the early years of LP Karajan completed his first superb cycle of the Beethoven symphonies, with the orchestra which in a very few years he had helped to make the finest in Britain. Only No. 8 was recorded in stereo. Here the others have been transferred in stereo transcription, with very satisfying results, so that this initial Karajan Beethoven cycle can be consistently enjoyed with little allowance needed for dated sound. As for the interpretations, they have the stamp of directness and authority which one recognizes in Karajan's

more recent Beethoven records. The *Eroica* and the *Ninth* may lack the overpowering sense of occasion which marks Karajan's Berlin recordings of the same works, but Nos. 5 and 7 are if anything even more exhilarating in their freshness, with no unwanted tensions. Elsewhere too Karajan allows a degree of warmth, seeks after polish and elegance rather less. At around £16 for the set of seven records this is formidable value.

Symphonies Nos. 1–9.
**(*) Decca Jubilee JBA 500/5. Vienna PO, Schmidt-Isserstedt (with soloists and chorus).
*(*) DG 2721 199 (9 discs). RPO, Dorati (with soloists and chorus).

Schmidt-Isserstedt's cycle of the Beethoven symphonies presents a consistently musical view, not lacking strength, and without distracting idiosyncrasies. All the symphonies are beautifully played – the character of the VPO coming over strongly – and well recorded. Apart from the *Pastoral*, clean and classically straightforward but entirely lacking in charm, there is no outright disappointment here, and the series culminates in a splendid account of the *Ninth*, one which does not quite scale the heights but which, particularly in the slow movement and the finale (with outstanding soloists), conveys visionary strength. For some a reservation may be that the performances are not so strikingly individual as to compel repeated hearings, although the *Fourth* must be excepted from this general comment. It is a symphony well suited to Schmidt-Isserstedt's thoughtful, poetic style. The *Fifth* – not a symphony that regularly gets successful performances on record – also stands out, with a first movement that has both bite and breathing space, a nicely measured *Andante* and a gloriously triumphant finale. Only the scherzo invites controversy in its slow tempo. The *Seventh*, similarly, is compelling throughout. Tempi are generally judged with perfect regard for the often conflicting requirements of symphony and dance – not too ponderous and not too hectic. The first movement of the *Eighth* is slower than usual, and although the *Allegretto* is crisp and light, the minuet is rather heavily pointed, with a Brahmsian touch in the trio. These are all performances that one can live with, but their mood is essentially serious: only rarely do they spark one off with fresh joy in Beethoven. The first two symphonies (again with generally slow tempi), although the playing is nicely detailed, are seriously lacking in charm. The nine works are presented consecutively on twelve sides, which means that Nos. 4 and 6 are split over separate discs, but the quality of the sound is excellent.

Dorati's Beethoven cycle generally lacks just the quality which made his great Haydn series so consistently compelling, a sense of spontaneity and new discovery, a feeling of live performance. Speeds are generally well judged, the style rarely if ever controversial, yet from Dorati one expected greater vigour. It is typical of his approach that the *Ninth Symphony* conveys, even in the first movement, an atmosphere of easy optimism, with little mystery or stress. Like the rest this is a performance which is enjoyable on its own terms but misses much of the greatness of Beethoven. The recording is not ideally refined or perfectly balanced, but is bright and full-ranging.

Symphony No. 1 in C major, Op. 21; Overtures: *Coriolan, Op. 62; Leonora No. 3, Op. 72b.*
   **(*) C.f.P. CFP 187. Berlin PO, Cluytens.

There is plenty of rhythmic life in Cluytens's account of the *First Symphony*, with no lack of vivacity in the outer movements and genuine high spirits in the finale. The *Andante* is kept moving, but the final impression here is of good musicianship rather than inspiration. The characteristic reverberant Berlin recording adds its own weight to the reading and tends to emphasize the conductor's accents. Of the two overtures, *Coriolan* is strongly dramatic and *Leonora No. 3* has both breadth and excitement: it begins with a fine sweep, and if Cluytens then lets the tension drop marginally, the closing pages are really exciting.

Symphonies Nos. 1; 2 in D major, Op. 36.
   *(**) RCA Victrola (m) AT 117. NBC SO, Toscanini.

The *First Symphony* brings one of the most convincing of Toscanini's Beethoven performances, characteristically fierce but full of youthful sparkle in the outer movements and with a finely phrased, unhurried account of the slow movement. The clarity of articulation in fast movements is superb. With just a little increase of tension, along with very fast speeds, the performance of the *Second Symphony* is not nearly so sympathetic. The strength of Toscanini remains, but the outer movements tend to be fierce and breathless. The mono recordings are limited but among the less shallow from the NBC Orchestra.

Symphonies Nos. 1; 8 in F major, Op. 93.
   *** DG Heliodor 2548 224. Bav. RO or Berlin PO, Jochum.

Jochum gives refreshingly unmannered readings of both symphonies, and the recordings sound very well indeed. As representative of the German tradition, these performances are very enjoyable, and the disc is very competitive. However, the cassette is not recommended. The transfer of No. 8 is successful, but No. 1 produces patches of ugly sound.

Symphony No. 2 in D major, Op. 36. Overtures: *The Creatures of Prometheus, Op. 43; The Ruins of Athens, Op. 113.*
 *** D G Heliodor 2548 214. Berlin P O or Bav. R O, Jochum.
Symphony No. 2; Overture: *Egmont, Op. 84.*
 **(*) C.f.P. CFP 193. Berlin P O, Cluytens.

Jochum gives a characteristically strong and refreshing reading of the *Second*, helped by beautifully balanced and pointed playing from the Berlin Philharmonic and recording (late-fifties vintage) that hardly shows its age. The two overtures are also given vivacious performances and balance the symphony satisfyingly.
  Cluytens is strong and direct and he too draws fine weighty playing from the Berlin P O. His recording is more modern and has a fuller, ample acoustic but no lack of clarity or detail. With an excellent account of the *Egmont overture* this makes an excellent alternative to Jochum.

Symphony No. 3 in E flat major (Eroica), Op. 55.
 *** C.f.P. CFP 40076 [TC-CFP]. Berlin P O, Cluytens.
 *(**) RCA Victrola (m) AT 121. NBC SO, Toscanini.

In its remastered form with the slow movement unbroken on side one the Cluytens performance is a fine bargain. Though the tempo at the start of the first movement is fast, Cluytens quickly

justifies it in strongly dramatic playing. The *Funeral march* is wonderfully hushed and intense, and the scherzo has tremendous rhythmic energy with superb horn playing in the trio. Indeed the last two movements show the Berlin orchestra in brilliant form, helped by the vividly atmospheric recording. The cassette, transferred at a high level, is a little rough in tutti in the first movement but seems cleaner in the *Adagio*. On side two the quality is excellent.
  The Victrola issue offers Toscanini's third recording of the *Eroica*, a live performance given at Carnegie Hall in 1953. It was this symphony above all which inspired Toscanini to supreme greatness in Beethoven, and it is sad that, like his other two recordings, this one is so obviously flawed. The first movement is clean of attack and tense but not at all hurried. The woodwind unfortunately is ill-matched. The *Funeral march* is taken spaciously, a superbly concentrated performance; the scherzo is spiky rather than playful, but intense in its clarity; the ebb and flow of the variations in the finale have one remembering Toscanini as an opera conductor, a great showman. The sound is predictably shallow, uncomfortably so in the opening chords.

Symphony No. 4 in B flat major, Op. 60. Overtures: *The Creatures of Prometheus, Op. 43; Fidelio, Op. 72c; The Ruins of Athens, Op. 113.*
 ** C.f.P. CFP 40001. Berlin P O, Cluytens.
Symphony No. 4; Overture: *Leonora No. 2, Op. 72a.*
 *** D G Heliodor 2548 225. Berlin P O, Jochum.

Jochum's Heliodor disc is the outstanding bargain recommendation, well played and well recorded. In Jochum's keenly alert interpretation the hushed tension of the slow introduction is most compelling, leading to a thrilling account of the *Allegro vivace* and a beautifully poised reading of the slow movement. In the overture Jochum brings out the massiveness of the inspiration, more original than *Leonora No. 3* in presenting the same material more expansively but without a formal recapitulation.

Cluytens, also with the Berlin Philharmonic, gives a vigorous performance, delightfully fresh and alert in the fast movements but marred by a somewhat pedestrian account of the sublime *Adagio*. A fair alternative to Jochum if the three overtures are more attractive as coupling.

Symphonies Nos. 4; 5 in C minor, Op. 67.
  *(**) RCA Victrola (m) AT 128. NBC SO, Toscanini.

The *Fourth Symphony* inspires Toscanini to one of his most sympathetic Beethoven recordings, for though the speeds are characteristically fast, there is a swagger and joyfulness in the outer movements, while the slow movement at a flowing tempo is beautifully phrased. The tautness of Toscanini's view of the first movement of the *Fifth* is exaggerated by the shallowness of the recording, but the relentlessness is not out of character with the music, and the *Andante* brings warm phrasing at an unrushed tempo. The scherzo is aggressive and unsprung, but the finale wears its militarism with a swagger and the braying brass is joyful. With such sound these performances may be hard to live with – particularly the *Fifth* – but they certainly have the stamp of greatness.

Symphony No. 5 in C minor, Op. 67.
  * DG Heliodor 2548 028. Berlin PO, Fricsay.

Symphony No. 5; Overture: *Coriolan, Op. 62.*
  * RCA Camden CCV 5023 [c4]. Chicago SO, Reiner.
Symphony No. 5; Overture: *Fidelio, Op. 72c.*
  *** DG Heliodor 2548 255 [3348 255]. Bav. RO, Jochum.

Although Jochum seems unduly restrained at the very opening, he launches into a finely vigorous reading, unmarred by any romantic exaggeration and gripping in a totally natural, unforced way. The finale is especially fine, and beautifully prepared with a dramatic dynamic change from pianissimo to a joyous fortissimo. The recording is very good, and it has transferred well to cassette, although the transfer level is rather low.

With relatively slow tempi the first two movements in Fricsay's reading are disappointingly heavy-handed, though the Berlin Philharmonic produces playing with excellent body of tone and fine detail. But this cannot compare with Jochum, or with Cluytens (see below).

Reiner's *Fifth* too is most disappointing, starting ponderously and then spurting forward to create synthetic excitement. The slow movement is over-romanticized in an unconvincing way. Inflated recording.

Symphonies Nos. 5; 8 in F major, Op. 93.
  *** C.f.P. CFP 40007 [TC-CFP]. Berlin PO, Cluytens.

With two symphonies offered at the lowest possible price, Cluytens's disc is outstanding value, with very good sound, considering the length of sides. The *Fifth* is an admirably refreshing reading, among the finest available, direct and urgent, unforcedly compelling, and (unlike many other versions on a single side) observing the exposition repeat. The Berlin horns in the finale are most exciting. The *Eighth* too is satisfying: despite a slowish tempo for the first movement, the point of the Berlin playing keeps the performance alert all through. The cassette originally had a restricted dynamic range but it has been remastered, and now it generally sounds well, although there are one or two passages with a hint of congestion.

Symphonies Nos. (i) *5;* (ii) *9 in D minor (Choral), Op. 125.*
    *** Decca DPA 599/600. Stokowski, (i) LPO (ii) Harper, Watts, Young, McIntyre, LSO Chorus, LSO.

Decca's recoupling of these recordings of the *Fifth* and *Ninth Symphonies* offers an excellent way to buy an outstanding version of the *Choral symphony* at less than the cost of one premium-price LP yet with ample groove space. Unmistakably Stokowski's is a great, compelling account of the *Ninth*, consistently conveying the sort of tension – not least in the hush of the slow movement – which marked live performances under the maestro. The first movement is strong and dramatic, taken at a Toscanini tempo; the scherzo is light and pointed, with timpani cutting through; the slow movement is warmly lyrical, and though the finale, with some strangely slow tempi, has its unevenness, this three-sided format allows for fuller, more immediate sound than on the original single-disc version. The fill-up is an almost equally compelling account of the *Fifth*, exceptionally strong in the outer movements and marred only by a sluggish tempo for the second-movement *Andante*.

Symphony No. 6 in F major (Pastoral), Op. 68.

    *** C.f.P. CFP 40017 [TC-CFP]. Berlin PO, Cluytens.
    *** RCA Camden CCV 5053 [C4]. Chicago SO, Reiner.
    ** DG Heliodor 2548 205 [3348 205]. Berlin PO, Maazel.

Cluytens's recording is intensely warm-hearted and atmospheric. On analysis alone one might object to the occasional idiosyncrasy, the very affectionate phrasing and a few speed changes. But the obvious spontaneity makes the whole performance most compelling, so that one finds oneself playing it again and again for sheer delight. Each movement has a glow which can only come from complete sympathy between players and conductor, and the final *Shepherds' hymn after the storm* shines out as an apotheosis. In the linking passage after the storm Beethoven's picture of a world freshened by rain is most vivid and from there to the end the sense of joyous release increases in triumphant crescendo. With good sound it makes a clear principal recommendation. The cassette is good too; the transfer to tape richly captures the warmth of the recording, yet there is no lack of upper range or detail. A splendid bargain.

Reiner's disc also offers an outstandingly fresh and enjoyable performance. Throughout Reiner adopts a straightforward, unmannered approach, his shading is subtle, and the recording, helped by the spacious Chicago acoustic, adds atmosphere without confusion of texture. The slow movement is particularly beautiful, but with the possible exception of a rather fast speed for the finale (justified in the firmness achieved) all the tempi sound utterly natural and unforced. The exposition repeat is observed in the first movement to add to the architectural strength which Reiner's freshness brings out. The remastered cassette has been transferred at the highest possible level, which has brought a slight lapse of refinement at fortissimos. The storm makes a superb impact, however, and the glorious slow movement is agreeably rich-textured.

There are no romantic eccentricities in Maazel's reading; indeed he is straightforward almost to a fault. He chooses fairly fast tempi for the first two movements, and although the Berlin Philharmonic plays well for him the result is efficient rather than warm-hearted. The scherzo bursts into life, but the finale returns to the refined mood of the first two movements. The recording is good on disc, but the cassette transfer is a little husky and unrefined in the more expansive moments.

Symphony No. 7 in A major, Op. 92.
*** C.f.P. CFP 40018. Berlin PO, Cluytens.
*** RCA Victrola (m) AT 153. NY PO, Toscanini.
Symphony No. 7; Overture: *Fidelio, Op. 72c.*
**(*) RCA Camden CCV 5026 [c4]. Chicago SO, Reiner.

The distinctive point about Cluytens's reading of the *Seventh* is his treatment of the main *Allegro* in the first movement. He uses his relatively slow tempo to point the 6/8 rhythm with a delectable lilt – almost another *Pastoral symphony* – but there is no lack of Beethovenian drama, with Beethoven's characteristic sforzandos sharply underlined. The *Allegretto* is beautifully moulded, and Cluytens more than is common succeeds in all four movements in combining Beethovenian unbuttonedness with the lilt of the dance. The recording, apart from some edginess on the violins – which helps to make this account of the finale the most exciting of any, if a little rough in places – is outstanding for its age. At bargain price this can hardly be

matched, and the disc is very competitive irrespective of price.

A powerful, understanding performance from Reiner, particularly impressive in the first and third movements, where the power is combined with fine rhythmic lift to confirm Wagner's 'apotheosis of the dance'. The fast tempo for the finale draws unscampering brilliance from the Chicago orchestra. Marginally less impressive are the symphony's slow introduction and the *Allegretto* second movement, where Reiner's manner at fastish speeds is cooler. The atmospheric Chicago recording hardly shows its age (late 1950s).

Toscanini's legendary reign as principal conductor of the New York Philharmonic has no finer memorial on record than this version of the *Seventh*. Already his manner in Beethoven was taut and intense, but his insistence on fast tempi did not at that time obtrude itself as it came to do later. Though the 1937 recording is obviously limited, this is an exhilarating performance, explaining Toscanini's dominance more convincingly than most of his NBC recordings.

Symphony No. 9 in D minor (Choral), Op. 125.
*** Decca Jubilee JB 1 [KJBC]. Sutherland, Horne, King, Talvela, Vienna State Opera Chorus, Vienna PO, Schmidt-Isserstedt.
**(*) C.f.P. CFP 40019. Brouwenstijn, Meyer, Gedda, Guthrie, St Hedwig's Cathedral Choir, Berlin PO, Cluytens.
** RCA Camden CCV 5021. Price, Forrester, Poleri, Tozzi, New England Cons. Chorus, Boston SO, Munch.

For a brief period Karajan's superb 1962 performance of the *Ninth* was available on a special-offer single L P, transferred to two sides from the original three, and losing remarkably little in quality of sound (DG 2563 999). Why DG have withdrawn this issue is inexplicable. It was made as the culmination of a complete cycle of the symphonies, recorded in an intensive series of sessions, and Karajan's commitment as well as that of the performers is consistently clear, with a concentrated account of the first movement and an exhilarating conclusion in the finale. The slow movement may seem a little reticent, but no orchestra has played it with more concern for tonal beauty than the Berlin Philharmonic on this occasion. It is to be hoped that DG will reissue this record during the lifetime of our book.

Otherwise first choice rests with Schmidt-Isserstedt on Decca, a medium-priced Jubilee issue but in every sense a bargain. Schmidt-Isserstedt gives a deeply satisfying reading, easier to live with than many that are more monumental. Unlike other conductors who have recorded complete cycles of Beethoven symphonies Schmidt-Isserstedt started with this most challenging of the series and at once established the effectiveness of his unforced, unexaggerated manner. The finale is outstandingly successful, with excellent choral and solo singing; and the 1966 recording still sounds excellent. The tape is also in every way first-class until the coda of the finale, where the entry of the bass drum muddles the texture and spoils the work's closing pages.

Cluytens's version competes strongly. The glory of the performance is the hushed and intense account of the slow movement, which makes it the more irritating that because of the one-disc format that movement has to break in the middle. But the other movements are finely concentrated too, showing – as the rest of Cluytens's cycle does – that in his lifetime he was seriously under-

estimated as a Beethoven interpreter. Soloists and chorus are first-rate – with the possible exception of the cavernous-sounding Guthrie – and considering the length of sides the recording, with ample Berlin reverberation, is most acceptable.

The first side of Munch's disc, lasting 38 minutes and 40 seconds, could well be the longest ever issued in stereo on 33 r.p.m. L P, and that points to the one big merit of this Camden issue: it is the only single-disc version of the *Ninth* that does not break the slow movement in the middle. With the first three movements on side one and only the finale on side two, one might almost complain that the opportunity for a fill-up has been missed. Naturally the penalty of the long side is a reduction in fidelity and frequency range, but as this is not a recent recording and the price is modest, that is hardly a point to labour. The performance is a dramatic one, and rather to one's surprise the third movement is taken quite slowly, with fine, expressive moulding by Munch. The first movement rather fails to get below the surface of the music, and the finale is marred by variable singing and too close a balance for the soloists.

(i) *Symphony No. 9.* Overtures: *Egmont, Op. 84; Leonora No. 3, Op. 72b.*

** D G Heliodor 2700 108 (2 discs). Berlin PO, Fricsay, (i) with Seefried, Forrester, Haefliger, Fischer-Dieskau, St Hedwig's Cathedral Choir.

Fricsay's account of the *Ninth* was the first to come out in stereo (in the late 1950s). It is a far from insignificant performance; generally it is well shaped and is full of vitality, though tempi are fairly broad, save in the scherzo. The *Adagio* is particularly beautiful, and only the finale seems lacking in weight. Here the recording, otherwise remarkably good for its age, lets the performance down with a diffuse focus for the chorus. Although a pair of overtures is included, the use of two discs means that this issue is considerably more expensive than Cluytens; but there is the advantage of not having a break in the slow movement.

CHAMBER AND INSTRUMENTAL MUSIC

Allegro and minuet for 2 flutes; Serenade in D major for flute and piano, Op. 41; Flute sonata in B flat major; 6 Themes and variations, Op. 105; 10 Themes and variations, Op. 107 (all for flute and piano); *Trio for 3 flutes in G major; Trio concertante in G major for flute, bassoon and piano.*
**(*) Everest 3468/3 (3 discs). Rampal; Veyron-Lacroix (with Larde; Marion; Hogne).

None of this music is great, but nearly all of it is pleasing, and these performances have charm and finesse. The recorded sound is a little restricted in range and body of tone, but it is genuine stereo and has sufficient presence and freshness. In every way this set gives pleasure. Ideal for early-morning listening on a summer's day.

String quartets Nos. 1–16; Grosse Fuge, Op. 133.
**(*) HMV sls 857 (10 discs). Hungarian Qt.
** DG 2721 071 (10 discs). Amadeus Qt.
* CBS gm 101 (10 discs). Juilliard Qt.
String quartets Nos. 1–16; String quartet in F major (transcription of *Piano sonata No. 9, Op. 14/1*);

Grosse Fuge; (i) *String quintet in C major, Op. 29.*
** D G 2721 130 (11 discs). Amadeus Qt, (i) with Aronowitz.

Apart from the full-priced versions by the Italian and Végh quartets, which offer deeper insights and greater artistic satisfaction, the Hungarian cycle of the Beethoven quartets is probably the best on the market. The performances are sound, well shaped and completely unmannered; they also have the merit of being well recorded. Although in the late quartets they do not scale the highest inspiration, the playing is conscientious and often perceptive. In the Op. 18 set, the Hungarians do not quite match the Amadeus in terms of polish and finesse, nor does their leader, Zoltan Szekely, always command the greatest beauty of tone. But these readings are far from undistinguished, and in terms of vitality and musicianship they serve the collector well.

The Amadeus set, recorded during the 1960s, is now available in two formats: one retailing at £22.00 and the other, offering the quartet transcription of the *E major Sonata*, Op. 14/1, and the *C major String quartet*, more expensive (£26.50). There is no doubt that the strongest things here are the Op. 18 set, where the tonal refinement and polish of this great ensemble tell. There is much to admire, too, in the *Rasumovsky* set, where the sumptuous tone and fine balance of the Amadeus are much in evidence. The weakest elements in the cycle are the late quartets, where over-familiarity may have weakened both the freshness and intensity of the readings. Norbert Brainin's vibrato will present problems here and there to all but his most fervent admirers, and his excessive sweetness (and perhaps too great a concern for sheer beauty of sound) undoubtedly robs the later masterpieces of something of their spiritual force. The Hungarians do not attempt to beautify,

17

and present these scores in a more direct and unadorned fashion. The D G recording still sounds truthful and realistic, and if some of the movements were a little less self-regarding, the set would be more impressive.

The Juilliard Quartet is a wonderfully accomplished body, and it goes without saying that there is much to admire in their playing. Generally speaking, however, the technical polish these performances exhibit is not matched by corresponding musical depths. There is too little humanity here, and scant feeling for the natural flow of the musical argument. Nothing is unforced, and the slow movements lack repose and spirituality. Not an enjoyable set, and its merits are not enhanced by the unsympathetic recording quality.

Piano music

(i) *Piano sonatas Nos. 1–32; Andante favori in F major, G.170; 6 Bagatelles, Op. 126; 6 Ecossaises in E flat major; Für Elise; Rondo à capriccio in G major (Rage over a lost penny), Op. 129; 6 Variations on Paisiello's duet 'Nel cor più' in G major; 2 Rondos, Op. 51/1–2.* (ii) *33 Variations in C major on a waltz by Diabelli, Op. 120.* (iii) *(Piano duet) Grosse Fuge, Op. 134; 3 Marches, Op. 45; Sonata for piano duet (Ich denke dein), Op. 6; 8 Variations on a theme by Waldstein.*
*** D G 2721 134 (14 discs). (i) Kempff; (ii) Anda; (iii) Demus and Shetler.

The bulk of this set – originally assembled for D G's Beethoven Edition in 1970 – is devoted to Wilhelm Kempff's fresh and exhilarating cycle of the sonatas, and it is a pity that Kempff was not persuaded to record the other items too. Anda's account of the *Diabelli variations*

is more than capable, but he lacks the spark of imagination which consistently holds the attention in Kempff's performances, with their diamond-sharp articulation and rhythmic point. Kempff's Beethoven has been providing a deeply spiritual experience for record collectors since the twenties and there is no doubt whatever of the inner compulsion which holds these performances together. He more than any pianist has the power to make one appreciate and understand Beethoven in a new way, and that is so however many times one has heard him. It makes a fascinating study to compare the interpretations not only with those of other pianists but with his own previous ones. Above all, these magnificent records never fail to reveal his own spontaneity in the studio, his ability to rethink the reading on each occasion.

The sonata recordings all date from the early to mid-1960s, and are to that decade what Schnabel's were to the pre-war years, in other words performances that are a yardstick by which all others are judged. The recordings have less bloom and freshness than Barenboim's, but they have a commanding stature. Kempff is occasionally fast (for example in the slow movements of Opp. 26 and 110) but he is invariably illuminating and has many felicitous touches. Of the boxed sets of Beethoven sonatas now before the public this would be first choice for many collectors, and so it should be.

Piano sonatas Nos. 1–32.
*** H M V SLS 794 (12 discs). Daniel Barenboim.

Barenboim's cycle of the Beethoven piano sonatas stands as one of the most compelling ever recorded, a superb memento of this artist's seemingly spontaneous insight into Beethoven even in his early twenties. Some of the tempi are controversial – in both directions, slow as well as fast – but no one can doubt that Barenboim's daring in adopting such slow tempi for the slow movements of the late sonatas reveals a concentration rarely caught on record. The recorded sound is warm and faithful, and the whole set has the enormous merit that each performance has one eager to go on listening in fresh discovery. At well under £2 per disc the records are unbelievably inexpensive.

Piano sonatas Nos. 7 in D major, Op. 10/3; 23 in F minor (Appassionata), Op. 57.
 **(*) RCA (m) VH 012. Horowitz.

Recorded in the late 1950s, the sound betrays its age, particularly at fortissimos. The performances, however, are incandescent, and their personality shines through any sonic defects. Both sonatas are viewed as a whole, and the *Appassionata* can rarely have been given with a stronger sense of line or a more powerful musical pulse. Yet at the same time no detail goes unremarked and every phrase vibrates with character. It goes without saying that not every feature of these readings will have universal appeal (and some may actively dislike them). However, these are performances of stature.

Piano sonatas Nos. 14 in C sharp minor (Moonlight), Op. 27/3; Piano sonata No. 21 in C major (Waldstein), Op. 53.
 *(*) RCA (m) VH 003. Horowitz.

Horowitz's account of the *Waldstein* will not be to all tastes. The first movement is very fast and impulsive, so much so that he pulls back for the second group. There is no want of fire and intensity, both here and in the rondo, nor is there any lack of depth in the slow movement, which has great inner feeling.

Many listeners will find the outer movements a shade overdriven and unrelenting, in spite of the moments of imposing artistry. The first movement of the *Moonlight* has superb control and repose, but the finale is too fast and dazzling for comfort. The dry, shallow recording dates from 1956.

Piano sonatas Nos. 15 in D major (Pastoral), Op. 28; 17 in D minor, Op. 31/2; 19 in G minor, Op. 49/1; 24 in F sharp major, Op. 78.
 ** DG Heliodor 2548 283 [3348 283]. Foldes.

Andor Foldes can often be coolly didactic and a shade sober, but these finely articulated performances have much to commend them. They are marvellously controlled and embrace a wider range of feeling than his (now deleted) *Appassionata* and *Waldstein*, and there are many sensitive touches. There is a certain lack of warmth but the clarity and finesse of the playing win admiration. The recording is clean and well-focused, and at Heliodor price the disc is worth considering. The cassette has been transferred at marginally too high a level, and although the sound is basically full and realistic, there is some distortion at peaks, particularly on side two (Nos. 17 and 19).

Andante favori in F major, G.170; Für Elise; Rondo à capriccio in G major (Rage over a lost penny), Op. 129; 2 Rondos, Op. 51/1–2; Piano sonata excerpts: No. 8 (Pathétique): 2nd movt; No. 14 (Moonlight): 1st movt; No. 20 in G major, Op. 49/2 (complete).
 ** DG Heliodor 2548 266 [3348 266]. Kempff.

The shorter pieces here are presented in Kempff's characteristically spontaneous manner. The inclusion of the sonata movements (although they are beautifully played) seems designed to attract the wider musical public rather than the specialist collector. Nevertheless this disc is well recorded and attractive for what it is. The tape transfer is clear and clean: side one seems to have a cooler atmosphere and sharper outline than side two, where there is marginally more bloom on the piano tone. But both offer good quality, even if the transfer is made at rather a low level.

Missa solemnis (Mass in D major), Op. 123.
> **(*)** RCA Victrola AT 200 (2 discs). Marshall, Merriman, Conley, Hines, Robert Shaw Chorale, NBC SO, Toscanini.

Toscanini directs a performance of Beethoven's choral masterpiece which brings out the single-minded concentration of the argument. It is particularly sad that the sound, as usual with Toscanini, is shallow, with the chorus badly focused, for from first to last this is unmistakably a great performance, one which in its severity allows no relaxation but brings out the spiritual intensity of the *Sanctus* and *Dona nobis pacem*. The choral singing is excellent and the solo quartet is outstanding, so that though the recorded sound would make this hard to live with, it is a performance which is required listening for the Beethovenian.

Berlioz, Hector
(1803–69)

Overture: *Le Carnaval romain, Op. 9.*
> ***RCA Victrola (m) AT 100. NBC SO, Toscanini – RES-

PIGHI: *Fountains and Pines of Rome.* ⊛***

A thrilling, exhilarating account of Berlioz's overture to add to the attractions of one of the maestro's finest commercial records.

'*Favourite composer*': (i) Overtures: *Le Carnaval romain, Op. 9; Le Corsaire, Op. 21. La Damnation de Faust: Hungarian march.* (ii) *Symphonie fantastique, Op. 14.* (iii) *L'Enfance du Christ:* Part 2, Scene 1. (iv; i) *Nuits d'été: Le spectre de la rose.* (v) *Les Troyens à Carthage: Je vais mourir.*
> ** Decca DPA 529/30 [KDPC 613/4], (i) Suisse Rom. Orch., Ansermet; (ii) Vienna PO, Monteux; (iii) Peter Pears, St Anthony Singers, Goldsbrough Orch., Colin Davis; (iv) Régine Crespin: (v) Josephine Veasey, ROHCGO, Kubelik.

These recordings, though not new, make up a generous cross-section of Berlioz's music for less than the cost of one full-priced issue. Josephine Veasey sings eloquently in the excerpt from *Les Troyens*, and the substantial excerpt from *The Childhood of Christ* (including the delightful *Shepherds' farewell*) is most welcome. Monteux's version of the *Symphonie fantastique* is a vital reading, lacking just a little in spontaneity, though with a gracious waltz and fine excitement in the last two movements. The sound is admirably vivid throughout, although in the symphony the upper strings have not quite the richness one would find in a modern recording. The cassette transfers are sophisticated, and there is much to enjoy here on both disc and tape.

Harold in Italy, Op. 16.
*** RCA Victrola (m) AT 112. Cooley, NBC SO, Toscanini.

Older collectors will recall Koussevitzky's pioneering record of *Harold in Italy* with William Primrose as soloist. The brooding power of its opening and the sheer incandescence of the finale would be difficult to surpass. Yet Toscanini's account, made in 1953 with Carlton Cooley as the eloquent soloist, is hardly less impressive. As in his complete *Roméo et Juliette*, the great Italian conductor is wholly attuned to every facet of Berlioz's temperament and sensibility. The recording, although it is obviously limited in range, is good for its age, and the disc takes its place among the finest *Harolds* to have been made.

Symphonie fantastique, Op. 14.
*** RCA Camden CCV 5048 [c4]. Boston SO, Prêtre.
*(*) C.f.P. CFP 40281. Hallé Orch., Loughran.

Dating from the earliest days of stereo, Prêtre's recording has been remastered. The sound is astonishingly full and vivid, and there is no slow-movement break. The performance is remarkably successful: Prêtre's choice and control of tempi are spontaneous and convincing. He dashes away capriciously soon after the opening, and the ebb and flow of the first movement are most convincingly handled. The waltz is warmly elegant with a blaze of neurosis at the end. But the heart of the interpretation lies in the beautiful slow movement, spacious and poised here, but with a spurt of high drama at the 'recitativo' climactic interchange between wind and strings. The *March to the scaffold* has a jaunty sense of melodrama, and the element of grotesque inherent in the finale is matched by the burst of adrenalin in the closing page. Beecham's

famous medium-price version must be the prime contender (HMV SXLP 30295 [TC-SXLP]), but Prêtre's disc remains a very satisfying version at the lowest possible price.

With sound less warm and bright than C.f.P. have generally given to the Hallé, Loughran's account is disappointing, heavy in places and rarely exciting, although there are touches which reveal Loughran's characteristic freshness of approach.

La Damnation de Faust, Op. 24.
*** DG Heliodor 2700 112 (2 discs). Rubio, Verreau, Roux, Mollet, Elisabeth Brasseur Choir, Lamoureux Orch., Markevitch.

Complete on four sides (at the expense of very few cuts and those only small ones), this set is very competitive indeed. The performance is dramatic and vivid, and the recording, which dates from the very end of the 1950s, sounds remarkably fresh, with an attractive overall bloom on the sound and no lack of atmosphere. The orchestral contribution emerges with fine colour, and Markevitch draws the full effect from Berlioz's quirky touches of scoring. Richard Verreau as Faust is especially impressive among the soloists, but Consuelo Rubio is good too and so is Pierre Mollet, with Michel Roux an effective Mephistopheles. The choral contribution is very French, not always too sophisticated, but committed and with plenty of character. In short this is very enjoyable, and one notices especially some lovely sounds from the orchestral strings in the score's more expressive moments.

Bizet, Georges
(1838–75)

L'Arlésienne (incidental music): Suites Nos. 1 and 2.
** RCA Camden ccv 5011 [c4]. Chicago SO, Martinon.
L'Arlésienne: Suites Nos. 1 and 2; Carmen: Suite No. 1.
*(*) C.f.P. cfp 40283. Paris Conservatoire Orch., Cluytens.

Anyone wanting just the two L'Arlésienne suites could do much worse than invest in this bargain Camden issue. The quality is bold and vivid (recorded in the characteristically resonant Chicago acoustic) and the playing is alive and nicely turned. The pressings are not without moments of pre-echo but on the whole are quiet-surfaced. The new tape transfer, made at a high level, is comparably lively and full-blooded, although the closing Farandole is slightly explosive. Nevertheless, this makes equally enjoyable listening.

Dating from the mid-sixties, Cluytens's disc is very well recorded: the quality is strikingly live and open. But the orchestral playing in the L'Arlésienne suites lacks the style that this music demands. Cluytens begins badly with a flabby rhythmic treatment of the striding opening theme, and although later the French timbre of the decorative bassoons has an individual character, the famous Farandole again lacks polish and crispness of ensemble. The Carmen music fares much better, and here the recording is really splendid. But at medium price Beecham offers this same coupling with truly memorable wind soloists in L'Arlésienne and an unforgettable swagger in the Carmen suite (HMV sxlp 30276). His recording is obviously less modern but is fully acceptable, and the cassette transfer (tc-sxlp 30276) is attractively crisp and lively.

'Favourite composer': (i) L'Arlésienne: Suites Nos. 1–2; Jeux d'enfants: Suite; La Jolie Fille de Perth: Suite; Symphony in C major: (ii) Carmen: highlights.
*** Decca dpa 559/60 [kdpc]. (i) Suisse Rom. Orch., Ansermet; (ii) Resnik, del Monaco, Krause; Schippers.

This is in every way a recommendable anthology of some of Bizet's finest music. The performances of the Symphony and orchestral suites are first-class, and the recording is clear, warm and vivid throughout, although the selection from Carmen does not give as much presence to the voices as one might expect. In this respect the tape set is to be preferred to the discs, as generally the cassette sound is marginally sharper-edged. Musically the items from the opera come up surprisingly well, with Resnik projecting convincingly, the Toreador song of Tom Krause suitably forthright, and the Don José of Mario del Monaco dramatically convincing with its plebeian lack of refinement.

Jeux d'enfants (Children's Games): Suite.
*** C.f.P. cfp 40086 [tc-cfp]. Scottish Nat. Orch., Gibson – SAINT-SAËNS: Carnival ⊛ ***; RAVEL: Ma Mère l'Oye.**(*)

From Classics for Pleasure and Sir Alexander Gibson a fresh recording and lively orchestral playing. The lyrical movements, shaped with gentle affection, give much pleasure and with good couplings this is an excellent disc in every way. The cassette sounds very well too, though rather less crisp in the upper range.

Boito, Arrigo
(1842–1918)

Mefistofele: Prologue.
*** RCA Victrola (m) AT 131.
Mascona, Columbus Boys'
Choir, Robert Shaw Chorale,
NBC SO, Toscanini – VERDI:
*Te Deum.****

Toscanini's 1954 Carnegie Hall
recording of the *Prologue* from *Mefistofele* is the only bargain account of any
part of the opera to be had. The alternatives are Bernstein's *Prologue*
coupled with Liszt's *Faust symphony* at
full price, and a first-class mid-price set
of the whole opera (with Cesare Siepi in
the principal role and Renata Tebaldi as
Margherita: Decca Ace of Diamonds
GOS 591/3). But there is a blazing intensity about Toscanini's performance
which shines through any sonic limitations and grips the listener from the first
bar to the last. Even at full price, this
disc would be worth the money.

Borodin, Alexander
(1833–87)

*In the Steppes of Central Asia.
Prince Igor: Overture; Polovtsian
dances; Polovtsian march.*
*(*) C.f.P. CFP 40309. LPO,
Susskind – MUSSORGSKY:
*Night on the Bare
Mountain.*(*)*

In the Steppes of Central Asia opens
poetically and atmospherically here, but
the performance is let down by Susskind's lack of imagination in matters of
tempi and rhythm (there is too little
contrast between the work's two principal themes), although the orchestral
playing is of a high standard. Similarly
he shows a lack of flair in the music from
Prince Igor, and the *Polovtsian dances*
never really catch fire at the end. The
recording is vivid and makes an excellent
impact, so that in spite of the conductor's
too studied approach the music does not
fail to communicate.

In the Steppes of Central Asia; Symphony No. 2 in B minor.
** DG Heliodor 2548 226. Dresden State Orch., Sanderling –
TCHAIKOVSKY: *Romeo and
Juliet.***

Sanderling's version of Borodin's
Second Symphony originally appeared
in the early 1960s, and has much to
recommend it. Not least of its advantages is the lively playing of the Dresden
orchestra, and Sanderling, as one would
expect, fashions the score in a
thoroughly dramatic and vivid fashion.
Particularly admirable are the effervescent scherzo and the poetic slow movement. The recorded sound is beginning
to show signs of age; it could be more
open at the top and richer in the bass
register. However, the balance is musically judged and the acoustic has
warmth: it can be thoroughly recommended at this price (but see also below
for Martinon's version in the Decca
collection).

'*The world of Borodin*': (i) *In the
Steppes of Central Asia:* (ii) *Symphony No. 2 in B minor;* (iii) *String
quartet No. 2: Nocturne;* (i; iv)
Prince Igor; Polovtsian dances.
*** Decca SPA 281. (i) Suisse
Rom. Orch., Ansermet, (iv)
with chorus; (ii) LSO, Martinon; (iii) Borodin Qt.

An extraordinarily successful
medium-price disc (costing under £3)

that will provide for many collectors an inexpensive summation of the art of Borodin. There can be few collections of this kind that sum up a composer's achievement so succinctly or that make such a rewarding and enjoyable concert. Martinon's performance of the *Symphony* is notable for its fast tempo for the famous opening theme, but the strong rhythmic thrust suits the music admirably, and the slow movement, with a beautifully played horn solo, is most satisfying. The recording has remarkable presence and sparkle, and only in the massed violin tone (which is good) is there a suggestion that the recording dates from the early sixties. Side two opens with *In the Steppes of Central Asia*, a vivid rather than an atmospheric reading; then follows the *Nocturne*, so effectively that one might have thought it the composer's own plan. The disc ends generously with the complete set of *Polovtsian dances*, reliably done, if not breathtakingly exciting, and very well recorded. A remarkable bargain indeed.

Prince Igor: Polovtsian dances.
** HMV 45 r.p.m. HMV 8. Orchestre de Paris, Rozhdest-vensky – RIMSKY-KORSAKOV: *Capriccio espagnol.***

A lively, straightforward account from Rozhdestvensky, with the 45 r.p.m. LP format emphasizing the brilliance rather than the depth of the sound. If you want the coupling this is good value though in no special way memorable. In spite of the faster speed this is a disc that will sound best on a small player.

Boyce, William (1710–79)

Symphonies Nos. 1 in B flat major; 2 in A major; 3 in C major; 4 in F major; 5 in D major; 6 in F major; 7 in B flat major; 8 in D minor.
*** C.f.P. CFP 40326. Menuhin Fest. Orch., Menuhin.

Boyce's set of eight symphonies was published in London in 1760. They are wonderfully inventive and entertaining. The orchestration is nicely varied: No. 5, for instance, opens with trumpets in a most regal manner, and in the diversity of its melodic and rhythmic patterns evokes the spirit of Handel, as do the broad opening of No. 1, the jollier No. 4 and the slow movement of No. 6. One feels these Handelian associations are especially relished by Menuhin, whose gracious phrasing and elegant manner are supported by alert orchestral playing, and warm yet transparent textures. However, Menuhin's approach tends to be lightweight, especially in the later symphonies, which he shows in divertimento terms. Their layout certainly draws on a mixed ancestry of forms, using the designs of both the Italian and French overture. But their freshness of inspiration is never in doubt, and that is fully conveyed by this excellent disc, beautifully recorded.

Brahms, Johannes (1833–97)

Concertos

There is currently no bargain version of the *First Piano concerto*, but the work is well served in the medium price-range, and many will feel that both the Concert Classics disc by Barenboim and Barbirolli with the Philharmonia Orchestra (HMV SXLP 30283) and the DG Accolade issue by Gilels and the Berlin Philharmonic under Jochum (DG 2542 126) are more than worth their cost. With

24

Barenboim and Barbirolli tempi are broad and measured, but the performance is sustained by the intensity of its concentration, and the slow movement is particularly fine. The Gilels version has a magisterial strength blended with a warmth and humanity that are altogether inspiring. Jochum is a superb accompanist and the only reservation is a recording which although warmly atmospheric does not focus the piano and orchestra in a completely truthful perspective. There is an excellent cassette transfer of the Gilels version [3342 126], whereas the HMV tape offers an unsatisfactory orchestral image.

Piano concerto No. 2 in B flat major, Op. 83.
   *** R C A Camden c c v 5042 [c4]. Gilels, Chicago SO, Reiner.
   *(*) R C A (m) v h 019. Horowitz, N B C SO, Toscanini.
   * D G Heliodor 2548 282 [3348 282]. Anda, Berlin PO, Fricsay.

Both Emil Gilels and his compatriot Sviatoslav Richter recorded this most powerful of piano concertos in Chicago (Richter's version is available on R C A medium-price g l 11267 [g k]). Although Gilels is markedly less individual he gives a firmer, less mannered reading, one which in the bargain price range is invincible. Though power and brilliance are the watchwords (no one has recorded the scherzo with more breathtaking command), the more relaxed side of the work is also managed well – the rich horn solos in the first movement, the sparkling Hungarian ideas of the finale. The recording too still sounds quite well. The cassette transfer is of excellent quality, generally clear, with lively orchestral sound and a clean piano image. The two final movements sound especially fresh.

Horowitz's recording is of a live performance given in 1940, so the sound (and one or two details of ensemble) calls for tolerance. Horowitz's playing has an Olympian grandeur, magisterial command and intellectual rigour, though the middle movements are a trifle unyielding. There is tremendous grip, as one would expect from this combination, but rather less spontaneity than one hopes for from a live performance. It is a version that all admirers of Horowitz and Toscanini will want to study, but it will leave many listeners unmoved.

Géza Anda's account of the concerto is nothing if not rhapsodic in feeling. He recorded the work twice, with Fricsay in the early 1960s and later in the same decade with Karajan. His view of the work is expansive and somewhat mannered, though he is not quite as idiosyncratic in the Fricsay version as in his remake (available on the D G Privilege label). There is much imaginative phrasing and no want of keyboard finesse, but this account is let down by the recording, which, though clearly focused and more transparent than Anda's later version, suffers from discoloration. This coarseness and some unpleasing tone in the upper strings diminish the appeal of what is at times an impressive reading.

Violin concerto in D major, Op. 77.
   *** R C A Camden c c v 5052 [c4]. Szeryng, L S O, Monteux.

Henryk Szeryng was born in Poland but later moved to live in Mexico. His playing on this early R C A recording (made at the end of the 1950s) combines typically East European brilliance and bite with a warmth and expressiveness recalling southern climates. Brahms had something of these opposites in his personality, for he loved the northern part of Germany yet enjoyed escaping to Latin latitudes. His concerto has its bleak, powerful moments and it also contains much that is intense and sunlit. Szeryng lives up to these changing moods, and displays a technique that is rock-steady and brilliant. If there is occasionally a little lack of depth this is compensated by the sparkle of the playing. He is well served by the orchestra, and if the recording is not of the most modern and is rather lopsided in balance, this remains a beautifully clean and heartfelt performance, well worth its modest price. The cassette transfer has been made at the highest level, and this leads to some lack of refinement in the orchestral tuttis on side one. On side two, the level rises further and the soloist's timbre is discoloured in the slow movement; there is congestion in the finale.

(i) *Double concerto in A minor for violin, cello and orchestra, Op. 102. Variations on a theme of Haydn (St Anthony chorale), Op. 56a.* (ii) *Gesang der Parzen (Song of the Fates), Op. 89.*
*** RCA Victrola (m) AT 125. NBC SO, Toscanini, with (i) Mischakoff, Miller, (ii) Robert Shaw Chorale.

An impressively taut account of the *Double concerto* from Mischa Mischakoff, Frank Miller and Toscanini. RCA have succeeded in taming some of the fierceness of the original, and the resulting sound is now perfectly acceptable. All concerned play quite superbly and much electricity is generated. Those who favour a more expansive view should look elsewhere (Oistrakh, Fournier and Galliera on medium-priced HMV Concert Classics SXLP 30185 would be a good choice). In certain moods, however, one could not surpass the present Toscanini issue for sheer exhilaration and grip. The *Haydn variations* are superbly played too, though some listeners would probably welcome slightly more relaxation. The choral piece *Gesang der Parzen* is something of a rarity

and is not otherwise available. It was written immediately after the *Second Piano concerto*, and this 1948 recording greatly adds to the undoubted attractions of this generously filled disc.

'*Favourite composer*': (i) *Academic Festival overture, Op. 80;* (ii; iii) *Hungarian dances Nos. 1 in G minor; 5 in G minor; 6 in D major; 12 in D minor; 13 in D major; 19 in B minor; 21 in E minor;* (ii; iv) *Symphony No. 1 in C minor, Op. 68;* (v) *Variations on a theme of Haydn, Op. 56a;* (vi) *Intermezzo in B flat minor, Op. 117/2; Rhapsody No. 2 in G minor, Op. 79/2; Waltz in A flat major, Op. 39/15;* (vii; i) *Alto rhapsody, Op. 53.*
** Decca DPA 553/4 [KDPC]. (i) Suisse Rom. Orch., Ansermet; (ii) Vienna PO; (iii) Reiner, (iv) Krips; (v) LSO, Monteux; (vi) Katchen; (vii) Watts, Chœurs de la Radio Suisse Rom.

A sound performance of Brahms's *First* from Krips and a first-rate one of the *Variations on a theme of Haydn* from Monteux. Helen Watts's account of the *Alto rhapsody* is boldly direct rather than melting, but Katchen is on excellent form in the piano music. The recording is good (if sometimes a little dated), and the tape transfers are well managed; but other anthologies in this series have been more imaginatively chosen.

Symphonies Nos. 1–4.
*** C.f.P. CFP 78252 (4 discs). Hallé Orch., Loughran.

No more satisfying cycle of the Brahms symphonies than Loughran's is available on record at whatever price. The reviews of the individual discs below discuss the particular qualities, strength and spontaneity, warmth in the phrasing coupled with unforced tempi steadily maintained. If the Hallé playing is not always as refined as it might be, the sound is excellent, needing none of the reservations usually taken for granted in bargain issues. The records are supplied in their sleeves within a robustly attractive box.

Symphony No. 1 in C minor, Op. 68.
*** C.f.P. CFP 40096 [TC-CFP]. Hallé Orch., Loughran.
**(*) RCA Victrola (m) AT 115. NBC SO, Toscanini.
*(*) RCA Camden CCV 5018 [c4]. Boston SO, Munch.

James Loughran provides an outstanding version, and he observes the exposition repeat in the first movement. The reading from first to last is as refreshing as any available, irrespective of price. The second and third movements both have a spring-like quality, and the slow movement is less sweet than usual, while the 6/8 trio of the third movement is taken for once at a speed which allows the climax not to sound breathless. The introduction to the finale is unusually slow, weighty and concentrated, while the great string melody is not smoothed over at all. The entry of the chorale at the end finds Loughran characteristically refusing to slow down to half speed. Though some of the woodwind playing is not ideally responsive, the whole orchestra, particularly the strings, shows a natural feeling for Brahms's style. The recording is a little light in bass but otherwise captures a ripe, clean Brahms sound, and the equivalent cassette is impressively full-blooded. Now remastered, it has a wide dynamic range and only fractional hints of strain at one or two of the most expansive climaxes.

Toscanini launches into the introduction to the first movement at a fierce tempo. He takes a modular view of the whole movement, keeping far steadier tempi than usual but without the inflexibility that too often marred his Beethoven on record. The slow movement is beautifully moulded, even if the failure of the recording to allow a pianissimo is a serious flaw. The third movement is somewhat charmless, but the finale shows Toscanini at full strength, with the main allegro strongly dramatic at an unforced tempo and the great main theme rich and warm. As always with Toscanini it is sad that the recording is so limited, but this is more acceptable than most.

Frenchmen conducting Brahms rarely sound idiomatic, but Munch comes near to being an exception, for his control over what was at the time of recording his own orchestra is very precise, and the result, if on the cool side, is unmannered and on the whole satisfying.

Symphony No. 2 in D major, Op. 73.
*** C.f.P. CFP 40219 [TC-CFP]. Hallé Orch., Loughran.
**(*) RCA Victrola (m) AT 132. NBC SO, Toscanini.

As a Brahmsian James Loughran is a master of transition, and his account of No. 2, like those in the rest of his excellent Brahms cycle with the Hallé, has a natural, warm flow, carrying the listener on, even while the basic approach is direct and unfussy. On interpretation his reading (with exposition repeat included) matches and even outshines any in the catalogue, at whatever price, and the modern C.f.P. recording is warm and naturally balanced, though there are one or two noticeable tape-joins. The Hallé ensemble and string tone are not always quite as polished as in versions from metropolitan orchestras, but the sense of spontaneity is ample compensation. The sound of the tape transfer is pleasingly fresh, and the remastered copies now available have an impressively wide dynamic range.

At the start of the RCA issue the edgy woodwind and coarse brass are unpromising, and the recording remains limited; but this is one of Toscanini's most warmly lyrical performances on record, one which, with steady tempi and affectionate phrasing, beautifully solves the many interpretative problems. There is nothing of the inflexible Toscanini here except in the slowish and heavy account of the third movement, not helped by a sour oboe. The finale is exciting without being rushed, though the coda brings a sudden jerk of acceleration. A fine example of Toscanini's Brahms despite the recording.

Symphony No. 3 in F major, Op. 90; Hungarian dances Nos. 1 in G minor; 3 in F major; 19 in B minor.
*** C.f.P. CFP 40237 [TC-CFP]. Hallé Orch., Loughran.

Loughran, so urgently spontaneous in the other three Brahms symphonies, takes an unexpectedly measured view of No. 3. Though initially the slow tempi for all four movements may seem to undermine tension, on repetition it emerges as an unusually satisfying reading, presenting this as an autumnal work with lighter scoring than in the other symphonies. The total impression is of toughness and restraint set alongside flowing lyricism. As is habitual with Loughran, the exposition repeat is observed in the first movement, an important point in this of all the Brahms symphonies. Full atmospheric recording, which has been admirably transferred to the clear, full-blooded cassette. This has been recently remastered and now offers a dynamic range to match the disc.

Symphony No. 4 in E minor, Op. 98.
*** C.f.P. CFP 40084 [TC-CFP]. Hallé Orch., Loughran.
** RCA Camden CCV 5032 [c4]. Boston SO, Munch.

Loughran's account, like Barbirolli's before him with the same orchestra, is outstanding, and with excellent sound it should not be missed. Loughran's approach is unobtrusively direct. He is rarely, if ever, concerned to underline interpretative points, yet as the concentration grows after the deceptively gentle start, so one more and more appreciates the satisfying assurance with which he solves every problem. His tempi – except perhaps for a relatively slow account of the scherzo – are unexceptionable, and like Barbirolli he believes in adopting expressive phrasing within a basically steady tempo. The Hallé strings are in excellent form, beautifully recorded, and so for that matter are all the sections of the orchestra. The cassette too is extremely successful, rich and clear on side one and strikingly brilliant in the last two movements.

Munch has some very fine moments. His speed for the opening movement is slow and the shaping is finely conceived and carefully executed. The slow movement shows the orchestra at its most affectionate, but the last two movements rather let down the standard, and the impression is of a distinct slackening of tension, so that the fragmentary construction of the finale becomes too apparent. The recording is clear enough, with more than a hint of the characteristic RCA hardness found in these early Boston recordings.

CHAMBER MUSIC

(i; ii) *Clarinet quintet in B minor, Op. 115;* (i; iii) *Clarinet sonatas Nos. 1 and 2, Op. 120;* (i; vi; vii)

Horn trio in E flat major, Op. 40;
(iii; viii) *Piano quartets Nos. 1–3,
Opp. 25, 26, 60;* (v; ii) *Piano quintet
in F minor, Op. 34;* (ix) *Piano trios
Nos. 1–3, Opp. 8, 87, 101;* (ii) *String
quartets Nos. 1–3, Opp. 51 and 67;*
(ii, augmented) *String quintets Nos.
1 and 2, Opp. 88 and 111; String
séxtets Nos. 1 and 2, Opp. 18 and
36;* (x) *Violin sonatas Nos. 1–3, Opp.
78, 100, 108;* (xi) *Violoncello sonatas
Nos. 1 and 2, Opp. 38 and 99.*
*** D G 2740 117 (15 discs). (i)
Leister; (ii) Amadeus Qt; (iii)
Demus; (iv) Donderer; (v)
Eschenbach; (vi) Seiffert; (vii)
Drolc; (viii) Drolc Qt; (ix) Trio
di Trieste; (x) Ferras, Barbizet;
(xi) Fournier, Firkusny.

A handsome and useful compilation
that works out at roughly £2.33 per
record. It draws on a number of fine
chamber music releases from the 1960s,
including the Amadeus versions of the
two *Sextets* (with Cecil Aronowitz and
William Pleeth), their fine versions of
the *Quintets*, Opp. 88 and 111, and much
else besides. Indeed some may feel that
the Amadeus are too generously represented: they take part in the *F minor
Piano quintet*, in which there is a vital
and sensitive account of the keyboard
part from Christoph Eschenbach, the
Clarinet quintet with a superbly eloquent
Karl Leister, as well as in the three
Quartets, made in the very early 1960s.
For the *Piano quartets*, D G have chosen
Joerg Demus and members of the Drolc
Quartet rather than their earlier (and in
some ways more sparkling) accounts by
Santoliquido, Pelliccia, Giuranna and
Amfitheatroff, which were much treas-
ured in the early sixties. The *Horn trio*
with Seiffert, Drolc and Eschenbach is
one of the best accounts on record, and
readers should have no cause for dissat-
isfaction with the Trio di Trieste's

keenly alert and vitally intelligent versions of the three *Piano trios*. Christian
Ferras gives finely controlled accounts
of the *Violin sonatas* with Pierre Barbizet, though they do not match the
Suk–Katchen partnership on Decca in
terms of warmth. In the *Cello sonatas*
Fournier and Firkusny are most distinguished; these performances have been
consistently underrated. Recordings
throughout are eminently well balanced
and surfaces are impeccable. This is a
valuable set and well worth the outlay.

(i) *Violin sonata No. 3 in D minor,
Op. 108. Intermezzo in B flat minor,
Op. 117/2; Waltz in A flat major,
Op. 39/15.*
*(*) R C A (m) v H 017. Horowitz,
(i) with Milstein – M U S S O R G-
S K Y: *Pictures.****

The sleeve bills Nathan Milstein
almost as an afterthought! The two
artists have made music together from
their youthful years onwards. This
present issue, however, disappoints a
little, for although Horowitz's playing is
commanding, it is unrelaxed and wanting in humanity in the slow movement.
By contrast, the *B flat minor Intermezzo*
is both delicate and moving. Although
there is playing of nobility and refinement from Milstein, neither artist generates the naturalness and warmth that
distinguish the Suk–Katchen version,
which remains the one to have in any
price category. This is on a medium-
priced Decca issue (Ace of Diamonds
S D D 542) which includes all three *Violin
sonatas*. There is a splendid equivalent
cassette [K D S C 542].

*Violoncello sonata No. 1 in E minor,
Op. 38.*
(**) Everest Olympic (m) 8140.
Rostropovich, Sviatoslav Rich-
ter – G R I E G: *Sonata.* (**)

29

BRITTEN

Commanding and eloquent playing from both artists, as one would expect; but the recording, presumably from the 1950s, does scant justice to Rostropovich's glorious tone. He is reticently balanced and the sound is blanketed. It is not clean on climaxes either. Both the label and the sleeve get the key of the sonata wrong.

(i) *A German requiem, Op. 45.* (ii) *Alto rhapsody, Op. 53. Nänie, Op. 82.*
> *(*) Decca DPA 583/4. Suisse Rom. Radio and Lausanne PA Choirs, Suisse Rom. Orch., Ansermet, with (i) Giebel, Prey; (ii) Watts.

The coupling here is apt and generous, with a real rarity in *Nänie*, and the recording is fresh and clear in the best Suisse Romande manner; but Ansermet's reading of the *German requiem* is sluggish and unimaginative, bringing out the foursquare qualities which led Bernard Shaw among others unfairly to stigmatize it as a prize bore among choral works. Klemperer's noble medium-priced version of the *Requiem*, coupled with the *Alto rhapsody* (Christa Ludwig in superb form) and the *Tragic overture*, is the one to have (HMV SLS 821).

Britten, Benjamin (1913–76)

(i) *Violin concerto, Op. 15;* (ii) *Serenade for tenor, horn and strings, Op. 31.*
> *** C.f.P. CFP 40250. LPO, Pritchard, with (i) Friend; (ii) Partridge, Busch.

With Pritchard directing performances which rival those under the composer's direction, this is an outstanding record of Britten's music. It was an imaginative idea to couple the most colourful of his song cycles with the still neglected *Violin concerto*, as warmly romantic in its way as the Walton masterpiece, written at exactly the same time (1939). It was an equally good idea to exploit the artistry of two outstanding performers. Rodney Friend, at the time leader of the LPO, later concert-master of the New York Philharmonic, proves a masterful soloist, magnificently incisive and expressive. As for Ian Partridge, one of the most consistently stylish of recording tenors, he gives a reading often strikingly new in its illumination, more tenderly beautiful and pure than Peter Pears's classic reading, culminating in a heavenly performance of the final Keats sonnet setting. Excellent recording in both works.

(i) *Matinées musicales, Op. 24;* *Soirées musicales, Op. 9;* (ii) *Variations on a theme of Frank Bridge, Op. 10.*
> *** C.f.P. CFP 40308. (i) Philharmonia Orch., Irving; (ii) Bath Fest. Orch., Menuhin.

This is an outstanding coupling of works which show Britten at his most approachable. Menuhin directs a deeply committed account of the virtuoso variations which Britten wrote for Boyd Neel and his string orchestra to play at Salzburg in the thirties. Menuhin does not miss the wit of the parody variations but allows full depth of expressiveness to the *Funeral march*. The recording quality is excellent, as is the much older sound (late-fifties vintage) of Robert Irving's infectiously rhythmic accounts of two colourful ballet scores based on late pieces by Rossini.

Simple symphony (for strings), Op. 4.

*** Decca DPA 627/8 [KDPC].
ECO, the composer – *Concert of English music.****

From the composer an infectious and beautifully recorded performance of his miniature masterpiece based on juvenilia. For all its simplicity the quality of the music is high, and the *Playful pizzicato* and *Frolicsome finale* are worthy of a young Mozart. This is part of an enjoyable concert reviewed under 'English music' in the Concerts section below.

The Young Person's Guide to the Orchestra (Variations and fugue on a theme of Purcell), Op. 34.
** C.f.P. CFP 185 [TC-CFP].
Richard Baker (narrator), N Philharmonia Orch., Leppard – PROKOFIEV: *Peter and the Wolf.***
* DG Heliodor 2548 284 [3348 284]. Monte Carlo Opera Orch., Frémaux – MILHAUD: *Le Carnaval d'Aix***(*): TURINA: Danzas fantásticas.***

Richard Baker's narrative, which details the orchestral instruments, is friendly to the point of being too cosy, and it tends to hold up the music's flow. However, the orchestral playing is lively and the recording admirably vivid. But one feels there are too many words here, and this is not a version to stand constant repetition, although it would be very suitable for school use.

The Monte Carlo performance under Frémaux is a welcome version without the narrative, but for such an orchestral showpiece the solo playing lacks polish and flair, although it is acceptable and quite well recorded on both disc and tape. But this issue is especially valuable for its couplings, which are much more successful as performances.

Bruch, Max
(1838–1920)

Violin concerto No. 1 in G minor, Op. 26.
** RCA Camden CCV 5017 [c4].
Laredo, Boston SO, Munch – MENDELSSOHN: *Concerto.***

Jaime Laredo's performance of Bruch's famous *G minor Concerto* is strongly romantic and has a youthful freshness which is appealing. He is well supported by the orchestra, and as the roughness in the recording which affects the Mendelssohn coupling seems less noticeable here, this is enjoyable. This is the cheapest good pairing of the Bruch and Mendelssohn concertos. The remastered cassette transfer is well managed, and has good range and detail, although the orchestral sound is not strikingly full-bodied. The musical notes are not included with the cassette.

Violin concerto No. 1 in G minor, Op. 26; Scottish fantasia for violin and orchestra, Op. 46.
** C.f.P. CFP 40248. Hasson, Scottish Nat. Orch., Gibson.

Maurice Hasson gives sympathetic performances of this ideal Bruch coupling. With understanding accompaniments and excellent modern recording, it makes an attractive record, but Hasson's tone is not uniformly beautiful. Even so, the *Scottish fantasia* is a work of much charm and this is an excellent way of making its acquaintance.

BRUCKNER

Bruckner, Anton
(1824–96)

Symphonies Nos. 1–9. (i) *Te Deum.*
**(*) DG 2740 136 (11 discs).
Bav. RO or Berlin PO,
Jochum, (i) with soloists and
chorus.
*Symphonies Nos. 0 in D minor and
1–9.*
**(*) Philips 6717 002 (12 discs).
Concertgebouw Orch., Hai-
tink.

Jochum's set of the Bruckner symphonies does not include the D minor,
No. 0; and he bases his cycle on the texts
prepared by Leopold Nowak, which do
not enjoy the approval of many admirers
of the composer. Like Haitink's, this
cycle appeared during the latter part of
the 1960s, and in terms of the quality of
recorded sound and the sensitivity of the
orchestral response, there is not a great
deal to choose between the two. Jochum
is a good deal freer in his approach to
the rhythmic shape of a movement, and
those who favour a more austere view
of the structure will stay with Haitink.
Yet Jochum brings a sense of mystery to
these scores that sometimes eludes his
Dutch rival. In terms of spirituality and
atmosphere, these readings are to be
preferred to Haitink's, though in their
architectural qualities they are weaker.
They are fractionally cheaper per disc,
and there is the bonus of the *Te Deum.*
But the honours are very evenly
divided between the two sets, and at less
than £2.50 per disc, Haitink's is well
worth considering. Its strengths have
been consistent: they are all well-shaped
readings, free from affectation and any
kind of agogic distortion. The grasp of
architecture could scarcely be stronger,
and yet Haitink's feeling for beauty of
detail is refined. The playing of the

Amsterdam Concertgebouw Orchestra
is throughout magnificent and listeners
will relish their responsiveness to all the
demands made upon them. Moreover,
Haitink has the distinct advantage of
textual merit: he employs the Haas
rather than the Nowak editions. The
appearance of a more recent Haitink
version of the *Seventh Symphony*, which
is more spacious and mysterious, suggests that in time the great Dutch conductor will re-record the whole cycle,
and with added insight; but the excellence of this set in terms of both performance and recording is not in dispute.
Brucknerians will not be without Karajan's version of No. 9 in the mid-price
DG Accolade series (2542 129 [3542
129]) or his inspired account from the
late 1970s of No. 7, but the collector
who needs a sensible, finely-wrought
view of the cycle need look no further.

Butterworth, George
(1885–1916)

The Banks of Green Willow (idyll).
*** Decca DPA 627/8 [KDPC].
ASMF, Marriner – *Concert of
English music.****

Butterworth's *Banks of Green Willow*,
like his *Shropshire Lad* rhapsody, represents the English folk-song school at
its most captivatingly atmospheric. Marriner's performance is beautifully made
and enjoys vivid, wide-ranging recorded
quality. It is part of a highly desirable
anthology discussed under 'English
music' in the Concerts section below.

Chabrier, Emmanuel (1841–94)

España (rhapsody).
*** D G Heliodor 2548 029 [3348 029]. Warsaw Nat. PO, Semkow – *Concert.****
España; Marche joyeuse.
(*) C.f.P. CFP 40312 [TC-CFP]. Hallé Orch., Loughran – *Concert.*

The Warsaw performance of Chabrier's rhapsody is as zestful as anyone could want, a little brash but undoubtedly exhilarating. It is brilliantly recorded and is part of a highly successful concert of French, Russian and Spanish orchestral showpieces. Loughran's performances have plenty of life too, but *España* has not quite as much zip in Manchester as it unexpectedly finds in Warsaw.

Cherubini, Luigi (1760–1842)

Medea (opera): complete.
**(*) Everest 437/3. Callas, Scotto, Pirazzini, Giacommotti, Chorus and Orch. of La Scala, Milan, Serafin.

First given in 1797, Cherubini's *Medea* was an opera ahead of its time. As one registers from this fine performance, it directly influenced Beethoven in *Fidelio*; but since then, until Maria Callas appeared, it had long come to be regarded as merely an interesting historical curiosity. The musical invention may often be undistinguished – few Cherubini melodies are really memorable – but with a fire-eating actress of the calibre of Callas the story of Medea in desperation murdering her children makes a vivid experience. When she recorded this set she was at the very peak of her career, and only a few flapping wobbles mar a superlative performance. It is good too to find the young Renata Scotto so fresh and stylish in the role of Glauce. The rest of the singing is much less distinguished, and documentation is limited to a brief synopsis of the plot. The sound is not quite so free on top as in other more expensive pressings, but the voices sound well and the stereo perspective is clean and undistracting.

Chopin, Frédéric (1810–49)

Piano concerto No. 1 in E minor, Op. 11; Krakowiak (concert rondo), *Op. 14.*
*(*) D G Heliodor 2548 066 [3348 066]. Askenase, Hague Residentie Orch., Otterloo.

Stefan Askenase offers good value, though there is a certain pallor about his playing. It is refined, stylish and neat but he is not strongly characterful. However, he is well served by the Hague Residentie Orchestra under Willem van Otterloo (and by the D G engineers). The sound is still remarkably fresh for its period and there is a nice, aristocratic feel to the solo playing. The tape transfer is of excellent quality. One must not forget, however, that Pollini's classic recording of the concerto is available on HMV at medium price. It offers playing of such total spontaneity, poetic feeling and refined judgement that criticism is silenced. It was given a rosette in the *Penguin Stereo Record Guide* (SXLP 30160 [TC-SXLP]).

CHOPIN

Piano concerto No. 2 in F minor, Op. 21; Polonaises Nos. 3 in A major, Op. 40/1; 6 in A flat major, Op. 53.
*(*) D G Heliodor 2548 124 [3348 124]. Askenase, Berlin PO, Ludwig.

Askenase's playing seems somewhat slack and lacking in character. His sensibility asserts itself in the slow movement, but in the last analysis this cannot be strongly recommended, even at Heliodor price; the *Polonaises* which act as a filler are disappointing too. The recording is well balanced, and the tape transfer is of first-rate quality, fresh, natural and with excellent piano tone.

PIANO MUSIC

Andante spianato and Grande polonaise brillante in E flat major, Op. 22; Ballades Nos. 1–4; Barcarolle, Op. 60; Berceuse, Op. 57; Boléro, Op. 19; Fantaisie, Op. 49; Impromptus Nos. 1–3; Fantaisie-impromptu, Op. 66; Mazurkas Nos. 1–51; Nocturnes Nos. 1–19; 3 Nouvelles études; Polonaises Nos. 1–7; Scherzi Nos. 1–4; Sonatas Nos. 2 and 3; Tarantelle, Op. 43; Waltzes Nos. 1–14.
**(*) RCA SER 5692 (12 discs). Rubinstein.

Rubinstein and Chopin are so closely identified that there seems little need to plead the claims of this anthology, surely one of the cornerstones of any Chopin collection. True, it is not entirely comprehensive: the *Preludes* and the *Studies* are not included, and Rubinstein's recordings of the two concertos are available separately (at medium price: RCA DPS 2034). His playing has unique authority, panache and imaginative flair, and many of the performances in this collection are inspired. The *Mazurkas* do not perhaps always eclipse memories of his superb set of 78s, made before the Second World War; their freshness and poetry remain incomparable. In the *Nocturnes* one admires Rubinstein's magical feeling for nuance and the inevitability of his rubato: the listener is left with the sense that there is no other way in which the rhythm could be inflected or a phrase shaped. The *Ballades* have tremendous fire and brilliance, and the *Polonaises* too have a virtuosity, freshness and control that put them almost in a class of their own. Nor is it likely that these accounts of the two mature sonatas will be surpassed in the recording studios, even if there are poetic details in other readings that move one more deeply. Supreme artist though he is, Rubinstein does not always convey the anguish that lies beneath the surface poetry of Chopin's art. The *Scherzi*, however, are stunning. The recordings are variable in quality: the *Nocturnes*, for example, are a good deal warmer than the *Ballades* (and much else in this compilation) where the tone is hard and shallow. However, this reservation should deter no one from acquiring this distinguished set.

Études, Op. 10/1–12; Op. 25/1–12.
*(**) Everest 3387. Ashkenazy.

These impressive performances were once available on Melodiya imports and on the French Chant du Monde label. The playing has enormous freshness and electricity, and in terms of dash and spontaneity is to be preferred to Ashkenazy's full-price Decca set. The recorded sound may be shallow and unpleasing – it was never distinguished – and the Op. 10 may reproduce slightly sharp; but this is well worth tolerating for the sake of some electrifying and poetic playing.

34

Études, Op. 10/1–12; Op. 25/1–12; Waltzes Nos. 1–19.
**(*) DG 2721 208 (2 discs).
    Vásáry.

In this price range Tamás Vásáry's set of the Opp. 10 and 25 *Studies* coupled with his *Waltzes* makes a most attractive proposition. He is an elegant pianist whose art is unfailingly instinctive yet disciplined by a fine musical judgement. Individual studies may be more strongly characterized by Pollini (at full price) or Ashkenazy, but Vásáry's playing is invariably fresh and conveys vivid musical feeling. He is authoritative and is particularly successful in the more reflective, thoughtful pieces, though there is no lack of brilliance elsewhere. The quality of the recorded sound is a shade wanting in bloom and richness, but this should not preclude a recommendation. We have perhaps underrated this set of *Études* in the past.

24 Preludes, Op. 28.
    (*) RCA Camden ccv 5003 [c4].
    Brailowsky.
24 Preludes, Op. 28; Prelude No. 25 in C sharp minor, Op. 45.
    * C.f.P. cfp 40284. Kerer.

Rudolph Kerer's record derives from the Melodiya catalogue. There are many musicianly touches that command admiration, but ultimately the reading falls short of the distinction and sensitivity that would justify its preservation in the recording studio. Poetic insight and imagination are of the essence in this repertoire, and there are many performances on and off record that have more of both. Alas, Alexander Brailowsky's is not one of them. He made this RCA recording (it is in 'stereo-enhanced' mono) at the end of his career when his technique was crumbling, and although his assumption of the grand manner is at times rather engaging, he

has too little that is memorable to say in the more lyrical music to compensate for the fluffs in the more demanding bravura passages. He is best remembered by his 78 r.p.m. records, some of which were outstanding.

Piano sonata No. 2 in B flat minor (Funeral march), Op. 35; Études, Op. 10, Nos. 3 in E major; 4 in C sharp minor; Impromptu No. 1 in A flat major, Op. 29; Nocturnes Nos. 2 in E flat major, Op. 9/2; 15 in F minor, Op. 55/1.
    **(*) RCA (m) vh 002. Horowitz.

Authoritative and electrifying performances from Horowitz. The main work here is the *B flat minor Sonata*, recorded in 1950 and sounding remarkably good for its age. Whatever one may think, this reading has outsize personality, even if its nervous tension may prove too much for some tastes. Yet Horowitz's lyricism is always intensely felt and highly personal, and his *Nocturnes*, recorded in the early 1950s, sing eloquently. The *Études* come from 1949 and 1936 respectively and have poise and inner fire.

Waltzes Nos. 1–14.
    *** DG Heliodor 2548 146 [3348 146]. Askenase.

Askenase's set offers playing of the utmost distinction. These performances show a most natural rubato, every bar illuminated by Askenase's natural feeling for the Chopin line and phrase. The extrovert waltzes have a sparkling precision, while the more intimate pieces have an unmatched poetic sensibility. Yet the playing is not introvert but outgiving, making a direct contact with the listener. Do not judge the recording quality by the opening *Waltz in A flat*, which sounds rather dry in timbre. The sound (both on tape and on disc) is not especially rich but it is clear and natural, and the ear can soon adjust to the lack of resonance when the playing is so masterly.

Collections

Andante spianato and Grande polonaise brillante in E flat major, Op. 22; Ballade No. 4 in F minor, Op. 52; Barcarolle in F sharp major, Op. 60; Polonaise (Fantaisie) in A flat major, Op. 61.
　　**(*) RCA (m) VH 008. Horowitz.

Classic accounts of Chopin, full of personality and nervous tension. The *Andante spianato* comes from 1945 and is a dazzling example of fiendish virtuosity. The *Polonaise Fantaisie* was recorded at a public performance in 1951 and has all the electricity of a live occasion, which offsets the odd miscalculation. The *Ballade* is wonderfully impressive and powerful, and the *Barcarolle*, the latest of the recordings, dating from 1957, has a searching, inward poetry that haunts the listener long after the turntable has come to a stop. Needless to say, the recorded sound betrays some shallowness, but the RCA engineers have done their best to refurbish it.

Ballade No. 1 in G minor, Op. 23; Mazurka in C sharp minor, Op. 30/4; Nocturnes: in F sharp major, Op. 15/2; in C sharp minor, Op. 27/1; Polonaise No. 6 in A flat major, Op. 53; Scherzo No. 1 in B minor, Op. 20; Waltz in A minor, Op. 34/2.
　　*** RCA (m) VH 011. Horowitz.

More stunning performances from Horowitz. The *B minor Scherzo* comes from 1950 and is breathtaking: a long-

treasured item in its early mono LP, it sounds smoother and slightly less clangorous in this new RCA transfer. As Chopin-playing it may seem too overwhelming to some listeners, for its dramatic brilliance is larger than life; but as piano-playing it is simply dazzling. The *G minor Ballade* is passionate, strongly characterized and full of aristocratic finesse, but the recording (from 1947) is, of course, a little wanting in body and bloom (to put it mildly). The *C sharp minor Mazurka* is a pre-war recording; most of the other performances date from the late 1940s. One distinguished critic wrote of these shorter pieces that Horowitz 'makes the music his own', and it is difficult to imagine any dissenting voice. A wonderful record.

Ballade No. 3 in A flat major, Op. 45; Études, Op. 10; Nos. 1 in C major; 12 in C minor (Revolutionary); Polonaise (Fantaisie) in A flat major, Op. 61.
　　(*) DG Heliodor 2548 223. Richter – DEBUSSY: *Estampes* etc.*

Sviatoslav Richter's Chopin recital (recorded at a public concert) opens with a wonderfully poetic account of the *Polonaise Fantaisie*, played with complete spontaneity and freshness. The *Étude in C major* which follows has rather too many accents, and the passagework is not especially clear, but the *Revolutionary study* is full of fervour (although there are some background noises), and the *Ballade* has a convincing individuality. The recording is rather dry, but at Heliodor price this disc is essential.

Ballade No. 3 in A flat major, Op. 47; Fantaisie-impromptu in C sharp minor, Op. 66; Impromptus Nos. 1 in A flat major, Op. 29; 2 in F sharp

major, Op. 36; 3 in G flat major, Op. 51; Mazurkas, Op. 41: Nos. 1 in C sharp minor; 2 in E minor; 3 in B major; 4 in A flat major; Scherzo No. 3 in C sharp minor, Op. 39.
  *** D G Heliodor 2548 215 [3348 215]. Askenase.

This is marvellously positive playing, full of personality and character. The recording too is bold and full, better than many of DG's more recent (and more expensive) piano recordings. Askenase always compels the attention, and his vigorous romantic style here makes a most attractive recital. The tape transfer is very good, offering a natural piano image, full and well balanced rather than especially brilliant.

Ballade No. 3 in A flat major, Op. 47; Mazurka in B flat minor, Op. 24/4; Nocturnes: in B major, Op. 9/3; in F major, Op. 15/1; in E minor, Op. 72; Scherzi Nos. 2 in B flat minor, Op. 31; 3 in C sharp minor, Op. 39.
  *** RCA (m) VH 018. Horowitz.

Horowitz's demonic virtuosity is so dazzling that it often blinds listeners to his sense of vision and poetic insight. This anthology offers some seemingly effortless brilliance allied to playing of the greatest delicacy and tenderness. The *B flat minor Scherzo*, recorded in 1958, is particularly impressive: the very opening figure does not bark urgently, as it so often can in insensitive hands, nor is the piece played at breakneck speed. Indeed, there is no playing to the gallery: every phrase is beautifully articulated and there is some magical lyricism. The *Nocturnes* that complete side one also come from the 1950s, one of them from a Carnegie Hall recital of 1953, and show exceptional range of tone-colour and great emotional eloquence. Perhaps the *C sharp minor Scherzo*

is a shade overdriven, but the *Ballade* (the earliest recording here, dating from 1949) and the *Mazurka* are masterly. There is some audience noise in the latter, and the sound is a little shallow by modern standards. But playing of this order is no everyday phenomenon and criticism must be silenced.

Barcarolle in F sharp major, Op. 60; Berceuse in D flat major, Op. 57; Fantaisie-impromptu in C sharp minor, Op. 66; Polonaise No. 3 in A major, Op. 40/1; Scherzo No. 2 in B flat minor, Op. 31; Waltzes Nos. 1 in E flat major. (Grande valse brillante), Op. 18; 3 in A minor, Op. 34/2; 14 in E minor, Op. posth.
  *(*) D G Heliodor 2548 276 [3348 276]. Askenase.

Askenase is at his best here in the *Berceuse* and the *Waltzes*; the *Grande valse brillante* is especially good. Elsewhere the effect of the music-making is less magical (the opening *Polonaise in A major* seems to lack grandeur), but the pianist is not helped by the dry recording, clear but rather lacking in timbre and inner colour.

'Favourite composer': (i) *Ballade No. 3 in A flat major, Op. 47; Barcarolle in F sharp major, Op. 60; Berceuse in D flat major, Op. 57;* (ii) *Études, Op. 10, Nos. 3 in E major; 5 in G flat major; Op. 25, Nos 1 in A flat major; 2 in F minor; 9 in B flat major;* (i) *Fantaisie-impromptu in C sharp minor, Op. 66; Impromptu No. 1 in A flat major, Op. 29;* (iii) *Mazurka No. 23 in D major, Op. 33/2;* (iv) *Nocturnes Nos. 2 in E flat major, Op. 9/2; 5 in F sharp major, Op. 15/2; 8 in D flat major, Op. 27/2; Polonaises Nos.* (v) *3 in A major, Op. 40/1;* (vi) *6 in A*

flat major, Op. 53; (vii) Prelude No. 15 in D flat major (Raindrop), Op. 28; (i) Piano sonata No. 2 in B flat minor (Funeral march), Op. 35; Scherzo No. 3 in C sharp minor, Op. 39; (iv) Waltzes Nos. 1 in E flat major (Grande valse brillante), Op. 18; 6 in D flat major (Minute); 7 in C sharp minor, Op. 64/1 and 2; 11 in G flat major, Op. 70/1.
** Decca DPA 563/4 [KDPC]. (i) Kempff; (ii) Backhaus; (iii) Magaloff; (iv) Katin; (v) Vered; (vi) Katchen; (vii) Gulda.

This is certainly a formidable set of Chopin favourites, but it is less attractive as a collection than some others in the *Favourite composer* series. The music is not laid out in the order above but in well-arranged groups. The first disc is given over to the distinctive but not always idiomatic playing of Kempff, and is let down a little by the piano recording, which in terms of colour has a certain pallor. The sound immediately perks up on side three with the performances by Peter Katin of some of the *Nocturnes*, and one is surprised to find that these are not true stereo, but transcriptions from mono. The uninformed ear would be easily taken in. Side four includes Ilana Vered's *Polonaise in A major*, and a selection of *Waltzes* nicely played by Katin, and here the recording is excellent. The quality is almost indistinguishable on disc and cassette.

Cimarosa, Domenico (1749–1801)

Oboe concerto in C minor (arr. Benjamin).
*** Pye GSGC 15011. Rothwell,

PA Orch., Barbirolli – ALBINONI and MARCELLO: *Concertos.***

This enchanting concerto, arranged by Arthur Benjamin from four single-movement keyboard sonatas, was given a quite ideal performance and recording by Evelyn Rothwell and her husband. The pastoral opening theme is phrased exquisitely, and after the gentle allegro which follows, the beautiful flowing Siciliana is played with a wonderful combination of affection and style. The gently rollicking finale is again caught to perfection, with Sir John sensitive to his wife's mood in every bar. The recording is excellently judged in matters of balance and tone. This is perhaps the most successful of all the six oboe concertos recorded by this memorable partnership.

Clementi, Muzio (1752–1832)

Piano sonatas: in F minor, Op. 14/3; in F sharp minor, Op. 26; in G minor, Op. 34/2.
⊛*** RCA (m) VH 007. Horowitz.

Masterly accounts of all three sonatas. Horowitz emphasizes their dramatic power and formal coherence, and they emerge as strongly prophetic of middle-period Beethoven. Composed during the 1780s, they embody the dark passionate intensity of the *Sturm und Drang* movement, and forge something of a link between Haydn and C. P. E. Bach on the one hand and Beethoven on the other. Rarely can these sonatas have enjoyed more committed and powerful advocacy than they do here. In terms of keyboard presence and sheer artistry, these performances are unlikely to be approached, particularly in view of the current preoccupation with period instruments. The recording dates from the mid-1950s and is a bit restricted in range, but this should not inhibit anyone from investigating repertoire of unusual interest in the hands of one of the very greatest keyboard executants. An indispensable issue, and a 'must' for all collections, large or small.

Coates, Eric
(1886–1958)

By the Sleepy Lagoon. Marches: The Dambusters; Knightsbridge (from *London suite*).
   *** H M V 45 r.p.m. H M V 1. Royal Liverpool P O, Groves – ELGAR: *Marches*.***

Sir Charles Groves and the Liverpool orchestra are on top form here; the march performances have splendid vigour and the waltz makes an attractive interlude between them. The recording is first-class – the combination of weight and brilliance at the end of the famous *In Town Tonight* march is very effective indeed.

Copland, Aaron
(born 1900)

Appalachian Spring (ballet).
   ** Everest 3002. L S O, Susskind – GOULD: *Spirituals*.

The restoration to the catalogue of this excellent record from the early days of stereo is most welcome. It still sounds astonishingly vivid. Although it is a

domestically made recording the American-style engineering, with a brightly lit upper range and wide dynamics, gives a touch of brashness to the sound. But with a slight treble cut it can be made to sound smoother without losing any of its impact and detail. Susskind's reading is both dramatic and sympathetic, and above all spontaneous. The unfolding of the Shaker variations is managed with affecting simplicity. With its attractive coupling, equally well done, this is worth investigating. However, our review copy had indifferent surfaces.

Billy the Kid (ballet): *suite; Statements for orchestra.*
   **(*) Everest 3015. L S O, the composer.

Copland's own coupling of *Billy the Kid* and *Statements for orchestra* is less successfully recorded than his other two Everest records of the mid-sixties. In fortissimos the focus tends to blur a little, and there is some minor distortion in *Statements*, although it is never serious enough to prevent the argument of the music from registering vividly. *Statements* is a major work, otherwise unrepresented in the catalogue. It was written between 1933 and 1935 for the Minneapolis Symphony Orchestra but did not receive its first complete performance until 1942, when it was premiered by the New York Philharmonic under Mitropoulos. In six terse movements, each subtitled, it is less obviously popular in style than the ballet, yet the music has an immediate communicative force. Particularly memorable are the eloquent fourth *Subjective* statement, the quirky following *Jingo* (somewhere between Shostakovich and Morton Gould in flavour), and the *Prophetic* finale with its enigmatic closing stroke on the tam-tam. The LSO plays with force and commitment throughout and is in equally good form in *Billy the Kid*, entering fully into the spirit of the gun battle and producing colourful wind solos. The recording, forwardly balanced, gives plenty of impact.

Symphony No. 3.
(*) Everest 3018. LSO, the composer.

Copland's first recording of his splendid *Third Symphony* was originally issued in the UK in the mid-sixties by World Record Club. Now it has reverted to its source label, Everest. It was always a good recording, slightly pungent, but not ineffectively so, with a resonant ambience, which the slow movement demands and which is essential in an expansive finale that draws on the famous *Fanfare for the Common Man* for its source material. The work opens with the same simple identification with the American soil that makes *Appalachian Spring* so memorable. Copland also marks the folk-like trio of the second movement *cantando semplice*, and his approach to the work as a whole is to convey a sense of expressive force without inflation. The LSO supports him with thoroughly committed playing, and if they are less polished in the scherzo than the Philharmonia Orchestra, which Copland used for his 1979 re-recording for CBS (mid-price: 61869), there is no lack of thrust, nor of repose in the fine slow movement. The finale has rather more breadth and gravitas on CBS, but by any standards this earlier record remains highly rewarding, and it provides an excellent introduction to a twentieth-century masterpiece.

Corelli, Arcangelo (1653–1713)

Oboe concerto (arr. Barbirolli).
*** Pye GSGC 15034. Rothwell, Hallé Orch., Barbirolli – HAYDN and PERGOLESI: *Concertos.****

Barbirolli's concerto is cunningly arranged from a trio sonata, and in its new form it makes one of the most enchanting works in the whole oboe repertoire. The performance here is treasurable. The opening, with its beautiful Handelian theme, is shaped with perfect dignity, and the gracious, stately allegro that follows has a touch of gossamer from the soloist. The perky finale is no less delectable, and the clean, clear recording projects the music admirably.

Debussy, Claude (1862–1918)

Images: Ibéria (only). *La Mer.*
⊛*** RCA Victrola (m) AT 111. NBC SO, Toscanini.

Ibéria is thrilling here in its rhythmic tautness and vitality; the only reservation concerns *Les parfums de la nuit*, which could afford to be more languorous and relaxed. (The version Toscanini recorded with the Philadelphia Orchestra during his 1941–2 season there is better in this respect, though the NBC sound is better focused.) Three Toscanini performances of *La Mer* survive, a 1940 NBC broadcast, a version with the Philadelphia Orchestra, and the present issue, made in 1950. All of them are atmospheric and powerful, but this is perhaps the most dramatic and inspired.

Never has the sea been whipped into such a demonic frenzy as in the *Dialogue du vent et de la mer*, whose spray almost drenches one. RCA have done wonders for the recorded sound. This is one of the classics of the gramophone, and an indispensable disc.

'Favourite composer': (i) *Images: Ibéria* (only). *La Mer.* (i; ii) *Nocturnes.* (i) *Prélude à l'après-midi d'un faune.* (iii) *Images: Reflets dans l'eau. L'Isle joyeuse.* (iv) *Petite suite: En bateau. Préludes, Book 1:* (v) *La fille aux cheveux de lin;* (vi) *La cathédrale engloutie.* (v) *Suite bergamasque: Clair de lune.*
** Decca DPA 619/20 [KDPC]. (i) Suisse Rom. Orch., Ansermet; (ii) with female chorus; (iii) Gulda; (iv) Eden, Tamir; (v) Joseph Cooper; (vi) Kars.

This compilation, which includes Ansermet's *La Mer, Ibéria* and the *Nocturnes*, is an attractive one, for although the SRO is not the finest of orchestras Ansermet's readings will not fail to give pleasure. The version of *La Mer* included here, however, is the 1965 recording (as distinct from the second, 1957 account), and the intonation (in the horns, for instance, and the cor anglais and cello melody in *De l'aube à midi*) is sometimes less than impressive, although the orchestral sound is faithfully captured by the more modern and sophisticated microphones. The piano music on the second disc is all well played. The opening *En bateau* (from the *Petite suite*), heard in its original piano duet version, is highly engaging, and the two Gulda performances, although impulsive, are full of character. The recording throughout is vivid and well detailed and the range of the tape transfer is impressive, with the percussive transients strikingly crisp.

La Mer.
*(*) RCA Camden CCV 5039 [c4]. Boston SO, Munch – RAVEL: *Rapsodie espagnole.**(*)
La Mer; Prélude à l'après-midi d'un faune.
* C.f.P. CFP 40231. LPO, Handley – FAURÉ: *Masques et bergamasques; Pavane.***

Munch secures playing of the highest efficiency and virtuosity from the Boston orchestra, but his reading of *La Mer* is a shade hard-driven. Atmosphere and sensitivity are not greatly in evidence, though the quality of the RCA recording is not as refined or sympathetic as in Munch's *Daphnis et Chloé*, also made in the mid-1950s. The sound tends to coarsen in climaxes, and in spite of the brilliant playing from this aristocrat of orchestras this account does not have strong appeal.

Vernon Handley's performances, though atmospherically recorded, are not really distinguished enough to merit a recommendation, even at bargain price, although the Fauré coupling is much more successful. One must not forget that at medium price Karajan's splendid 1965 recording of *La Mer* and *L'après-midi* is available on DG Accolade 2542 116 [3342 116], coupled to Ravel's *Boléro*, while Giulini's Philharmonia recording of *La Mer*, coupled to the three *Nocturnes*, is on HMV Concert Classics: SXLP 30146 [TC-SXLP].

Piano music

Estampes; Préludes, Book 1: 2, Voiles; 3, Le vent dans la plaine; 5, Les collines d'Anacapri.
*** DG Heliodor 2548 223. Richter – CHOPIN: *Ballade No. 3 etc.***(*)

Richter's recital offers wonderful Debussy playing, subtly characterized, the spontaneity of a live performance entirely compensating for the few audience noises. The recording itself is on the dry side, but there is no lack of brilliance, witness the glittering close of *Les collines d'Anacapri*. This inexpensive record offers masterly performances: try the magical *Jardins sous la pluie* or the gentle exoticism of *Pagodes*. Richter's complete recording of Book 2 of the *Préludes* is available at medium price on Turnabout (TVS 34360 [KTVC]).

Préludes, Book 1: 1, Danseuses de Delphes; 2, Voiles; 3, Le vent dans la plaine; 5, Les collines d'Anacapri; 8, La fille aux cheveux de lin; 9, La sérénade interrompue; 10, La cathédrale engloutie; 11, La danse de Puck; Book 2: 3, La puerta del vino; 4, Les fées sont d'exquises danseuses; 6, General Lavine – eccentric; 7, La terrasse des audiences; 8, Ondine; 9, Hommage à S. Pickwick Esq. P.P.M.P.C.; 11, Les tierces alternées; 12, Feux d'artifice.
   **(*) DG Heliodor 2548 285 [3348 285]. Haas.

Monique Haas's collections of *Préludes* is generous, with eight items from each book, and this is likely to prove an attractive anthology for those with a limited budget. Refined classical playing, well if somewhat dryly recorded; Monique Haas is a trifle cool, perhaps – she is not so imaginative or atmospheric as Richter – but eminently sound and recommendable. The more extrovert items come off especially well: *La cathédrale engloutie* is vividly imaginative, and *Feux d'artifice* really sparkles. Like the disc, the cassette offers clean, clear piano timbre.

Delibes, Léo (1836–91)

Coppélia (ballet): complete.
   **(*) Decca DPA 581/2 [(***) KDPC 2 7045]. Suisse Rom. Orch., Ansermet.

Delibes's masterpiece makes admirable gramophone listening. *Coppélia* in the theatre gives the impression of an unending succession of colour and memorable tunes. Tchaikovsky admired the score, and rightly so, for it has not a dull bar. Ansermet's classic recording emerges with astonishing freshness in this very successful reissue.

Ansermet's authoritative hand is always apparent, and his power of evocation (especially in the first scenes of Act 2) makes some delightful effects. The *Dance of the Automatons* sparkles like a musical-box, and the passage where Swanhilda pretends to be Coppélia coming to life and dances her stiff little waltz is pointed with loving care. The *Divertissement* is brilliantly played. One must accept the French quality of the woodwind, but the recording is very good, and this set will give much pleasure. The cassette transfer is poorly managed. The strings are dry and lustreless and there is some congestion in Act 1, where the bass drum muddies the orchestral texture.

Coppélia (ballet): suite; *Sylvia* (ballet): suite.
   *(*) RCA Camden CCV 5030 [c4]. Boston SO, Monteux.

Monteux conducted for Diaghilev, and he knew just how to bring the sparkle to the eyes and the bloom to the cheeks of Delibes's prettiest ballet music. He points the *Valse de la poupée* in *Coppélia* deliciously and there is plenty of vigour in the lively music for the corps de ballet. In *Sylvia* the *Intermezzo* and *Valse lente* are played gently, with tender warmth. All this music comes over well, but the recording, which is very reverberant, blurs the moments of orchestral spectacle, especially the *Prélude* and *Cortège de Bacchus* in *Sylvia*, which seriously lack bite and crispness of outline. On Decca SPA 314 an excellent selection from Ansermet's complete *Coppélia* is coupled to an equally vivacious suite from *Sylvia*, and this is a much better buy at medium price, but the equivalent cassette is not recommended because of transfer problems.

La Source (ballet): *Act 2* (complete).
*** C.f.P. CFP 40298. ROHCGO, Mackerras – MESSAGER: *Deux Pigeons.****

La Source (1866) was the ballet score that established Delibes's reputation. It was written in collaboration with Leon Minkus (each supplied half the music), and the success of Delibes's contribution was immediately obvious. He wrote Act 2 (as included here) and the first part of Act 3, and was to use these sections again (with more music added) for a later ballet called *Naïla*. The music is characterful and tuneful, often reflecting the oriental background of the story. The scoring, with colourful woodwind, crisp brass and swirling strings, is marvellous, and Mackerras is just the man for it. He secures sparkling playing from the Covent Garden Orchestra and directs with consistent panache. The recording, made in the mid-sixties, is fresh and clean, with a vivid palette and a fine bite from the brass.

Delius, Frederick (1862–1934)

Fennimore and Gerda: Intermezzo; Irmelin: Prelude; Koanga: La Calinda (arr. Fenby); *On Hearing the First Cuckoo in Spring; Sleigh Ride; A Song before Sunrise; Summer Night on the River; A Village Romeo and Juliet: The Walk to the Paradise Garden* (arr. Beecham).
*** C.f.P. CFP 40304 [TC-CFP]. LPO, Handley.

All Delius conductors are haunted by the ghost of Beecham, whose close identification with the composer has deterred challenging batons. While his readings remain an indispensable cornerstone for any library, it is good to welcome more up-to-date recordings. Recent anthologies by Norman Del Mar and Neville Marriner have won much acclaim but are at full price. Here Vernon Handley covers much the same ground as Marriner (though he throws in the *Irmelin Prelude* for good measure), while there is also duplication with Del Mar. Some collectors may find Handley's *Walk to the Paradise Garden* a little overheated in sentiment; but, generally speaking, this is a successful anthology, with expansive and imaginative phrasing, and the LPO responds with some fine wind playing. The quality of the recorded sound is admirable; the acoustic is appropriately warm and open, while the engineers succeed in meeting the diverse claims of tonal homogeneity and clarity of texture. At times the wind seem a trifle too close, but there need be no serious reservation on technical grounds. The tape transfer is as successful as the disc, clear in detail with plenty of warmth and body and offering complete security from background rustles and clicks. Although this collection falls short of the special distinction Beecham brought to this repertoire, it can be recommended with confidence.

It can be happily supplemented at medium price with HMV's splendidly recorded Beecham/ RPO Concert Classics reissue including the *Florida suite* (a delightful early work dating from 1886), the *Dance rhapsody No. 2* and *Over the Hills and Far Away*: SXLP 30415 [TC-SXLP].

Donizetti, Gaetano
(1797–1848)

Lucia di Lammermoor (opera): complete.
**(*) Everest S 439/2. Scotto, Di Stefano, Bastianini, Vinco, Ricciardi, Malagu, Chorus and Orch. of La Scala, Milan, Sanzogno.

On four well-filled sides this performance of *Lucia di Lammermoor* from La Scala follows the stage text with normal cuts. The cast is an outstanding one, with Scotto in the first flush of freshness. This is a youthful heroine, and though the coloratura is not always elegant and some top notes are raw, she is no less moving for being a little gauche. The playing under Sanzogno is at times unpolished, but there is plenty of dramatic fire. Giuseppe di Stefano was still at the peak of his career when the recording was made; his legato is never ideally smooth, but this is a superbly characterful voice used with great flair. At the period Bastianini too was in superb voice, and the recording is attractively bright, clean and forward, though surfaces can be noisy. The minimal notes on the back of the box disagree with the record labels in detailing which act is which.

Sutherland's first 1961 complete recording of the role of Lucia is, of course, also available at medium price (Decca Ace of Diamonds GOS 663/5), but bargain-hunters might like to consider supplementing the Scotto version with Sutherland's début recording of the Mad scene, which was first issued in November 1969, and which she did not surpass later in either of her complete recordings of that opera. In fact this disc (which includes arias from *Linda di Chamounix*, Verdi's *Ernani* and *I Vespri siciliani*) must be set on a pedestal as one of the finest and most thrilling displays of coloratura ever recorded (Decca Jubilee JB 97 [KJBC]).

Other medium-priced recordings of Donizetti include a good DG Privilege set of *Don Pasquale* (2709 039 – 2 discs), which is strongly cast, although none of the singers is a star name. The recording is faithful if not especially atmospheric, but the conductor, Ettore Gracis, misses the kind of sparkle that is needed to bring this delightful opera fully to life. However, there is no lack of sparkle in Decca's first stereo set of *L'Elisir d'amore*, which dates from the mid-fifties. With Hilde Gueden at her most seductive and Giuseppe di Stefano's contribution headily sweet-toned, this version brings out all the charm of Donizetti's comic masterpiece. Capecchi as Belcore and Corena as Dulcamara are both splendid, and Molinari-Pradelli finds the lightness of touch that eludes Gracis in *Don Pasquale*. Fitted on to two discs (Ace of Diamonds GOS 566/7), this set, still sounding well, is good value by any reasonable standards.

Dukas, Paul
(1865–1935)

L'Apprenti sorcier (The Sorcerer's Apprentice).

** C.f.P. CFP 40312 [TC-CFP].
Hallé Orch., Loughran – *Concert.***
** RCA Camden CCV 5031 [c4].
Boston SO, Munch – IBERT:
*Escales***; RAVEL: *Boléro*
etc.*(*)

The obvious recommendation for *The Sorcerer's Apprentice* is Ansermet's 1964 Decca recording. The performance is slightly relaxed but has a fine cumulative effect, and if the recording lacks the last degree of brilliance it has plenty of atmosphere. This is available on a splendid medium-priced Jubilee disc (and cassette), coupled with Honegger's *Pacific 231* and recommendable performances of Ravel's *Boléro* and *La Valse*: JB 36 [KJBC]. Ansermet's version is also included in a marginally less expensive Decca collection called '*Danse macabre*' together with other colourful genre pieces, the rest of the programme being conducted by Sir Alexander Gibson (SPA 175).

Munch's account is in the cheapest price bracket, and at the bargain end of the catalogue it is highly competitive, especially if one considers the unusual coupling of Ibert's evocative *Escales*. The remastered cassette offers acceptable sound, although the dynamic range is not impressively wide and the work's climax lacks impact and brilliance. Loughran is much better recorded, and his performance is also a good one, if lacking the last degree of flair. The rest of his programme is attractive (see the Concerts section below).

Dvořák, Antonin
(1841–1904)

'*Favourite composer*': (i; ii) *Carnaval overture, Op. 92; Scherzo capric-*

cioso, Op. 66; (iii; iv) *Serenade for strings in E major, Op. 22;* (v; vi) *Slavonic dances Nos. 1 in C major; 8 in G minor, Op. 46/1 and 8; 10 in E minor, Op. 72/2;* (v; ii) *Symphony No. 9 in E minor (From the New World), Op. 95;* (vii) *Rusalka: Invocation to the moon.*
*** Decca DPA 539/40 [KDPC].
(i) LSO; (ii) Kertesz; (iii) Israel PO; (iv) Kubelik; (v) Vienna PO; (vi) Reiner; (vii) Lorengar.

In every way this is an outstanding set, by any possible standards a bargain. We are offered Kertesz's splendid LSO performances of the *Carnaval overture* and the *Scherzo capriccioso* (the latter unsurpassed in the present catalogue), together with his excellent 1961 VPO version of the *New World symphony*. Kubelik's account of the *String serenade* relies on virility rather than charm to make its appeal, but it is certainly splendidly alive and brilliantly recorded. Reiner's *Slavonic dances* are also given plenty of projection by the engineers, and his readings are polished and sparkling. Pilar Lorengar's *Invocation to the moon* from *Rusalka* makes a welcome sampler of Dvořák as an operatic composer. On the cassettes (which are also technically very successful) the symphony is given a whole side to itself, and thus can be listened to without a break in continuity.

Serenade for strings in E major, Op. 22.
** DG Heliodor 2548 121 [3348 121]. North German RO, Schmidt-Isserstedt – TCHAIKOVSKY: *String serenade.***

A lyrical account of Dvořák's engaging *String serenade*, truthfully recorded. This was originally coupled to an indifferent account of the Brahms *Serenade No. 2* but it is now paired with an attractive account of the Tchaikovsky. The recording too is first-class, clean and clear, yet with no lack of body. The cassette transfer is well managed, although on tape the Tchaikovsky coupling is much less clear, although acceptable.

Slavonic dances Nos. 6 in D major; 7 in C minor; 8 in G minor, Op. 46/6–8; 9 in B major; 16 in A flat major, Op. 72/1 and 8.
(*) C.f.P. CFP 40290. Hallé Orch., Loughran – SMETANA: *Vltava* etc.(*)

Bright, vivacious performances with many affectionate touches, and they are strongly projected here by a vividly brilliant recording. The orchestral percussion makes a great impact, and at times one wishes the balance was slightly more reticent in this respect.

Symphonies Nos. 7–9; Scherzo capriccioso, Op. 66; Legends, Op. 59, Nos. 4, 6 and 7.
** Pye Collector GGCD 304 (2 discs). Hallé Orch., Barbirolli.

This set is published on only two discs, and with such long sides (up to 38 minutes in Symphony No. 7) the sound is hardly refined. But these are rich, spontaneous-sounding performances which will give great pleasure both to newcomers, attracted by an amazing bargain, and to committed Dvořákians, who will relish Barbirolli's unusual combination of expressiveness in detailed phrasing and strongly architectural control of longer spans. None of the performances is now available separately.

Symphony No. 7 in D minor, Op.

70; Slavonic rhapsody No. 3, Op. 45.
*** C.f.P. CFP 40314. LPO, Davison.

Davison's is a highly engaging performance of Dvořák's delightful *D minor Symphony*. He chooses fast tempi for the first three movements, but with warmly committed playing from the LPO the result is never forced or unfeeling. There are many felicitous touches of wind phrasing, and the conductor often demonstrates his sympathy for Dvořák's scoring. The finale, though less incisive, erupts infectiously, and with vivid yet atmospheric recording, naturally balanced, this is very attractive indeed. The record is made even more competitive by the vivacious account of the *Slavonic rhapsody* (which opens the disc), although the ear is conscious that this recording – made in 1979, whereas the symphony dates from 1974 – although brighter and clearer, is less agreeable in ambience, with sharper, less natural string timbre.

Symphony No. 8 in G major, Op. 88; Carnaval overture, Op. 92.
*(*) C.f.P. CFP 40303. LPO, Susskind.

This was one of the last recordings made by Walter Susskind before he died. It readily shows his qualities as a conductor, his care for detail, his ability to secure good orchestral balance and sympathetic phrasing. With excellent playing from the LPO there is a good deal to enjoy here, but the reading as a whole lacks spontaneity and forward thrust. The delightful scherzo is bland (when the woodwind echo the famous lyrical tune of the trio they sound curiously subdued). The finale generates more adrenalin, but even here the ebb and flow of tension are not wholly successful. The recording is excellent, clear but with an attractive degree of resonance and bloom. The overture is more satisfying. But with Karajan's performance of the symphony, somewhat idiosyncratic but richly expansive, available at medium price, splendidly recorded on Decca's Jubilee label (JB 71 [KJBC]) and generously coupled to Tchaikovsky's *Romeo and Juliet overture*, the Susskind issue cannot receive a very strong recommendation, in spite of its modest price.

Symphony No. 9 in E minor (From the New World), Op. 95.
**(*) RCA Victrola (m) AT 114. NBC SO, Toscanini.
Symphony No. 9; Carnaval overture, Op. 92.
** C.f.P. CFP 104 [TC-CFP]. Philharmonia Orch., Sawallisch.
*(*) RCA Camden CCV 5012 [c4]. Boston SO, Fiedler.

Toscanini's *New World* has long been famous – a yardstick against which later recordings have been judged. The triangle in the scherzo rings like an insistent electric bell, and the timpani is as hard as a board; but this is one of the most successful of the maestro's later NBC recordings, for it genuinely conveys the spontaneous vitality and energy which gave him a unique place in music over so many decades. The tempi tend to be fast, the manner more rigid than is common in Dvořák, but the result remains persuasive and always exciting. Despite the abrasive qualities the recording is more vivid than most given to this conductor.

Sawallisch's approach is straightforward, exciting, and without mannerisms. There is more poetry in the slow movement than he finds, but overall the orchestral playing is sensitive, and the conductor's conception consistent and well integrated. The stereo recording is excellent, and with a brilliant and idiomatic performance of *Carnaval* thrown in, this is among the best buys in the

lowest price-range. The cassette offers splendid sound to match the disc, with a wide dynamic range, plenty of body and warmth, yet no lack of brilliance and detail.

A strong, professional account from Fiedler, well played and brightly recorded, but with no special individuality. As so often happens in this coupling, the overture goes splendidly, with spontaneity and atmosphere.

String quartets Nos. 1–14; String quartet in F major: fragment; Waltzes, Op. 54/1 and 4.
*** DG 2740 117 (12 discs). Prague Qt.

This is not the first time that the Dvořák quartets have been recorded complete (they were previously available on Vox played by the Kohon Quartet), but it is undeniably the most successful. Dvořák's quartets span a longer period even than his symphonies; the first, in A major, Op. 2, was written as early as 1862, thus preceding *The Bells of Zlonice* by three years, while the last dates from 1895. The advantages of this collection are obvious and can be briefly stated: one is able to view the growth and development of an artistic personality, as well as his growing responsiveness to and mastery of the quartet medium. If you put one of the late quartets alongside the remarkable *D major String quartet* of 1869–70, a sprawling piece some seventy minutes long, and full of interesting things, his greater concentration becomes evident. Needless to say, the ideas encountered in this work, and its companion in B flat, lack the profile and presence of the mature master, though there are always imaginative and heart-warming episodes. The familiar Dvořák shines through in the *D minor Quartet*, Op. 34, and his quartet output after this (1877) is *terra cognita*. The Prague Quartet are

47

on the whole sympathetic advocates, though they are not the equal of the Smetana or Janáček Quartets during the 1960s. Nor is the recording always in the demonstration bracket, but it is still very good indeed, and it would be absurd to withhold a strong recommendation on either artistic or technical grounds. Indeed this is a splendid investment for any lover of Dvořák and/or chamber music.

Elgar, Edward
(1857–1934)

(i) *Chanson de matin; Chanson de nuit, Op. 15/1 and 2; Cockaigne overture, Op. 40;* (ii) *Pomp and Circumstance marches, Op. 39/1 and 4;* (i) *Serenade in E minor for strings, Op. 20.*
** C.f.P. CFP 40235 [Pye ZCCCB 654]. Weldon, (i) RPO; (ii) PA Orch.

This collection, well played and splendidly recorded, is well worth its modest price. The *Marches* lack something in gusto and the *Serenade* is rather under-characterized (it has more expressive depth than Weldon finds), but *Cockaigne* goes really well and the two *Chansons* are nicely shaped. Unexpectedly the cassette version is issued by Pye, with quite good transfers, well balanced, if lacking the last degree of sparkle.

'*Favourite composer*': (i) *Chanson de matin: Chanson de nuit, Op. 15/1 and 2;* (ii) *Introduction and allegro for strings, Op. 47;* (iii; iv) *Pomp and Circumstance marches, Op. 39/1–5;* (v) *Serenade for strings in E minor, Op. 20;* (iii; vi) *Variations*

on an original theme *(Enigma), Op. 36.*
**(*) Decca DPA 537/8 [KDPC]. (i) LPO, Boult; (ii) ASMF, Marriner; (iii) LSO; (iv) Bliss; (v) RPO, Cox; (vi) Monteux.

A successful set, with Bliss's *Pomp and Circumstance marches* and Monteux's *Enigma* the highlights. Boult's two *Chansons* are stereo transcriptions of good mono recordings, but they sound well, and the only performance here that is slightly under-characterized is the *Serenade*. The tape transfers are of very good quality indeed: the *Enigma variations* (complete on one side with the five *Pomp and Circumstance marches* on the reverse) sound freshly minted – in many ways the sound here (as elsewhere in this collection) is preferable to the equivalent disc. The *Chansons* lean heavily towards the right channel but the sound itself is excellent.

Cockaigne overture, Op. 40; Falstaff (symphonic study), *Op. 68.*
⊛*** C.f.P. CFP 40313 [TC-CFP]. LPO, Handley.

Vernon Handley directs a superb performance of *Falstaff*, one of Elgar's most difficult works, and the achievement is all the more remarkable because his tempi are unusually spacious (generally following the composer's markings), making the contrasted episodes more difficult to hold together. The playing of the LPO is warmly expressive and strongly rhythmic, and the recording is one of the finest to come from Classics for Pleasure. *Cockaigne* is also given a performance that is expansive yet never hangs fire. This is a richly enjoyable coupling, and the cassette transfer is of first-rate quality to match the disc closely.

Violin concerto in B minor, Op. 61.

**(*) C.f.P. CFP 40322. Bean, Royal Liverpool PO, Groves.

Hugh Bean offers us the only modern recording of the Elgar concerto on a bargain label. The medium-priced alternative recordings are by Albert Sammons (World Records SH 288) and the youthful Menuhin (HMV HLM 7107). They come from 1928 and 1933 respectively and their claims on Elgarians remain strong. Hugh Bean has not the outsize personality of his most eloquent rivals but there is much to be said for his playing. He studied with Albert Sammons and his reading has a nobility and reticence well attuned to this composer, and his selfless artistry is wholly dedicated to the music rather than to ego projection. The recording has great warmth and fidelity, and its perspective perhaps underlines the undramatic yet convincing view of the concerto Mr Bean gives. His version may not have the authority of Sammons, Heifetz or (at full price), Pinchas Zukerman, but given the up-to-date recorded sound and the excellence of Groves's support, it is well worth considering. Indeed, in the quieter, more reflective passages, Hugh Bean has something quite special to say.

(i) *Violoncello concerto in E minor, Op. 85; Elegy, Op. 58; In the South overture, Op. 50.*
*** C.f.P. CFP 40342 [TC–CFP].
(i) Robert Cohen; LPO, Del Mar.

(i) *Violoncello concerto in E minor, Op. 85. Variations on an original theme (Enigma), Op. 36.*
*(*) Pye GSGC 15005. Hallé Orch., Barbirolli, (i) with Navarra.

This C.f.P. disc and cassette at last provide a fully recommendable bargain version of Elgar's *Cello concerto*. The performance is strong and intense with steady tempi, the colouring more positive, less autumnal than usual, relating the work more closely to the *Second Symphony*. Del Mar's accompaniment underlines this impression and he also directs an exciting account of *In the South* (recorded in a single take), with the *Elegy* an eloquent bonus. The sound is excellent in both media.

André Navarra's is also a strong and firm view of the concerto and Barbirolli's early version of the *Enigma variations* is, as ever, rich and red-blooded. But the Pye recording now sounds its age, with a restricted range (in both works) and a degree of buzziness in the cello sound for the *Concerto*.

Introduction and allegro for strings, Op. 47; Variations on an original theme (Enigma), Op. 36.
** C.f.P. CFP 40022 [TC-CFP]. LPO, Boult

Boult's earlier stereo account of the *Enigma variations* dates from the 1960s. It is enjoyable enough but seems a little under-characterized. This is partly caused by the recording, which is vivid and clear but lacks inner warmth and atmosphere. This also affects the *Introduction and allegro*, which comes over as athletic and strong but lacking in expansive qualities, although it is effective enough in its way. The tape has been remastered and sounds splendid, clear and detailed, wide in range. It is if anything slightly fuller in sound than the disc.

Pomp and Circumstance marches Nos. 1 and 4, Op. 39.
*** HMV 45 r.p.m. HMV 1.

49

Royal Liverpool P O, Groves –
COATES: *Marches.****

This attractive compilation shows
H M V's 12-inch 45 r.p.m. disc format at
its most impressive. Groves's way with
Elgar's pomp and circumstance is genial,
perhaps somewhat phlegmatic but not
lacking a proper feel of pageantry. The
recording has striking brilliance and
weight and makes a splendid impact.
But one must remember Del Mar's outstanding medium-priced Privilege issue
with the R P O, which couples all five
Pomp and Circumstance marches with a
memorably fine version of the *Enigma
variations* (D G 2535 217 [3335 217]).

*Symphony No. 1 in A flat major,
Op. 55.*
*** C.f.P. CFP 40331. LPO,
Handley.
*** Lyrita REAM 1. LPO, Boult
– VAUGHAN WILLIAMS: *Tallis
fantasia.****

Vernon Handley directs a beautifully
paced performance of Elgar's *First.* The
LPO has recorded this symphony many
times before, but never with more poise
and refinement than here, and the Elgar
sound is gloriously captured, particularly the brass. Not surprisingly Handley, as a former pupil of Sir Adrian
Boult, takes a direct view. As in his fine
recording of *Falstaff,* there is sometimes
a hint of restraint which then opens up,
with power in reserve. It is in the slow
movement, more spacious and lovingly
expressive than Sir Adrian allows, that
Handley scores above all. Even making
no allowance for price (and Sir Adrian's
Lyrita disc, although it has a generous
coupling, costs about a pound more than
the C.f.P. issue) this is outstanding
among current versions.

However, the inclusion on the Lyrita
issue of the Vaughan Williams *Tallis
fantasia* as a bonus makes it very striking

value for money, particularly as it offers
the finest recording Sir Adrian ever
made of the Elgar *First.* The opening
movement is fierce and biting (reflecting
perhaps the conductor's irritation at
being pressured into having all the
violins on the left); the scherzo is delicate in the fairy-like scampering at the
start and in the trio, while the slow
movement is light and tender, with the
emotion understated before the heroic
culmination of the finale. With its apt
and particularly generous coupling it
makes a fine alternative recommendation, brightly recorded.

Falla, Manuel de
(1876–1946)

El amor brujo (Love, the Magician;
ballet): *Ritual fire dance; Pantomime. La vida breve* (opera): *Interlude and Spanish dance. The Three-
cornered Hat (El sombrero de tres
picos;* ballet): *3 Dances.*
*** Decca DPA 629/30 [KDPC].
Suisse Rom. Orch., Ansermet
– *Concert.***(*)

Ansermet's performances have colour
and spirit and the Decca sound is excellent. This is part of an attractive if
lightweight concert discussed under
'Spanish music' in our Concerts section.
There is an outstanding H M V medium-
priced disc coupling the complete *Amor
brujo* with the two orchestral suites from
The Three-cornered Hat conducted by
Giulini. The Philharmonia playing is
both civilized and atmospheric, and Victoria de los Angeles is the distinguished
soloist: S X L P 30140.

Fauré, Gabriel
(1845–1924)

*Masques et bergamasques: suite,
Op. 112; Pavane, Op. 50.*
** C.f.P. CFP 40231. LPO, Hand-
ley – DEBUSSY: *La Mer* etc.*

These performances under Vernon
Handley are very enjoyable, fresh and
sympathetic, and the C.f.P. recording
is excellent. But unfortunately the
Debussy couplings are undistinguished.
On Decca there is an excellent
medium-priced compilation of Fauré's
music, with sympathetic and stylish
accounts of *Masques et bergamasques*
and the delightful suite of the incidental
music for *Pelléas et Mélisande* by Ansermet and the Suisse Romande Orchestra.
This anthology also has the advantage
of including the noble *Prélude* to the
opera *Pénélope*, the *Harp impromptu*,
Op. 86, elegantly played by Osian Ellis,
and a sensitive version of the familiar
Pavane conducted by Raymond Agoult:
Eclipse ECS 805.

Requiem, Op. 48.
*** C.f.P. CFP 40234 [TC-CFP].
Los Angeles, Fischer-Dieskau,
Elisabeth Brasseur Choir,
Paris Cons. Orch., Cluytens.

The reissue on C.f.P. of the Los
Angeles/Fischer-Dieskau version of
Fauré's *Requiem* recorded by EMI with
the late André Cluytens in the early
1960s makes claims on the collector's
pocket that are so modest as to be
irresistible. It has always been a good-
sounding version, with great expressive
eloquence in its favour, and the remastered pressings are remarkably fresh,
with plenty of atmosphere and good
detail. There are those who may prefer
other (full-priced) versions – King's College Choir on HMV, for instance, show

greater restraint – but by any standards
this is a memorable performance, with
the comparatively romantic approach
bringing out the riches of colour in both
the orchestral and the vocal writing.
This is not to say that Cluytens misses
the liturgical character of the work:
indeed the *In Paradiso* projects a gentle
vision of heaven in which the spirituality
of the conception is in no way diminished
by the radiance of the physical sounds.
The tape transfer is of excellent quality,
and Los Angeles's solo on side two is
given striking tonal freshness.

Gay, John
(1685–1732)

The Beggar's Opera (arr. Frederick
Austin).
** Argo DPA 591/2. Noble,
Prietto, McAlpine (singers);
Westbury, Shelley, Lawson,
Samson, Chorus and Orch.,
Austin.

The Beggar's Opera was the eighteenth-century equivalent of the modern
American musical. It was first produced
in 1728 and caused a sensation with
audiences used to the stylized Italian
opera favoured by Handel. Its impact
produced a whole series of inferior ballad operas, culminating a century later
in works like *Maritana* and *The Bohe-
mian Girl* which are far removed from
Gay's piece in spirit as well as social
content. This Argo version is conducted
by Richard Austin, son of the musician
who in the 1920s again made a popular
hit with his revised score. It is a period
performance, rhythmically not as vital
as it might be, but with strong characterful contributions from actors and
singers alike. The actors come from the
BBC Repertory Company and are well

produced by Douglas Cleverdon, so that, although musically this could be more polished, the whole entertainment holds together well, conveying the vivacity of the piece. However, on HMV Concert Classics, and costing only about a pound more, there is an altogether superior version conducted by Sir Malcolm Sargent with a singing cast including artists of the calibre of Elsie Morison, John Cameron, Owen Brannigan, Ian Wallace, Constance Shacklock and Alexander Young. This performance is in every way first-class. EMI chose *Let us take the road* for inclusion on their original stereo demonstration disc and indeed the sense of presence and atmosphere throughout is highly compelling; it is just as demonstration-worthy on cassette as it is on disc: HMV ESDW 704 [TC2-ESDW].

Gershwin, George
(1898–1937)

An American in Paris.
  ** RCA Victrola (m) AT 129. NBC SO, Toscanini – GROFÉ: *Grand Canyon suite.* (*)

Toscanini's Gershwin is unexpectedly mellow. It is lively and vivid too but not overdriven. Although the great central blues tune is taken fairly briskly, the orchestral players manage to retain its idiomatic quality. The whole performance is refreshing, and the recording, if lacking in range, is not spoilt by being too brightly lit. Nevertheless, at medium price Decca offer a splendid modern stereo version by the Los Angeles Philharmonic, conducted with considerable panache by Zubin Mehta. As the same issue includes a distinguished account of the *Rhapsody in Blue* by Julius Katchen with the LSO under Kertesz and has

Copland's *Fanfare for the Common Man* as a bonus, it merits a strong recommendation, either on disc or on the equally successful cassette: SPA 525 [KCSP].

Piano concerto in F major; Rhapsody in Blue.
  **(*) C.f.P. CFP 40005. Binns, Sinfonia of London, Alwyn.

The performance of the *Rhapsody* has a thoughtful contribution from Malcolm Binns and a more exuberant one from Kenneth Alwyn (a much under-rated British conductor). The performance of the *Concerto* has fine vitality and plenty of bravura in the outer movements, though not at the expense of lyrical warmth. In the slow movement, however, the opening trumpet solo (played unmuted) is not very idiomatic in style. Nevertheless the disc is very well recorded, and the music-making does not lack spontaneity.

Ginastera, Alberto
(born 1916)

Estancia; Panambi (ballet suites).
  ** Everest 3041. LSO, Goossens – VILLA-LOBOS: *Bachianas Brasileiras No. 2.***

These characteristic ballet scores by the Argentinian composer Ginastera are notable for their exotic orchestral colouring. The music is alive if not especially substantial, and it is effectively presented by Sir Eugene Goossens with the immediacy of Everest sound. Indeed the recording, which is atmospheric as well as vivid, still sounds remarkably well; if the resonance clouds the detail a little, it suits the music.

Gluck, Christoph
(1714–87)

Orfeo ed Euridice (opera): Act 2 (complete).
> **(*) RCA Victrola (m) AT 127. Merriman, Gibson, Robert Shaw Chorale, NBC SO, Toscanini.

Toscanini makes the opening chord of Gluck's Act 2 sound like Beethoven's *Egmont overture*, and the style of performance is in places inappropriately romantic, but this is one of Toscanini's most purposeful and compelling performances on record. If the *Dance of the Furies* is as relentless as the storm in Beethoven's *Pastoral symphony*, the tenderness of the playing in the *Dance of the Blessed Spirits* gives the lie to the idea of this conductor as inflexible. Nan Merriman, a fine mezzo who made far too few records, gives a superb performance, well supported by the boyish soprano of Barbara Gibson as Amor and by the Robert Shaw Chorale. The sound is limited in range, particularly that of the chorus, but it is one of the better recordings from NBC.

Gould, Morton
(born 1913)

Spirituals for string choir and orchestra.
> ** Everest 3002. LSO, Susskind – COPLAND: *Appalachian Spring.***

It is unexpected to find an English performance of this essentially American piece, but the Everest engineers bring a veneer of transatlantic brilliance to the recording with its brightly lit string timbres, so that it sounds much like an American product, especially as the LSO playing is so perceptive and idiomatic. Indeed this slight but rewarding score has never sounded better on disc. There are five movements, and the elegiac quality of *Sermon* is nicely balanced with the drama of *Protest* and the ambivalent exuberance of *Jubilee*. The sly humour of *A little bit of sin* (with its melodic hint of *Shortnin' bread*) is wittily underplayed. Although our review copy looked immaculate the surfaces were rustly (although not too distractingly so) and there is more than usual background noise, inherent in the master recording.

Grieg, Edvard
(1843–1907)

Piano concerto in A minor, Op. 16.
> *** C.f.P. CFP 40255 [TC-CFP]. Solomon, Philharmonia Orch., Menges – SCHUMANN: *Concerto.****
> **(*) Pye [ZCCCB 656]. Cherkassky, LPO, Boult– SCHUMANN: *Concerto.***(*)
> (**) Everest (m) 3434. Gieseking, Berlin PO, Furtwängler – SCHUMANN: *Concerto.* (**)

Current pressings of Solomon's performance provide greatly improved quality compared with the original full-priced issue. The mellow piano tone is matched by a truthful if not brilliant orchestral picture, and the overall balance is excellent. Solomon's poetic lyricism has a special appeal in this work, and although the orchestral contribution is sound rather than inspired, there is some sensitive string playing in the *Adagio*. At C.f.P. price this is a rewarding and worthwhile investment. The cassette transfer is of excellent quality, clear and clean with no lack of body, matching the disc very closely.

Shura Cherkassky's account on Pye has an EMI source. It was originally issued on World Record Club and later on Music for Pleasure. Both are deleted now and at present this fine performance is not available on disc. It is coupled to a wonderfully poetic account of the Schumann *Concerto*. Cherkassky's reading of the Grieg is bold and extrovert: he is particularly commanding in the slow movement, which has considerable depth. The transfer to tape is generally clear, with plenty of warmth in the orchestral strings. The last degree of bloom is missing from the upper range, but the balance is good.

It is good to welcome Gieseking's unfailingly fresh and original thoughts on Grieg back into the catalogue, particularly as he is so warmly supported by the Berlin Philharmonic Orchestra under Furtwängler. However, this recording must be approached strictly as a historical document. Like its coupling it dates from the war years, and the reader is warned that the sound quality is extremely poor. The musical interest outweighs the sonic limitations, but the latter are greater than one would expect from a commercial recording of this period, and this cannot be recommended for normal listening purposes.

(i) *Piano concerto in A minor, Op. 16. Peer Gynt: Suites Nos. 1 and 2, Opp. 46, 55.*
* RCA Camden CCV 5019 [c4]. (i) Gruner-Hegge, Oslo PO, Baekkelund, (i) with Gruner-Hegge.
(i) *Piano concerto. Peer Gynt Suites 1 and 2:* excerpts: *Morning; Anitra's dance; In the Hall of the Mountain King; Arab dance; Solveig's song.*

*(*) C.f.P. CFP 160 [TC-CFP]. LPO, Pritchard, (i) with Katin.

The RCA Camden is the more generous of these two discs and it is well recorded. But it is not very competitive, in spite of the attractive coupling. The *Peer Gynt* performances are idiomatic (although with some curiously slow speeds here and there), but in the concerto neither the soloist, whose style is unrefined, nor the orchestra offers very polished playing. Katin's approach to the concerto is much fresher, but this performance is unmemorable, and the presentation of the *Peer Gynt* music seems equally faceless and matter-of-fact. The recording is excellent both on tape and on disc. Katin recorded the concerto earlier for Decca with the LPO under Colin Davies, and that performance (at medium price) is much more successful. The outer movements are most enjoyable, with Davis's brisk and masterly conducting adding to the freshness. The slow movement does not relax quite enough, but there is the compensation that it is utterly unsentimental. The couplings are generous, the *First Peer Gynt suite* in a distinguished performance by the LPO under Fjeldstad and a brilliant account of the engaging *Scherzo* from Litolff's *Concerto symphonique* (Decca SPA 170 [KCSP]).

'Favourite composer': (i) *Piano concerto in A minor, Op. 16;* (ii) *Holberg suite, Op. 40;* (iii; iv) *Lyric suite, Op. 54;* (iii; v) *Peer Gynt: Suites Nos. 1 and 2, Opp. 46, 55; Prelude; Dance of the Mountain King's Daughter; Sigurd Jorsalfar (suite), Op. 56.*
*** Decca DPA 567/8 [KDPC]. (i) Katchen, Israel PO, Kertesz; (ii) Stuttgart CO, Münchinger; (iii) LSO; (iv) Black; (v) Fjeldstad.

An outstanding anthology. The only item below the remarkable high overall standard is Münchinger's rather unsmiling account of the *Holberg suite*. But this can be forgiven when the discs are generously full and the *Peer Gynt* and *Lyric suites* are so successful; indeed Stanley Black's performance of the latter work is one of the more memorable items. Katchen's version of the *Piano concerto* is a strong one, a hint of wilfulness tempered by a natural flexibility, and a feeling for the work's poetry. Kertesz provides plenty of life in the accompaniment and this performance has its own kind of spontaneity and is very attractive in its way. The recording is vivid and powerful in Decca's more spectacular manner, although some ears perceive a reverberant twang in the acoustic which is not entirely natural. On tape the sound matches the excellence of the discs (its imagery slightly brighter) except in the *Piano concerto*, where, for some reason, the treble seems accentuated, giving a slightly brash effect to the orchestral tuttis.

Violoncello sonata in A minor, Op. 36.
> (**) Everest Olympic (m) 8140. Rostropovich, Sviatoslav Richter – BRAHMS: *Sonata No. 1.* (**)

An impassioned and full-blooded account of this sonata from both artists, very dimly and inadequately recorded. There can indeed have been no finer performance of this work on record, particularly from the pianist, which makes the sonic limitations most distressing. There is neither range nor body here.

Peer Gynt (incidental music), *Op. 23:* complete.
> **(*) Pye [ZCCCB 655]. Cantelo, RPO, Gibson.

This Pye tape offers a recording originally issued by World Record Club and later reissued (on disc only) on Music for Pleasure's short-lived classical Fanfare label. The selection is complete and although Gibson (unlike some full-priced rivals) does not have the advantage of a chorus, April Cantelo's contribution is a striking one (she sings both *Solveig's song* and the *Cradle song* with appealing freshness). The performances generally show Gibson at his very best; they are spontaneous and full of character. The recording too offers rich string textures and brings out the warmth of the music-making. Although it lacks the very last degree of range and sparkle the transfer is well balanced and makes very agreeable listening. One single drum roll causes a moment where the refinement slips, but otherwise the quality is consistently excellent.

Grofé, Ferde
(1892–1972)

Grand Canyon suite.
> (*) RCA Victrola (m) AT 129. NBCSO, Toscanini – GERSHWIN: *American in Paris.* **

The piercing piccolo at the opening of *Sunrise* has a stereoscopic projection here, and the exaggerated balance and dry acoustic do little to enhance Grofé's technicolour pictorialism. Everything is glaringly, painfully clear, and only *On the trail* is redeemed by its geniality and wit, which come over in spite of the unkind acoustic. At medium price there is a most attractive account of the *Grand Canyon suite*, warmly and perceptively played by the Utah Symphony Orchestra under Maurice Abravanel. The appropriate coupling is Copland's tourist image of a Mexican dance hall, *El salón*

Mexico, and the recording is splendidly evocative and atmospheric both on disc and on tape: HMV Greensleeve ESD 7073 [TC-ESD].

Handel, George Frederick (1685–1759)

Harp concerto in B flat major, Op. 4/6.
*** DG Heliodor 2548 281 [3348 281]. Zabaleta, Paul Kuentz CO, Kuentz – MOZART: *Flute and harp concerto*; RAVEL: *Introduction and allegro.***(*)

Zabaleta's fine performance of the *Harp concerto* makes a delightful effect on this remastered Heliodor disc. The sound itself is delicately crystalline, but the texture has warmth too and does not lack substance. The performance, with its subtlety in matters of light and shade, is highly imaginative, and the couplings are generous, though not quite as attractive as the Handel. Unfortunately the tape transfer is much less well focused than the disc, which is an altogether safer recommendation.

Harp concerto in F major, Op. 4/5; Concerto for lute and harp in B flat major, Op. 4/6; Concerto grosso in C major (Alexander's Feast); Water music: suites Nos. 1–3 (complete).
*** Oiseau-Lyre DPA 597/8 [KDPC 2 7056]. Philomusica, Granville Jones or Dart, with Ellis, Dupré.

This most welcome compilation happily joins together two outstanding discs from the early days of stereo. The performances of the two solo concertos are admirably fresh, and the recording is beautifully balanced. Both come from the Op. 4 set of works for organ, but they are no less attractive in this alternative form. The *Concerto grosso* associated with the oratorio *Alexander's Feast* is given a vigorous, alert performance; here the early date of the recording is slightly more noticeable. The performance of the three suites which make up the complete *Water music* is no less distinguished. Scholarship and spontaneity make a very happy partnership here and the recording hardly shows its age. On tape there is a moment of congestion when the trumpets enter regally in the third suite; otherwise the sound throughout is both robust and clear.

'*Famous composer*': (i) *Organ concerto No. 2 in B flat major, Op. 4/2.* (ii) *Royal Fireworks music: suite; Water music: suite* (arr. Harty and Szell). *The Faithful Shepherd: Minuet* (arr. Beecham). (iii; iv) *Solomon: Arrival of the Queen of Sheba.* (ii) *Xerxes: Largo* (arr. Reinhardt). (v) *Coronation anthem: Zadok the Priest. Messiah:* highlights: (vi) *Ev'ry valley;* (vii) *O thou that tellest;* (vi) *For unto us a child is born; I know that my Redeemer liveth; The trumpet shall sound; Hallelujah chorus.* (iii; viii) *Rodelinda: Dove sei (Art thou troubled).*
*** Decca DPA 551/2. [KDPC]. (i) Karl Richter, CO; (ii) LSO, Szell; (iii) ASMF; (iv) Marriner; (v) King's College Choir, ECO, Willcocks; (vi) Sutherland, McKellar, Ward, LSO Chorus, LSO, Boult; (vii) Ferrier, LPO, Boult; (viii) Greevy, cond. Leppard.

With such a distinguished roster of singers and musicians and a sensibly and imaginatively chosen programme this pair of discs (or tapes) cannot fail to give pleasure, and the performances are matched by the consistent excellence of recording. Szell's versions of the suites arranged by Sir Hamilton Harty from the *Fireworks* and *Water music* date from a short but particularly successful Decca recording period in the early sixties, when he also made a record of Tchaikovsky's *Fourth Symphony*. Like that disc these performances are highly recommendable. The orchestral playing is outstanding; the strings are wonderfully expressive in the slower pieces, while the horns too excel in their lively roulades. The vocal items are also very successful; the inclusion of Kathleen Ferrier's *O thou that tellest* within the selection from the Boult recording of *Messiah* was a happy idea.

Music for the Royal Fireworks; Concerti grossi, Op. 3, Nos. 2 in B flat major; 5 in D major.
** C.f.P. CFP 105 [TC-CFP]. Virt. of England, Davison.
Music for the Royal Fireworks; Water music: suite (original versions).
**(*) DG Heliodor 2548 169 [3348 169]. Schola Cantorum Basiliensis, Wenzinger.
Music for the Royal Fireworks; Water music: suite (arr. Stokowski).
* RCA Camden CCV 5002 [c4]. RCA Victor SO, Stokowski.
Water music: suites Nos. 1–3 (complete).
** C.f.P. CFP 40092 [TC-CFP]. Virt. of England, Davison.

Davison's pair of C.f.P. discs offers performances that are reasonably authentic in style if rhythmically somewhat unresilient. The playing itself is fresh and stylish, but it lacks the kind of imaginative force that can make this music glow and almost overwhelm the listener by its spontaneity and originality. Nevertheless the recording is modern and well balanced (if rather forward), although the *Fireworks music* is rather light in the bass in the more spectacular tuttis. The tape transfers are flawless, matching the discs closely.

The playing of the Schola Cantorum Basiliensis shows a splendid feeling for the open-air style of the music, with crisp buoyant rhythms. The use of original instruments in the *Fireworks music* gives a suitably robust effect (complete with less than perfect intonation), while a fuller orchestra is used in the *Water music*. The recording on disc is excellent, but the cassette transfer is not wholly successful, rather dry in timbre, and with moments of congestion.

By any possible standards of baroque scholarship Stokowski's record with its souped-up spectacular orchestrations is hopelessly unauthentic. Yet it is easy to feel a sneaking admiration for the sheer personality of his presentation. His warmth is obvious in the lyrical music, and even with the use of organ-inspired swell effects as well as the echo devices in the phrasing, there are moments when the listener can be seduced in spite of himself. The recording has some coarseness in *fortissimo*, which appears to stem from the master tape, but it sounds opulent at *mezzo-forte*. There are genuine moments of grandeur in the *Fireworks music*, and at the end (reasonably enough, but only Stokowski would dare to do it) fireworks effects and enthusiastic crowd noises are introduced momentarily, laminated to the closing tutti. One cannot but smile at the effective ingenuousness of such an interpolation. A collector's item, and an attractive reminder of a great musician who made his own rules.

Coronation anthems: 1, Zadok the Priest; 2, The King Shall Rejoice; 3.

My Heart Is Inditing; 4. Let Thy Hand Be Strengthened. Solomon: From the censer curling rise (chorus).
*** C.f.P. CFP 40321. Ambrosian Singers, Menuhin Fest. Orch., Menuhin.

Although not as refined as the famous Argo full-priced King's College recording of the coronation anthems, this is still an impressive account of some of Handel's finest ceremonial music. The chorus sings with striking vigour in the famous *Zadok the Priest*, and they are at their incisive best in *My Heart Is Inditing*. No. 4 is let down just a little by its middle section, but the chorus from *Solomon* makes a splendid culmination to an attractive collection. The orchestral playing is imaginatively phrased with a well-judged sense of balance and style, and the 1970 recording is admirably vivid.

Messiah: excerpts.
*(*) C.f.P. CFP 40020 [TC-CFP]. Morison, Thomas, Lewis, Huddersfield Choral Soc., Royal Liverpool PO, Sargent.

Many will undoubtedly want a sampler of Sir Malcolm Sargent's traditional account of *Messiah*. This contains some fine solo singing, notably from Elsie Morison and Richard Lewis, but the choruses are disappointing, heavy in style and recorded in a curiously muffled way which cannot entirely be the fault of the singing itself. The tape is no more successful than the disc. We badly need a recommendable bargain version of the complete *Messiah*, though until it arrives the Mackerras version on HMV (SLS 774 [TC-SLS]) with Elizabeth Harwood, Janet Baker, Paul Esswood, Robert Tear, and Raimund Herincx, is a first-rate medium-price recommendation.

58

Haydn, Josef (1732–1809)

Oboe concerto in C major.
(*) Pye GSGC 15034. Rothwell, Hallé Orch., Barbirolli – CORELLI and PERGOLESI: *Concertos.**

Of the three concertos on this delectable disc the Haydn, because of its very positive classicism, suits Evelyn Rothwell's style marginally less well than the other two. But Sir John's strong opening has all the classical verve anyone could want, and in the first movement his wife's delicacy makes a delicious foil for the masculine orchestral sound; in particular the phrasing of the second subject is enchanting. The slow movement too is well brought off, and it is only in the finale that, for all the pleasure of the feminine tessitura, others have shown that a stronger style is even more effective. But the rest of this collection is treasurable and, taken as it is, the performance offers much pleasure in its own way.

'Favourite composer': (i) *Trumpet concerto in E flat major;* (ii; iii) *Symphonies Nos. 94 in G major (Surprise); 101 in D major (Clock).* (iv) *String quartet No. 77 in C major (Emperor), Op. 76/3:* 2nd movt. (v) (Piano) *Andante with variations in F minor.* (vi; ii) *The Creation:* highlights.
*** Decca DPA 611/2 [KDPC]. (i) Stringer, ASMF, Marriner; (ii) Vienna PO; (iii) Monteux; (iv) Aeolian Qt; (v) Backhaus; (vi) Ameling, Spoorenberg, Krenn, Krause, Fairhurst, Vienna State Opera Chorus, Münchinger.

Monteux's performances of the *Surprise* and *Clock symphonies* are captivating. He turns a genial eye on a genial composer at his most civilized, and he secures very polished playing throughout, with many a turn of phrase to delight the ear. Highlights are the delicious *Andante* of the *Surprise* and the contrasting finale of the same work, bustling with vigour and high spirits. In the *Clock* he sets a perky mood in the second movement, and a very pointed tick-tock emphasizes Haydn's gentle humour. The recordings are excellent, warm-toned to suit the conductor's approach. By contrast Alan Stringer's view of the *Trumpet concerto* is more robust, and no doubt a conscious attempt was made to stimulate the forthright open tone of the primitive keyed instrument Haydn would have been used to. The orchestral playing has striking finesse, however, and with beautiful recorded sound this performance is very successful. It is a pity that room could not be found for the complete *Emperor quartet* rather than just the famous slow movement. (Readers are reminded that the outstanding Amadeus performance of this work, coupled to Mozart's *Hunt quartet*, K.458, is available on a DG medium-priced Accolade issue, splendidly recorded on both disc and cassette: 2542 122 [3342 122].) The Decca set concludes with generous excepts from Münchinger's distinguished account of *The Creation*, which are especially valuable. The recording throughout is of Decca's usual high standard, but the tape transfers have not been uniformly successful. The symphonies sound well, but there is an element of coarseness in the concerto and some roughness at peaks in the vocal music.

Symphonies Nos. 88 in G major; 98 in B flat major.
  ⊕*** DG Heliodor 2548 241. Berlin PO, Jochum.

Splendid accounts of both symphonies which wear their years lightly. Indeed, comparison of No. 98 with the more recent version Jochum made with the LPO reveals only marginally greater freshness in the upper strings in the newer disc. The playing of the Berlin orchestra is more polished and homogeneous than that of the LPO, and Jochum brings to both works a warmth and humanity (as well as the necessary vitality) and also a sweetness of tone and sensitivity of phrasing that put these among the most desirable recorded performances in the Haydn discography. Outstanding value.

Symphonies Nos. 94 in G major (Surprise); 101 in D major (Clock).
  *(*) RCA Victrola (m) AT 120. NBC SO, Toscanini.

In the 1920s Toscanini made a classic recording of the *Clock symphony*, but its felicity was not matched in this 1947 studio recording, which is faster and less persuasive and has distressingly dry sound. The *Surprise* on the reverse is more sympathetic, not just in sound but in performance too, with fizzing accounts of the outer movements.

Symphonies Nos. 94 in G major (Surprise); 103 in E flat major (Drum Roll).
  *** C.f.P. CFP 40269. LPO, Leppard.

Leppard directs beautifully stylish and resilient readings of two favourite Haydn symphonies which stand comparison with any rivals at whatever price. At well-chosen tempi – never rushed or forced – Leppard is consistently persuasive, not least in the slow movements, which are spaciously and affectionately presented without ever falling into unwanted romantic manners. The texts used are scholarly (as one would expect with Leppard) and include an extra sixteen bars in the finale of No. 103 which – probably without Haydn's approval – were excised in the regularly published version. Well-balanced modern recording.

Symphonies Nos. (i) 100 in G major (Military); (ii) 101 in D major (Clock).
** D G Heliodor 2548 218. (i) Leipzig Gewandhaus Orch., Suitner; (ii) Berlin R O, Kleinert.

These are thoroughly musical performances, nicely played and warmly recorded. Indeed the sound in the *Military symphony* is rather over-resonant and bass-heavy, but it yields to the controls and is fully acceptable. Both readings are stylish in the German manner, a little heavy, but with elegant, polished strings and notably fine wind playing. The percussion effects in the *Military symphony* make their proper effect in spite of the reverberation. The slow movement of the *Clock* (where the recording, although still mellow, is better balanced) is particularly felicitous, with a beautifully judged basic tempo. In short there is much to enjoy here, although this record will not suit those who prefer brilliance to body in orchestral recording.

Piano sonata No. 52 in E flat major.
(*) R C A (m) v H 010. Horowitz – MUSSORGSKY: *Pictures.*(*)

Horowitz's performance of the great *E flat Sonata* comes from 1951 and is not to be confused with his pre-war set of 78s made in the early 1930s. Perhaps that had the edge on this later version, in terms of lightness and (in the finale) wit. The articulation is no less astonishing but the outer movements are a shade too tense and hurried. But this is still

marvellous playing, and its character and brilliance survive the somewhat shallow recording.

Mass No. 7 in C major (Missa in tempore belli; Paukenmesse).
** D G Heliodor 2548 229. Morison, Thomas, Witsch, Kohn, Bav. Radio Choir and Orch., Kubelik.

The mixed team of soloists here works well, and Kubelik's dramatic yet lyrical approach brings direct and forthright music-making, while not missing the colour and atmosphere in which this score abounds. With a spacious recording which wears its years lightly, this is excellent value at Heliodor price.

Holborne, Anthony (died 1602)

Short airs, both grave and light (suite).
C.f.P. CFP 40335 [TC-CFP]. Praetorius Consort, Ball – PRAETORIUS: *Terpsichore*; LAMBRANZI: *Dances.*

An engaging selection from Holborne's collection of 'Pavans, Galliards, Almains and other Short Airs, both grave and light', published in 1599. (There were sixty-five items altogether.) As in the *Terpsichore* coupling, Christopher Ball's arrangements are recorder-dominated, and occasionally the ear craves a consort of viols, and perhaps voices too. But the skill of the scoring (*The last will and testament* is a poignant example) and the freshly alert and sympathetic performances are matched by the excellent C.f.P. sound. There is no appreciable difference between the disc and the excellent cassette. Highly recommended in both formats.

Holst, Gustav (1874–1934)

The Perfect Fool (ballet music), *Op. 39.*
   *** Decca DPA 627/8 [KDPC]. LPO, Boult – *Concert of English music.****

This suite comes from Holst's comic opera of the same name, which opens with a ballet danced by the Spirits of Earth, Water and Fire. They are summoned by an arresting trombone invocation which is one of Holst's most unforgettable ideas, and the ballet music has the diversity of colour and rhythmic originality which have made *The Planets* so popular. It is superbly played here and is given a vintage Decca recording of demonstration quality. This is part of an anthology discussed under 'English music' in our Concerts section.

The Planets (suite), *Op. 32.*
   **(*)C.f.P. 40343 [TC-CFP]. Hallé Orch. and Chorus, Loughran.

The Planets is exceptionally well represented in the catalogue at full price (Boult, Previn and Solti) and medium price (Karajan's Decca Jubilee disc and tape – JB 30 [KJBC] – is of outstanding quality); but this is the only bargain version currently available on disc. Loughran finds plenty of atmosphere in Holst's score, sometimes taking a more measured approach than usual. But the orchestral playing is often very fine, and is splendidly projected by the recording, which is ripely vivid and marvellously refined in detail. The brass are given splendid bite and sonority, and as sound

this is among the finest versions. The tape matches the disc in its vividness and clarity.

Sargent's more traditional view of the work used to be available on C.f.P., but it has now been reissued on HMV's new Ideal cassette label (with no disc equivalent). An hour of music is offered by this medium-priced series, costing just under £3; and here the bonus is an attractively ebullient performance of the *St Paul's suite* for strings. Sargent's *Planets* have plenty of character too; their highlight is an exuberant version of *Jupiter*, with a richly expansive central melody. The tape transfer is excellent until the side-turn, and then at the beginning and close of *Saturn* and again in *Neptune* the pianissimo textures are somewhat lacking in focus and security. At the end of the main work the *St Paul's suite*, which is transferred at a higher level, positively bursts on the listener; but once the volume is turned down the sound is first-class: TC-IDL 507.

Honegger, Arthur (1892–1955)

Le Roi David (oratorio).
   (*) Decca DPA 593/4. Audel (narrator), Danco, De Montmollin, Martin, Hamel, Suisse Rom. Orch. and Chorus, Ansermet – MARTIN: *In terra pax.**

Le Roi David is better described as a dramatic mosaic rather than a symphonic psalm. It was for many years Honegger's best-known work (with the sole exception of *Pacific 231*), largely on account of its pageantry and atmosphere. This Decca recording, made under the authoritative guidance of

61

Ernest Ansermet, dates from the mid-1950s and originally appeared in mono only. The sound lacks the range and body of the most modern recordings, but it wears its age lightly, and given the enormous interest and invention this score offers, and the interest of its coupling, readers need not hesitate to invest in it. Judged by the highest standards, the orchestral playing is a little wanting in finish, but there is now no alternative at any price, and no collector is likely to be dissatisfied with the distinguished cast, or this richly inventive tapestry of sound. A thoroughly rewarding set.

Ibert, Jacques
(1890–1962)

Escales (symphonic pieces).
*** RCA Camden ccv 5031 [c4].
Boston SO, Munch – DUKAS:
L'Apprenti sorcier**; RAVEL:
Boléro etc.*(*)

Escales remains Ibert's most popular orchestral work, and the evocation of Tunis that forms the central movement of the three is haunting. Much of the inspiration derives from the North African musicians Ibert heard on a visit immediately after the First World War. The three pieces were finished in 1922 and established the composer virtually overnight. They are enormously colourful, and although Munch's performance is not so atmospheric as some recent accounts, the Boston Symphony play with superb aplomb. The recording does not expand as one might wish and is a trifle hard. However, it is acceptable, and so is the remastered cassette transfer, although the sound is rather confined and the climaxes fail to expand as vividly as they should. Also there are no

musical notes with the cassette, surely essential for a work of this nature.

Janáček, Leoš
(1854–1928)

Sinfonietta; Preludes: *The House of the Dead; Jenůfa; Kátya Kabanová; The Makropoulos Affair.*
*** Pye GSGC 15033. PA Orch.,
Mackerras.

Charles Mackerras has established an international reputation as an authority on the music of Janáček with his superb complete Decca recordings of *Kátya Kabanová* and *The Makropoulos Affair*; and this record, dating from 1960, explains why. The performance of the *Sinfonietta* is splendidly vibrant, abrasive in its rhythmic energy, yet with an underlying lyric intensity. The famous opening brass fanfare (which uses twelve trumpets) has an almost medieval spareness in its sonority and atmosphere, and the second movement *Allegretto* is given a rhythmic incisiveness to recall the *Battle on the Ice* from Prokofiev's *Alexander Nevsky*. The slightly dry acoustic seems ideal and although the recording sounds slightly dated the force and impact of the performance are unsurpassed in the present catalogue. The four operatic preludes make an ideal coupling, creating a kind of suite. The darkly eloquent *Kátya Kabanová* and *The House of the Dead*, with its concertante violin solos, make a superb foil for *The Makropoulos Affair*, which comes first, and the pungent *Jenůfa* introduction, which closes the disc. Again the performances have striking character and passionate feeling, and the somewhat brightly lit, unexpansive sound gives an extra edge to the music-making.

Khachaturian, Aram (1903–78)

Gayaneh (ballet): extended excerpts.
*** Everest 3052. LSO, Fistoulari.

Apart from the complete set of the original 1942 score on RCA, this Everest disc provides the most extensive selection from *Gayaneh* available in stereo, and Fistoulari imparts his usual inimitable touch, especially in the quieter music, where there is some melting orchestral playing. Even the famous *Sabre dance* gains from the slight degree of understatement inherent in his reading. Without loss of energy it avoids the breathless abandon of some performances (which can sound like a traction engine running downhill out of control). This is not to suggest that the score's exciting moments lose their spectacular quality here. Indeed the *Russian dance* which begins side two and the spectacular *Fire* sequence are both splendidly unbuttoned. The recording is reverberant but does not in the least sound its age. Our review copy had a patch of noisy surface on the second side.

Kodály, Zoltán (1882–1967)

Dances of Galánta; Dances of Marosszék; Háry János: suite.
*** C.f.P. CFP 40292. LPO, Susskind.
Háry János: suite.
** RCA Victrola (m) AT 122. NBC SO, Toscanini – PROKOFIEV: *Symphony No. 1;* SIBELIUS: *Finlandia.***

Susskind's attractive performances of Kodály's three most popular orchestral works are treated to sound of superb demonstration quality. In depth of focus and fidelity this compares with the very best recordings of the seventies, and although Susskind's direction could be more resilient the playing of the LPO is excellent. Susskind's overriding attention to detail generally made him a more successful exponent of shorter rather than large-scale works in the recording studio and this record, one of several he made for C.f.P. not long before he died, is a fitting memento of his musicianship.

Toscanini rarely displayed a sense of humour in his conducting. Verdi's *Falstaff* provides a notable exception, and so does this delightful, crisp account of Kodály's colourful suite, well coupled with other music not generally associated with this conductor. The recording is limited and rather rough.

Lambranzi, Gregorio (fl. *c.* 1640)

Dances from the School of Gregorio Lambranzi (arr. Ball).
*** C.f.P. CFP 40335 [TC-CFP]. Praetorius Consort, Ball
PRAETORIUS: *Terpsichore;* HOLBORNE: *Airs.****

Gregorio Lambranzi was an Italian dancing master of whom very little is known. But the dances he used, which are arranged here by Christopher Ball into three short pot-pourris, are delightfully infectious and tuneful. Surprisingly they seem to show some evidence of English derivation, even including a piquant reminder of *The British Grenadiers*. With sparkling performances and excellent recording this is in many ways the most interesting of the three groups

63

of dances on this enterprising record. The cassette transfer is of outstanding quality, offering sound identical with the LP.

Lehár, Franz
(1870–1948)

The Merry Widow (Die lustige Witwe; operetta): complete.
** Decca DPA 573/4. Gueden, Grunden, Kmentt, Loose, Dönch, Vienna State Opera Chorus and Orch., Stolz.

Hilde Gueden makes a charming Widow, and this 1958 recording offers a more complete text than is usual on record, including the delightful *Zauber der Häuslichkeit* duet, which too often is omitted. It is good to have a tenor Danilo in Per Grunden. The conducting of Robert Stolz, himself an operetta composer, is sound rather than inspired; the rest of the cast supports Gueden well. With good early stereo and first-rate production, it makes a fair bargain, although at only about a pound more one can have the classic set made by EMI a few years earlier, with Schwarz-kopf, Gedda, Kunz, Loose, and the Philharmonia Chorus and Orchestra under Ackermann. This is a stereo transcription of mono, but a very successful one (on both disc and tape), and it shows Schwarzkopf at her freshest and most beguiling: HMV SXDW 3045 [TC2-SXDW], awarded a rosette in *The Penguin Cassette Guide.*

The Merry Widow (abridged, in an English version by Christopher Hassall).
**C.f.P. CFP 40276 [TC-CFP]. Wilson, Blanc, Hay, Hillman,

McCue, Sandison, Scottish Opera Chorus, Scottish Phil-harmonia Orch., Gibson.

Gibson is at his freshest and most inspired in this magic operetta. The 1977 recording is warm and full, and the selection of items is admirable, with several passages included which have often been missed in 'complete' recordings, the duet *Zauber der Häuslichkeit* and the Act 3 *Cakewalk.* Much of the singing is not distinguished, but it is the teamwork which makes this a sparkling entertainment, and at the price it can be warmly recommended. The cassette version is rather less clean in focus than the LP, but the solo voices are clear and there is no lack of bloom on the sound.

Liszt, Franz
(1811–86)

Piano concertos Nos. 1 in E flat major, G.124; 2 in A major, G.125.
*** RCA Camden CCV 5047 [c4]. Pennario, LSO, Leibowitz.
(i–iii) *Piano concerto No. 1 in E flat major;* (ii; iv) *Hungarian rhapsody No. 2, G.359;* (v) *Les Préludes* (symphonic poem), *G.97.*
*** DG Heliodor 2548 235. (i) Vásáry; (ii) Bamberg SO; (iii) Prohaska; (iv) Kraus; (v) Berlin RO, Fricsay.

Pennario gives extremely brilliant, virtuoso performances, perhaps not pen-etrating too far beneath the surface of the music, but very enjoyable in their extrovert spontaneity. The recording is sparkling to match, with very vivid stereo to bring everything forward. The result is highly effective, with some superb, glittering bravura from the pianist and plenty of excitement from the orchestra too. The sound itself (mid-sixties vintage) is surprisingly fresh, and the closing pages of the *A major Concerto* are splendidly exhilarating, with the brashness put to the service of the music.

Vásáry's recording of No. 1 still sounds very well indeed and his performance is distinguished by considerable subtlety and refinement, yet with no loss of impact. It is as satisfying an account as almost any available. But what makes this disc doubly attractive is the inclusion of Fricsay's superb *Les Préludes*. Fricsay had just the temperament for this fine piece: he plays it with enormous feeling and conviction and the recording is splendidly vivid. This is among the finest versions of *Les Préludes* currently available, and as Richard Kraus's account of the *Hungarian rhapsody* has both sparkle and panache, this disc makes a really excellent bargain.

whom this technique appeals will not be disappointed with these versions on musical grounds, and certainly the recording is demonstration-worthy in its way. Davis points the close of the first movement of No. 1 with both humour and magic, a delectable moment. Pascal Rogé is very well recorded too, and he gives a brilliant and commanding performance of the *Sonata*. Simon Preston's version of the *Prelude and fugue on BACH* is undoubtedly distinguished, and the other solo piano items are well done (Joseph Cooper's account of the *Valse oubliée* is notably stylish). The only real drawback to this compilation is Bernard Herrmann's rather laboured reading of *Les Préludes*. This also causes problems in the tape transfer, producing a degree of roughness at the climax; otherwise the cassettes match the discs closely in quality.

'Favourite composer': (i) *Piano concertos Nos. 1 in E flat major, G.124; 2 in A major, G.125;* (ii) *Les Préludes, G.97.* (Piano) (iii) *Hungarian rhapsody No. 2, G.244; Liebestraum No. 3 in A flat major, G.541;* (iv) *Piano sonata in B minor, G.178;* (v) *Valse oubliée No. 1, G.215.* (Organ) (iv) *Prelude and fugue on the name BACH, G.260.*

**(*) Decca DPA 621/2 [KDPC].

(i) Ivan Davis, RPO, Downes; (ii) LPO, Herrmann; (iii) Vered; (iv) Rogé; (v) Cooper; (vi) Preston (organ of Hull City Hall).

Ivan Davis's performances of the two concertos are among the finest available. They are vividly characterized and they show real poetic feeling. The original recording used Decca's Phase Four system, which brings vivid spotlighting of solo orchestral instruments and a forward balance for the piano. But those to

Années de Pèlerinage, 1st year (Switzerland): Au bord d'une source, G.160/4; 2nd year (Italy): Sonnetto del Petrarca, G.161/6. Harmonies poétiques et religieuses: Funérailles, G.173/7. Hungarian rhapsodies (arr. Horowitz) *Nos. 2, 6 and 15, G.244. Valse oubliée No. 1, G.215.*

*** RCA Victrola (m) VH 006. Horowitz (piano).

These performances come from the period 1947–53. Horowitz's virtuosity is always at the service of wholly musical ends, and although the playing is not always well served by the engineers, enough of the phenomenon is conveyed to do him justice. As with all electrifying, transcendental pianists, the sheer strength of his personality will alienate some listeners, but most will surely find this pretty breathtaking. There is great delicacy, poetry, and, of course, the most effortless wizardry.

Litolff, Henri
(1818–91)

Concerto symphonique No. 4 in D minor, Op. 102: Scherzo (only)
*** C.f.P. CFP 115 [TC-CFP]. Katin, LPO, Pritchard – TCHAIKOVSKY: *Concerto No. 1.* *(*)

A scintillating performance, brilliantly recorded; if only the concerto which forms the coupling had the same kind of panache this would be a world-beater. The cassette transfer is of demonstration quality.

Mahler, Gustav
(1860–1911)

Symphonies Nos. 1–9.
**(*) CBS GM 15 (15 discs). NYPO or LSO, soloists, including Armstrong, Baker (No. 2), Lipton (No. 3), Grist (No. 4), chorus, Bernstein.

Bernstein, for all his idiosyncrasies, often amounting to self-indulgence, directs what is clearly the most red-blooded and characterful cycle of Mahler symphonies on record. Dedicated Mahlerians may resist on points of detail, but the overall richness and urgency make this a most compelling set. The more recent of Bernstein's two recordings of the *Second Symphony* is preferred; recorded in Ely Cathedral, it has obvious shortcomings but many vivid qualities. In place of the Mahler reminiscences originally coupled with the *Sixth*, Bernstein's expressive account of the opening *Adagio* of No. 10 is included. Though the recordings were

made over a span between the early sixties and mid-seventies, they generally provide big bold sound, with forward balances that are not always apt – as in the monumental *Eighth Symphony*.

Symphony No. 1 in D major (Titan).
**(*) C.f.P. CFP 40264. LPO, Delogu.
** DG Heliodor 2548 123 [3348 123]. Dresden State Orch., Suitner.

Delogu directs a youthfully fresh reading of Mahler's *First Symphony*, one which points the *Wayfaring Lad* themes in particular with fine delicacy. The recording, with its wide dynamic and tonal range, enhances the excellent playing of the LPO, and though this may not be so perceptive and stylish in detail as the finest versions, it makes an excellent bargain.

Suitner's is a lightweight performance – in the interpretative sense – but spontaneous and enjoyable. Suitner does not always show a feeling for the overall structure, but he certainly creates a sense of atmosphere, and in this he is helped by the DG recording, which also has a wide dynamic range. The slow movement is not very sombre, but the mood created fits well into the extrovert nature of the performance overall, with its jubilant conclusion. The tape transfer matches the disc, clear and well balanced.

Symphony No. 4 in G major.
*(*) C.f.P. CFP 159 [TC-CFP]. Price, LPO, Horenstein.

Horenstein's characteristic simplicity of approach seems too deliberate here (the rhythms of the second movement, for instance, are curiously precise) and even the great slow movement sounds didactic, though it is not without atmosphere. Margaret Price's singing in the finale is beautiful but cool, in line with the rest of the interpretation. The recording is clear but unatmospheric; the cassette transfer is very successful. It has excellent detail, and the sound throughout is extremely vivid (if rather dry in acoustic).

Marcello, Alessandro (1684–1750)

Oboe concerto in C minor (arr. Bonelli).
*** Pye GSGC 15011. Rothwell, PA Orch., Barbirolli – ALBINONI and CIMAROSA: *Concertos*.***

Sir John's subtlety in matters of light and shade within an orchestral phrase brings the music immediately alive and at the same time prevents the rather jolly opening tune from sounding square. There is a beautiful *Adagio* and a gay finale, both showing the soloist on top form, and the well-balanced recording adds to one's pleasure.

Martin, Frank (1890–1974)

In terra pax (oratorio).
*** Decca DPA 593/4. Buckel, Höffgen, Haefliger, Mollet, Stämpfli, Suisse Rom. Orch. and Chorus, Ansermet – HONEGGER: *Le Roi David*.**(*)

Frank Martin's beautiful score was commissioned by the Swiss Radio in preparation for the announcement of the end of the 1939–45 war, and it was

first performed by Ansermet. Originally this score occupied a whole disc but it has been accommodated without appreciable loss of quality on a side and a half. Martin's music has an appropriate eloquence and spirituality, and he is admirably served by these fine soloists. The score falls into four short sections, all of biblical texts, and its sincerity and sense of compassion leave a strong impression. Coupled to Honegger's atmospheric pageant *Le Roi David* in an almost equally fine performance, this is an outstanding bargain. The recording, from the mid-1960s, is of high quality.

Mendelssohn, Felix (1809–47)

Violin concerto in E minor, Op. 64.
** RCA Camden CCV 5017 [c4]. Laredo, Boston SO, Munch – BRUCH: *Concerto No. 1*.**

Jaime Laredo's tone is small and precise, but this is a fine performance; the soloist's technique is matched by sensitivity, and the slow movement is tenderly phrased. The recording has a tendency to roughness in the tuttis and there is some lack of substance in the finale, but this is the cheapest recommendable coupling of the Bruch and Mendelssohn concertos. The remastered tape transfer is made at a high level and there is some slight roughness in the orchestral tuttis, most noticeable in the slow movement. Otherwise the sound is clear and has a good range.

'*Favourite composer*': (i; ii) *Violin concerto in E minor, Op. 64;* (ii; iii) Overture: *The Hebrides (Fingal's Cave), Op. 26;* (iv) *A Midsummer Night's Dream: Overture, Op. 21; Incidental music, Op. 61: Scherzo;*

Nocturne; Wedding march; Symphony No. 4 in A major (Italian), Op. 90. (v) (Piano) *Songs without words Nos. 30 in A major (Spring song), Op. 62/6; 34 in C major (Bees' wedding), Op. 67/4.* (vi) *Hear my prayer (O for the wings of a dove).*

** Decca DPA 557/8. [KDPC]. (i) Ricci, Gamba; (ii) LSO; (iii) Maag; (iv) Suisse Rom. Orch., Ansermet; (v) Backhaus; (vi) Roberts (treble), St John's College, Cambridge, Choir, Guest; White (organ).

Ricci's performance of the *Violin concerto* is first-class, and Ansermet's *Italian symphony* is more than serviceable. The same conductor's account of the *Midsummer Night's Dream* music is not one of his finest performances, but it is well recorded. Backhaus's rather brittle *Songs without words* and the slightly self-conscious account of the choral piece are acceptable enough. The transfers to tape are well managed.

Symphony No. 3 in A minor (Scottish), Op. 56; Overture: *The Hebrides (Fingal's Cave), Op. 26.*

*** C.f.P. CFP 40270 [TC-CFP]. Scottish Nat. Orch., Gibson.

It was an attractive idea to record Scotland's premier orchestra and most distinguished conductor in a coupling of the two engaging works conceived during Mendelssohn's Scottish visit in 1829. The opening bars of the symphony were inspired by his first sight of Holyrood Palace with its historical and romantic associations, which set his imagination working strongly. Yet he had some problems with the composition and the symphony was not completed until 1842. The writing has less obvious spontaneity than the companion *Italian symphony*,

and it needs a committed performance to make its full effect on the listener. Gibson and his orchestra are on top form and they play the piece with warmth and eloquence. The string phrasing is strikingly fresh and among the wind soloists the clarinets distinguish themselves (as also in the overture). The reading is agreeably relaxed and its presentation is helped by the rich glowing recording, with its full body and natural perspective. The (high-level) tape transfer has marginally less range and transparency than the disc but is still very good.

Symphony No. 4 in A major (Italian), Op. 90.

(*) RCA Victrola (m) AT 101. NBC SO, Toscanini – SCHUBERT: *Symphony No. 8.(*)

Symphony No. 4; A Midsummer Night's Dream: Overture, Op. 21; Incidental music, Op. 61: Scherzo; Nocturne; Wedding march.

** C.f.P. CFP 40224. LPO, Lockhart.

The *Italian symphony* was one of the very last recordings which Toscanini made in 1954, and though, characteristically, he did not relax as much as some would want, this is an electrifying performance, exhilarating in the outer movements, with sound rather better than usual from this source.

James Lockhart's performances are given an excellent modern recording, and they are well played too. However, the music is not strongly characterized, and in the symphony (where the first-movement repeat is observed) the two central movements sound a little bland.

At medium price the *Italian symphony* is splendidly served by Previn's LSO performance (dating from 1971), fresh, beautifully articulated and with a spontaneous, well-controlled vitality. The couplings are the *Ruy Blas overture* and an equally recommendable account of Prokofiev's *Classical symphony*. The recording is excellent on disc; the tape is compressed, with the upper range more restricted too: RCA Gold Seal GL 12703 [GK].

The *Overture* and *Incidental music* from *A Midsummer Night's Dream* are extremely well served in the medium price-range. Raphael Frühbeck de Burgos's Jubilee record and tape, with excellent soloists, the Ambrosian Chorus and New Philharmonia Orchestra, is absolutely complete and beautifully recorded: Decca JB 72 [KJBC]. Fairly generous selections, including all the key numbers, are also available from Maag (Decca SPA 451 [KCSP]), which is the cheapest, Haitink (Philips Festivo 6570 021 [7310 021]), Kubelik (DG Privilege 2535 393 [3335 393]) and Klemperer (HMV SXLP 30196 [TC-SXLP]). Each of these recordings has its own special character and it is very difficult to suggest a 'best buy', although Kubelik's version has a captivating lightness of touch.

Symphonies Nos. 4 in A major (Italian), Op. 90; 5 in D minor (Reformation), Op. 107.
   * RCA Camden CCV 5035 [c4]. Boston SO, Munch.
Symphony No. 5.
   (*) RCA Victrola (m) AT 123. NBC SO, Toscanini – SCHUBERT: *Symphony No. 5.

A disappointing pair of performances from Munch, over-driven and charmless, and not helped by a recording which glares to the point of distortion. Toscanini, on the other hand, directs a performance of the *Reformation symphony* full of such keen conviction that one forgets the obvious weaknesses of material and structure. Mendelssohnian lightness was not Toscanini's forte, but the playing of the NBC orchestra at the very end of the maestro's career is brilliant, and the

recorded sound is not quite so limited as it usually is from this source.

Andante and rondo capriccioso, Op. 14; Song without words No. 34 (Spinning song), Op. 62/4; Scherzo, Op. 16/2 (arr. Rachmaninov).
   *(*) RCA Camden CCV 5037 [c4]. Brailowsky (piano) – RACHMANINOV: *Piano concerto No. 2.**

Brailowsky's technique had slipped considerably by the time he made these recordings in the autumn of his career. But the underlying articulation is characterful and stylish, and much of the playing is persuasive, in spite of the variable recording.

Messager, André (1853–1929)

Les Deux Pigeons (ballet): suite.
   *** C.f.P. CFP 40298. ROHCGO, Mackerras – DELIBES: *La Source.****

This gay and pretty score represents French ballet music at its most vivacious. The story is slight but it has the background of a gipsy encampment to give it colour and temperament. The music is insubstantial but highly engaging, and charmingly tuneful. Mackerras conducts it with a perfect mixture of warmth and élan, and the sparkling stereo projects the lively orchestral playing vividly.

Milhaud, Darius
(1892–1974)

Le Carnaval d'Aix (fantasy for piano and orchestra).
(*) DG Heliodor 2548 284 [3348 284]. Helffer, Monte Carlo Opera Orch., Frémaux – BRITTEN: *Young Person's Guide**; TURINA: *Danzas fantásticas*.

Milhaud's delightful *Carnaval d'Aix* was written for a visit to America in 1927. It was an arrangement of an earlier work, the ballet *Salade*, which he had composed for Massine three years previously. Although very French in flavour the score also shows influences of Stravinsky's *Pulcinella*. It is wittily good-natured throughout and is in essence a set of variations, producing twelve delightfully vivacious miniatures. The performance here is spirited and stylish: Claude Helffer is an excellent soloist, and the orchestral playing has such verve that one is hardly aware that the Monte Carlo is not one of the outstanding orchestras of Europe. The playing is much less distinguished in Britten's *Young Person's Guide to the Orchestra*, but the Turina *Dances* are attractively played, and this modestly priced disc is well worth having for two works out of the three. The recording is clear and quite well balanced, and it has transferred cleanly and vividly to cassette.

Millöcker, Karl
(1842–99)

Der Bettelstudent (The Beggar Student; operetta): complete.
*** Everest s 466/2. Schock, Gueden, Ollendorf, Schaedle, Konetzni, Minich, Pratsch-Kaufmann, Berlin Opera Choir and SO, Stolz.

Unlike the Strauss operetta issues in the same series this one includes a complete text (but no translation), which helps in elucidating the typically complicated and unbelievable operetta plot about love and petty politics, with the 'beggar student' ending up a genuine count. The performance under Robert Stolz fizzes from beginning to end, and the singing is generally very good, not only from such famous principals as Gueden, Schock and Konetzni but also from Kurt Pratsch-Kaufmann, an archetypal operetta singer, tunelessly characterful in a way that G. and S. addicts will warm to. Millöcker's invention may not always be memorable, but he never lacks charm, and the exuberance of this performance is helped by vividly atmospheric recording.

Mozart, Wolfgang
(1756–91)

Andante in C major for flute and orchestra, K.315: see under *Flute concertos.*

'Favourite concertos': (i; ii) *Clarinet concerto in A major, K.622;* (ii; iii) *Flute and harp concerto in C major, K.299;* (iv–vi) *Flute concerto No. 2 in D major, K.314;* (vii; v; viii) *Horn concertos Nos. 2 and 4 in E flat major, K. 417 and 495.*
*** Decca DPA 521/2 [KDPC]. (i) Prinz; (ii) Vienna PO, Münchinger; (iii) Tripp, Jellinek; (iv) Claude Monteux; (v)

LSO; (vi) Pierre Monteux, (vii) Tuckwell; (viii) Maag.

These are all first-class performances and this two-disc album is very competitively priced. The only snag is that by including only two of the *Horn concertos* this anthology cuts across all the discs offering the complete set. However, for anyone investing in Dennis Brain's full-priced LP this Decca set should make a useful supplement in containing modern stereo recordings of two favourites. The cassette transfers are generally well managed.

'*Favourite composer*': (i; ii) *Clarinet concerto in A major, K.622;* (iii) *Piano concerto No. 21 in C major, K.467;* (iv) *German dance, K.605/3: Sleighride;* (ii; v) *Overture: Le Nozze di Figaro;* (ii; vi) *Serenade No. 13 in G major (Eine kleine Nachtmusik), K.525;* (vii) *Symphony No. 40 in G minor, K.550.*
> ****(*)** Decca DPA 541/2 [KDPC]. (i) Prinz, Münchinger; (II) Vienna PO; (iii) Vered, LPO, Segal; (iv) Vienna Mozart Ens., Boskovsky; (v) Erich Kleiber; (vi) Kertesz; (vii) N Philharmonia Orch., Giulini.

The Prinz/Münchinger account of the *Clarinet concerto* (also available above) cannot be faulted. Refinement and beauty of tone and phrase are a hallmark throughout, and the sound is excellent. Ilana Vered's recording of what, thanks to the film *Elvira Madigan*, is now Mozart's most popular piano concerto is also recommendable, although the recording – originally Phase Four – is very closely balanced. But Miss Vered plays with the spontaneity of youth, phrasing most persuasively, and she is attentively accompanied by Segal and the LPO. Giulini's account of the *G minor Symphony* is beautifully played and recorded, but it is curiously lacking in vitality, neither classically poised nor romantically charged. But the other short items come off well, especially Kertesz's thoroughly musical *Eine kleine Nachtmusik*, and as a set this is generally recommendable, with good cassette transfers to match the discs (the sound on tape occasionally needs a little smoothing in the treble).

(i) *Clarinet concerto in A major, K.622;* (ii) *Clarinet quintet in A major, K.581.*
> ***(*)** RCA Camden CCV 5006 [c4]. Goodman, with (i) Boston SO, Munch; (ii) Boston Symphony String Qt.

Benny Goodman's flirtations with Mozart date from the later thirties, when he made his first 78-r.p.m. discs of the *Quintet* with the Budapest Quartet. The idea of a jazz musician playing 'correct clarinet' (Goodman's own term) was something of a novelty then; today American musicians move from the 'popular' to the 'serious' field more easily. The present coupling is not really a good example. The playing is all too correct and stiff. In both works the only movements that come fully to life are the finales, where Goodman finds an easy, flowing lyricism. Elsewhere he seems over-prudent in matters of expressiveness. The recording dates from 1956 and is rather mushy in texture. But this issue certainly has a place in the catalogue.

Flute concertos Nos. 1 in G major, K.313; 2 in D major, K.314.
> **⊛***** Pickwick SHM 3010. Galway, New Irish Chamber Ens., Prieur.

Andante in C major for flute and orchestra, K.315; Flute concertos Nos. 1 and 2.

MOZART

**(*) C.f.P. CFP 40072 [TC-CFP].
Adeney, ECO, Leppard.

To have modern recordings of Mozart's two *Flute concertos* played by James Galway available in the cheapest price range is bounty indeed. Moreover the accompaniments, ably directed by André Prieur, are polished and stylish, and the recording (although it gives a rather small sound to the violins) is excellent, clear and with good balance and perspective. It might be argued that Galway's vibrato is not entirely suited to these eighteenth-century works, and that his cadenzas too are slightly anachronistic. But the star quality of his playing disarms criticism. The slow movement of the *First Concerto* is beautifully paced; the timbre and phrasing has exquisite delicacy, and the pointed articulation in the finale (nicely matched by the orchestra) is a delight. In No. 2 Galway again floats the melodic line of the first movement with gossamer lightness, and after another enchanting slow movement the finale sparkles joyously, with the orchestra once more on top form.

The Classics for Pleasure alternative offers also the *Andante in C major*, no mean bonus, and Adeney's fine performances (though less imaginative and charismatic than Galway's) are matched by Leppard's crisply turned accompaniments. The only snag here is the recording, which, although admirably clear, is lacking in inner warmth and bloom: the orchestral strings are not very attractively caught by the microphones. However, the recently issued tape version has a much smoother treble without loss of transparency, and the middle response is strikingly warmer. So those collectors who, for whatever reason, resist James Galway will find this C.f.P. cassette an excellent alternative.

Flute and harp concerto in C major, K.299.

72

(*) DG Heliodor 2548 281 [3348 281]. Zöller, Zabaleta, Berlin PO, Märzendorfer – HANDEL: *Harp concerto**; RAVEL: *Introduction and allegro.***(*)

The outer movements of this performance have an attractive rhythmic buoyancy. Karlheinz Zöller is a most sensitive flautist and his phrasing is a constant pleasure, ensuring the success of the slow movement, while Zabaleta's poise and sense of line knit the overall texture of the solo-duet together most convincingly. Märzendorfer conducts expressively yet with a firm overall control. The sound is good, although it has an element of thinness which betrays the recording date (the early sixties). But with a little treble cut-back a very acceptable quality can be achieved. The tape transfer, however, is fuzzy and poorly focused on top.

Horn concertos Nos. 1 in D major, K.412; 2 in E flat major, K.417; 3 in E flat major, K.447; 4 in E flat major, K.495.

*** C.f.P. CFP 148 [TC-CFP]. Brown, Virt. of England, Davison.

James Brown's performances have plenty of life and spirit and are enjoyably spontaneous. Arthur Davison's contribution is a major one. Using a small group of genuine Mozartian dimensions, he achieves crisply sprung accompaniments and he is always attentive to the soloist's style. This is straightforward and musical. The cassette version has been remastered and now has virtually demonstration sound, clean and clear, with plenty of dynamic contrast, and a convincing balance for the soloist.

Piano concertos Nos. 1–6; 8–9; 11–27 (complete).
*** DG 2720 030 (12 discs).

Anda, Camerata Academica of Salzburg Mozarteum.
Piano concertos Nos. 1–6; 8–9; 11–27; Concert rondo No. 1 in D major, K.382.
*** HMV SLS 5031 (12 discs). Barenboim, ECO.

Géza Anda's recordings of the Mozart concertos mostly originate from the 1960s, and his set represents an astonishingly economical way of collecting this repertoire. His readings are invariably poised and blend spontaneity of feeling with well-considered sentiment, so that the impression Anda conveys is of emotion recollected rather than impulsively arrived at. His playing has great finesse and sparkle, when this is called for, and in slow movements, such as those of K.466 and K.453, no mean depth and poetry. He seems to have good rapport with his players, and the occasional untidiness of ensemble is rare enough to be of no importance. There are numerous felicities to mention: K.595, one of the last recordings of the cycle to appear, is particularly distinguished. Apart from its searching slow movement, it has a quality of resignation without ever indulging in the poeticized sentiment that one encounters elsewhere (including Barenboim's ECO reading). Anda has the measure of the varied responses this music calls for, and elsewhere (in the heavenly slow movement of K.413, for example) he never succumbs to the temptation to underline pathos at the expense of an overall grip on its momentum. The *G major Concerto*, K.453, is one of the best recorded versions to be had, with an unfailing sense of sparkle. Inevitably there are some less commanding performances: the *E flat Concerto*, K.271 (Jeunehomme), is not as distinguished as many of its rivals, and K.482 in the same key is slightly lacking in grandeur. Yet on the whole Anda rarely misses a point.

His readings have a sense of line and a classical feeling for proportion. Some of the earlier recordings are beginning to show their age: there is a certain want of bloom and freshness in the upper strings in the *G major Concerto*, K.453, and greater warmth and richness would not come amiss. In this respect Barenboim's EMI set has the advantage, for the sound has greater body and the textures are more transparent. None the less, given the excellence of the DG transfers (the surfaces are impeccable) and the highly competitive price (approximately £2 per disc) this set is well worth considering.

Daniel Barenboim's recordings with the English Chamber Orchestra are slightly later than Anda's. They began appearing in 1967 and were completed by the mid-1970s. The cycle has an engagingly impulsive quality, and whatever reservations one may feel about individual concertos, the sense of joy and spontaneity always shines through. There is an authority as well, total commitment to Barenboim's particular view of a movement, so that the listener feels persuaded that this is the *only* view. As piano playing, it goes without saying that these performances are masterly; the range of colour, the brilliance and the sensitivity of Barenboim's musical equipment are a constant source of admiration. At times he responds to the surface beauties of the music with too ready a display of feeling or colour (the minuet section in the finale of K.271 and the slow movement of the *B flat*, K.595, are a little too much of a good thing), but for the most part the perspectives are well maintained, and there is hardly a bar in the whole set that does not radiate personality. Particularly strong are the performances of K.414, 450 and 451, and if the tempi in the *G major*, K.453, are a little extreme (the first movement is just a shade too rushed), there is no doubting the character and distinction of the playing. If anything,

MOZART

Barenboim seems to have a closer rapport with his players than does Anda, and the ECO wind seem unfailingly responsive to his demands. There are occasional moments that approach preciosity (for example, the slow movement of the *A major*, K.488), and the *B flat Concerto*, K.595, almost steps outside the sensibility of the period; but there are far too many strengths for these to weigh too heavily in the balance. Take, for example, the marvellously articulate way in which Barenboim phrases the second group of the first movement of the *C major Concerto*, K.415: this surely leaves no doubt of his imaginative vitality. There are artists (mostly at full price) whose insights or spirituality in individual concertos Barenboim may not match – Gilels in K.595 and Perahia in K.413, to take only two examples – but this set remains highly distinguished.

Piano concertos Nos. 15 in B flat major, K.450; 25 in C major, K.503.
* D G Heliodor 2548 193. Foldes, Berlin PO, Ludwig.

These recordings come from the early 1960s and sound admirably fresh in their Heliodor transfers; indeed the sound quality shows much greater definition and vitality than the D G originals. The readings have plain virtues. The first movement of the *B flat Concerto* could do with more sparkle, though there is admirable clarity and lack of affectation. Had this playing more spontaneity and warmth and less self-conscious rectitude, it would be more enjoyable. The competition in this repertoire is so strong nowadays that only the most distinguished readings survive.

Piano concertos Nos. 17 in G major, K.453; 26 in D major (Coronation), K.537.
* C.f.P. CFP 40310. Richter-Haaser, Philharmonia Orch., Kertesz.

This record dates from the early 1960s, and an earlier edition of the *Stereo Record Guide* spoke of its 'restrained elegance'. Hans Richter-Haaser is closer to Ingrid Haebler than any other pianist in this respect and seems deliberately to inhibit the range and variety of keyboard colour (and dynamics) in an attempt to scale down his responses to those that would be possible on a period instrument. The result will strike some listeners as prim and wanting in real sparkle and joy. Having much enjoyed Richter-Haaser's Beethoven and Brahms, one has no pleasure in returning such an unenthusiastic response to this issue, but there are so many fine versions clamouring for one's allegiance that this cannot be recommended.

Piano concerto No. 21 in C major, K.467.
** D G Heliodor 2548 287 [3348 287]. Brancart, RTB SO, Hoffman – RACHMANINOV: *Rhapsody on a theme of Paganini.***

Anyone buying this disc or cassette on impulse should be quite well satisfied with it. The recording is vivid and well balanced and the performance is fresh and spontaneous. The famous string cantilena in the slow movement is elegantly phrased without being over-romanticized, and the alert wind playing is another attractive feature of the orchestral contribution. Tempi in the outer movements are brisk but not hurried. With such good sound (the cassette transfer is first-class in every way) this cannot fail to give pleasure.

(i) *Piano concerto No. 21 in C major, K.467. Serenade No. 13 in G*

major (Eine kleine Nachtmusik), K.525.
**(*) C.f.P. CFP 40009 [TC-CFP].
Virt. of England, Davison, (i) with Lympany.

Although this issue was obviously inspired by the *Elvira Madigan* film, the performance is in no way over-romanticized. It is of authentic Mozartian proportions, neat, small in scale, but with plenty of character. The account of *Eine kleine Nachtmusik* is robust yet elegant, not polished to the final degree but crisply articulated, with a beautifully judged *Romanze*, spontaneous and graceful. The recording is clear and vivid to suit the performances, although the forward balance (as with other recordings by this group) brings a limited dynamic range in the serenade. The recording of the concerto has a more natural balance. Both works have been splendidly transferred to cassette (the issue has been remastered), which is an altogether superior bargain to the record, for it includes a delightful bonus, a first-class performance of the *Oboe quartet* from Ian Wilson and the Gabrieli Quartet. The recording here is admirably fresh and clean.

(i) *Double piano concerto in E flat major, K.365;* (ii) *Triple piano concerto in F major, K.242.*
**(*) C.f.P. CFP 40291. Yehudi Menuhin cond. (i) Fou Ts'ong, Hephzibah Menuhin, Bath Fest. CO; (ii) Hephzibah, Yaltah, and Jeremy Menuhin, LPO.

One would have to pay quite a lot more to do better than this. The recording is of mid-1960s vintage and sounds remarkably fresh and vivid, even if the pianos are too forward in the *Double concerto*. The playing in the *Triple concerto* is thoroughly musical and vital

even though it falls short of its main rival version (Ashkenazy, Barenboim, Fou Ts'ong) in refinement and distinction. There is no current version of the *Double concerto* at less than full price that is quite as satisfactory (the Brendel–Klien version sounds its age), though again these soloists, musicianly and spontaneous though they are, do not sound as assured and imaginative as Emil and Elena Gilels, Brendel and Imogen Cooper, or Ashkenazy and Barenboim – all of whom, however, cost much more.

Concert rondos (for piano and orchestra) *Nos. 1 in D major, K.382; 2 in A major, K.386.*
*** D G Heliodor 2548 238. Fischer, Bav. State Orch., Fricsay – BEETHOVEN: *Piano concerto No. 3.* ***

Annie Fischer gives charming performances of Mozart's two brilliant concertante *Rondos*, an excellent fill-up for her outstanding version of Beethoven's *Third Concerto*. The recording is not quite so open as in the Beethoven coupling but it is pleasing, with good piano tone.

Violin concerto No. 3 in G major, K.216.
**(*) RCA Camden CCV 5041 [c4]. Laredo, Washington Nat. SO, Mitchell – BACH: *Violin concerto No. 1.*(*)

A first-class account of Mozart's delightful *G major Concerto* from Jaime Laredo. The slow movement is very beautiful; its success is partly due to the restrained yet eloquent introduction from the Washington orchestra. Indeed Howard Mitchell makes a major contribution throughout, and if the orchestral tuttis are slightly woolly in the bass the soloist is naturally caught and well balanced. The tape transfer has been remastered and generally sounds well, although it benefits from a slight bass cut. But the upper range is free and clear. There are no musical notes with the cassette.

At medium price one must remember David Oistrakh's outstanding performance with the Philharmonia Orchestra, vividly recorded and attractively coupled to Gilels's equally memorable version of Beethoven's *Fourth Piano concerto* (HMV SXLP 30086 [TC-EXE 156]). In the same price-range Philips are currently reissuing the recordings by Szeryng with the New Philharmonia Orchestra under Sir Alexander Gibson. Szeryng plays with great purity of style and musical insight, and the orchestral support is beautifully shaped and responsive. No. 3, K.216, is coupled with No. 5 (the so-called *Turkish*), K.219, on Festivo 6570 024 [7310 024]; Nos. 1 in B flat major, K.207, and 4 in D major, K.218, are on Festivo 6570 109 [7310 109], and this latter issue generously also includes the *Adagio*, K.261, and the *Rondo*, K.269, so is a bargain in the fullest sense of the word. The sound is fresh and clean on disc and tape alike.

Divertimento for wind in B flat major, K.196f.
   ** D G Heliodor 2548 122. Detmold Wind Sextet – SCHUBERT: *Trout quintet.***

This attractive *Divertimento* is given a lively performance and is well recorded. It makes an agreeable makeweight for a good bargain version of Schubert's *Trout quintet*.

Serenade No. 7 in D major (Haffner), K.250.
   ** C.f.P. CFP 40275. Bath Fest. Orch., Menuhin.

Mozart's serenade written for the

wedding celebrations of Elise Haffner in July 1776 is an entirely delightful eight-movement divertimento, of considerable substance. Three of the central movements (starting with an *Andante*) act as a miniature violin concerto, and with such a distinguished soloist they cannot fail to make their effect here. The performance as a whole is vigorously alert, with scrupulous attention to matters of style, but it is somewhat unsmiling. The recording is partially at fault, for, although clear and vivid, it is almost aggressively forward and needs taming to sound wholly congenial. Once this is done there is much to admire and enjoy here.

Serenade No. 13 in G major (Eine kleine Nachtmusik), K.525. Overtures: *Le Nozze di Figaro; Don Giovanni.*
   ** HMV 45 r.p.m. HMV 3. RPO, Colin Davis.

Colin Davis's performance of the well-known *Nachtmusik* is relaxed and stylish, and the recording sounds only slightly dated (the strings in the first movement are not as rich as we would expect today). One wonders if this recording from the early sixties is a suitable candidate for the enhancement of range possible with the 45 r.p.m. presentation. However, the layout seems admirable, with the *Serenade* complete on one side backed by the two fine overture performances, alert, sparkling and dramatic.

Symphonies Nos. 36 in C major (Linz), K.425; 38 in D major (Prague), K.504.
   *** C.f.P. CFP 40336. LPO, Mackerras; Sillem (harpsichord).

Mackerras's coupling has appeared before on C.f.P. and was withdrawn.

Now in this reissue it sounds freshly minted. The inclusion of harpsichord continuo may seem slightly eccentric to some, but these are fine, stylish performances, splendidly played.

Symphonies Nos. 36 in C major (Linz), K.425; 39 in E flat major, K.543.
**(*) RCA Camden ccv 5050 [c4]. Boston SO, Leinsdorf.

Outside the Heliodor catalogue it is rare to find Mozart playing of the calibre provided on this Camden reissue in the lower price ranges. The Boston orchestra's contribution is superbly polished as well as highly sensitive. The recording too is transparent enough to reveal the music's inner detail. The readings are strong and characterful (the first movement of No. 39 especially so), and by playing the repeats Leinsdorf gives extra structural weight to the finales. With such alive and committed music-making any minor reservations are swept aside.

Symphonies Nos. 40 in G minor, K.550; 41 in C major (Jupiter), K.551.
*** C.f.P. cfp 40253 [tc-cfp]. LPO, Mackerras.
* RCA Victrola (m) at 110. NBC SO, Toscanini.

Mackerras directs excellent clean-cut performances. He observes exposition repeats in the outer movements of the *G minor* but not in the *Jupiter* (uncomfortably long for a single side), which is a pity in so majestic a work. Some may prefer a more affectionate style in slow movements, but with clean, modern recording this can compete with records costing more than twice as much. The cassette transfers were originally limited in dynamic range, but they have been remastered with excellent results: the

sound is now full and clear and has plenty of dynamic contrast.

Toscanini was never much of a Mozart stylist – Furtwängler was a supreme classicist next to him – and these are two of the maestro's least sympathetic recordings.

Symphony No. 41 in C major (Jupiter), K.551; Serenade No. 13 in G major (Eine kleine Nachtmusik), K.525.
**(*) RCA Camden ccv 5000 [c4]. Boston SO, Leinsdorf.

A very rewarding account of the *Jupiter* from Leinsdorf to match his excellent performances of Nos. 36 and 39. The strong first movement (exposition repeat included) is matched by the power of the finale, and the slow movement has intensity without being pushed too hard. The minuet and trio are used to lighten the tensions between the other movements, so that the effect of the finale is the more forceful. *Eine kleine Nachtmusik* is also well played, but although Leinsdorf is not ungracious, he is rather too serious here, and the music is not allowed to smile as it can. Nevertheless this is a very worthwhile issue, and the recording has plenty of body, if not always complete transparency of texture.

String quartets Nos. 17 in B flat major (Hunt), K.458; 19 in C major (Dissonance), K.465.
*** C.f.P. cfp 40302. Lindsay Qt.

A highly competitive issue at this price. The *Hunt* is available in a medium-price DG Accolade issue with the Amadeus, and the Lindsay Quartet well withstand the comparison. They play with unforced expressiveness and an alert and vital sensitivity. In the slow movement some readers may even prefer them to their more celebrated rivals, for

they play most beautifully and without
the slightest affectation. Their recording,
too, is more recent and is wider in range.
In the *Dissonance quartet*, so called
because of its bold opening, they face
competition from the Fine Arts Quartet
on Saga (coupled with the *D minor Quartet*, K.421); again there is much sensitivity
here, and they hold their own against the
undoubtedly formidable American
ensemble. In any event, the Fine Arts disc
costs roughly a pound more. We assume
that the small editing error in the minuet
has been cleared up on copies offered for
sale.

OPERA

Don Giovanni: complete.
(**) Everest Olympic (m) 9109/4.
Gobbi, Schwarzkopf, Welitsch,
Seefried, Dermota, Kunz,
Greindl, Vienna PO, Furt-
wängler.

With a cast of legendary quality under
the baton of Furtwängler (in Mozart an
unswerving classicist) this is as much a
historic performance as that of Wagner's
Ring cycle recorded at La Scala in the
same year, 1950. As in the *Ring* the
recording quality is limited and at its
worst is very dim indeed, except that the
prompter is generally heard clear as a
bell. There is similarly a sense of atmosphere in the tension of live performance,
but in Mozart (unlike Wagner) inevitable flaws of ensemble are seriously
distracting, particularly when, as here,
the low ceiling of frequencies means that
the coloration of voices is falsified. It is
splendid to have the enormous tonal
range of a Gobbi applied to Don Giovanni's music – who else can match this
singer's proud defiance? – but at times
he is given a bottled nasal quality
because of the recording. Schwarzkopf
too – the most positive of the women –
loses some of her bloom, and her cry of

'*Perfido mostro*' before the Act 1 quartet
comes at a sudden dimming of sound.
Ljuba Welitsch is made to sound raw
from lack of transients, and only Irmgard
Seefried's voice has its natural sweetness, though among the men Dermota's
tenor has purity and poise. At the price
it is a set well worth hearing but the
flaws will tend to bar frequent repetition.

It hardly needs saying that the four
key Mozart operas are an essential cornerstone for any serious record collection, however modest. *Die Zauberflöte*
is well served in the bargain range by
the splendid Fricsay mono set (see
below); any consideration of the other
three, *Così fan tutte, Don Giovanni* and
Le Nozze di Figaro (of which only *Don
Giovanni* is available on bargain label)
must take into account the classic Walter
Legge productions of the early sixties.
All have been reissued by HMV at
medium price on both disc and tape (the
cassettes admirably clear, but slightly
less rich than the LPs). Elisabeth
Schwarzkopf (at the peak of her vocal
powers) and Giuseppe Taddei are common to all three sets; Boehm conducts
Così fan tutte (SLS 5028 [TC-SLS]), Giulini *Don Giovanni* (SLS 5083 [TC-SLS])
and *Figaro* (SLS 5152 [TC-SLS]). The
famous Kleiber set of *Nozze di Figaro*
must also be remembered, with Hilde
Gueden and Lisa della Casa both at their
finest. This Mozart bicentenary recording from the mid-1950s still sounds well
on disc (Decca Ace of Diamonds GOS
585/7), but the cassette transfer [K 79
K 32] is one of the great achievements of
the tape catalogue. With each act heard
unbroken on a single side, and miraculously natural sound quality, the cassette format brings a completely new
dimension to the performance as a
whole. Another outstanding *Figaro*
recording is the exceptionally generous
selection of highlights from the Leinsdorf Vienna set, with Lisa della Casa
again in the role of the Countess, Rob-
erta Peters a sparkling Susanna, and

78

Rosalind Elias an excellent Cherubino. It is the ladies who shine rather than the men, but this single disc (or cassette) containing fourteen numbers is by any standards a bargain: Decca SPA 514 [KCSP].

Finally there is the two-disc Beecham set of *Die Entführung aus dem Serail. Il Seraglio* (as it is more affectionately known to many Mozartians) is perhaps less commanding a stage work than the other four – the weakness of the ending a dramatic drawback, however attractive its optimism is to the audience – but it contains some of Mozart's most enchanting music and creates in Osmin one of the most appealing of all opera's buffo characters. In the Beecham set Gottlob Frick is unforgettable in this role and if the set is otherwise flawed in its casting, there is much to delight the ear in a performance that is as stylish as it is vivacious: HMV SLS 5153 [TC-SLS].

La finta giardiniera (Die Gärtnerin aus Liebe): complete.
(**) Everest s 444/3. Guillaume, Plumacher, Hohmann, Neidlinger, Stuttgart Chorus and Orch., Reinhardt.

This is infinitely preferable to the set of another early Mozart opera, *Il Re pastore*, on the same label, for though here too the recording is limited, the freshness and sparkle of the performance defy any scrubbiness of sound. Rolf Reinhardt's direction is lively, the playing of the Stuttgart Orchestra is well sprung, and the very good team of soloists includes Gustav Neidlinger, later to establish himself as the supreme Alberich in the *Ring*. Here in the bass role of Nardo he is magnificent, a most stylish Mozartian. The piece itself is a real charmer, the most appealing of the juvenile Mozart operas, and though cuts are made and no spoken dialogue is included (with justification this perform-

ance uses the German text) the comedy comes over well. Words and translation are included.

Il Re pastore: complete.
(*) Everest s 449/2. Giebel, Nentwig, Plumacher, Hohmann, Weikenmeier, Stuttgart Tonstudio Orch., Lund.

Mozart's early pastoral opera is among the most charming products of his teens, but this is too rough a performance to give much pleasure, particularly as the recording is limited and the string tone seedy. Presumably this was a performance done for radio, and none of the soloists is flattered. The best of them, the contralto Hetty Plumacher, has the bloom taken from her voice by the recording, and though she and the others cope with the abundant florid music, intrusive aitches abound. Despite good intentions the piece fails to sparkle as it should. Unlike most other issues from this source this one provides the complete text and translation.

Die Zauberflöte (The Magic Flute): complete, with dialogue.
⊛*** DG Heliodor (m) 2701 015 (3 discs). Stader, Streich, Otto, Haefliger, Vantin, Fischer-Dieskau, Greindl, Borg, Berlin RIAS Chamber Choir, Berlin Motet Choir, RIAS SO, Fricsay.

Zauberflöte drew from Fricsay one of his very finest opera performances on record, fresh and alert, with superb choral singing and some outstanding contributions from the soloists. It is in every way a classic set, and the mono recording from the mid-fifties still sounds astonishingly well. There has never been a more dazzling account of the Queen of the Night's role in a complete set than this one from Rita

Streich, and the recording balance disguises any lack of size, bringing out the sweetness and phenomenal brilliance. Fischer-Dieskau – like his great predecessor Gerhard Hüsch, Papageno to Beecham – treats the role of Papageno in Lieder-style, and very compelling it is, the more valuable because, conscious of his physical size, Fischer-Dieskau never sang the part on stage. For these two performances alone the set is indispensable. The other singers are more variable, and Josef Greindl's Sarastro is disppointing; but overall the performance is unforgettable. This is a great deal more than just a historic reissue.

Mundy, William
(*c*. 1529–*c*. 1591)

Vox Patris caelestis.
> *** C.f.P. CFP 40339 [TC–CFP]. Tallis Scholars, Phillips – ALLEGRI: *Miserere****; PALESTRINA: *Missa Papae Marcelli.***(*)

William Mundy's *Vox Patris caelestis* was written during the short reign of Queen Mary (1553–8). While it is almost exactly contemporary with Palestrina's *Missa Papae Marcelli*, its florid, passionate polyphony is very different from that of the Italian composer. This is emphasized by Peter Phillips' eloquent performance, which presses the music onwards to reach an exultant climax in the closing stanza with the words: '*Veni, Veni, veni caelesti gloria coronaberis*'. The work is structured in nine sections in groups of three, the last of each group being climactic and featuring the whole choir, with solo embroidery. Yet the music flows continuously, like a great river, and the complex vocal writing creates the most spectacular effects, with the

trebles soaring up and shining out over the underlying cantilena. The imaginative force of the writing is never in doubt, and the Tallis Scholars give an account which balances linear clarity with considerable power. The recording is first-class and the reverberant acoustic adds bloom and richness without blurring the detail.

Mussorgsky, Modest
(1839–81)

Night on the Bare Mountain (arr. Rimsky-Korsakov).
> **(*) DG Heliodor 2548 267 [3348 267]. Berlin PO, Maazel – RESPIGHI: *Pines of Rome*; RIMSKY-KORSAKOV: *Capriccio espagnol.****
> *(*)C.f.P. CFP40309. LPO, Susskind – BORODIN: *In the Steppes* etc.*(*)

Mussorgsky wrote his *Night on the Bare Mountain* in 1867 but never heard it played. The piece we know, although it uses some of Mussorgsky's basic material, is more a work of Rimsky-Korsakov, who added much music of his own, including the contrasting lyrical section at the end. The original has undoubted power and fascination, but its construction is a good deal less polished and there are few who would argue that Rimsky's piece is not more telling and vividly dramatic, even if it is so little like the original. Maazel's version is part of an outstanding Berlin Philharmonic triptych which dates from the early days of stereo. The acoustic here is slightly less expansive than in the rest of the programme (especially on tape), but there is no lack of electricity.

Susskind's account is well played and is given a vivid modern recording; but the performance refuses to catch fire, and only really comes to life in Rimsky's lyrical coda. One must remember that in the lower-medium price-range there is a superb collection of Russian music played by the Berlin Philharmonic under Sir Georg Solti. This includes not only a gripping account of *Night on the Bare Mountain* but also the beautiful *Khovantschina Prelude*, with the *Persian dance* from the same opera for good measure. The other items – no less recommendable – are Glinka's overture for *Russlan and Ludmilla* and Borodin's for *Prince Igor*. The recording is first-class in every way: Decca SPA 257 [KCSP].

Night on the Bare Mountain; Pictures at an Exhibition (orch. Ravel).
**(*) RCA Camden CCV 5038 [c4]. Chicago SO, Reiner.

Reiner's account of *Pictures at an Exhibition* dates from the earliest days of stereo but it still sounds astonishingly vivid, lacking something in sheer brilliance, but having fine weight and atmosphere. *Night on the Bare Mountain* is slightly more recent, but both are splendid performances, finely characterized and superbly played. The Chicago brass has always been famous, and listening to this record one can see how well the reputation is deserved; but the whole orchestra is on top form. The early RCA stereo, however, lacks something in sharpness of focus.

Pictures at an Exhibition (orch. Ravel).
(*) RCA (m) AT 107. NBC SO, Toscanini – RAVEL: *Daphnis et Chloé Suite No. 2.*(*)
** C.f.P. CFP 40319 [TC-CFP]. LPO, Pritchard – PROKOFIEV: *Symphony No. 1.**(*)

Although time has not improved the quality of this RCA recording, which is somewhat shallow and strident, the performance remains undimmed. Toscanini brings his highly charged temperament to this score, which hums with atmosphere and electricity under his baton. Whether in the brilliance of *Baba Yaga* or the delicacy of the *Unhatched chicks*, the sheer virtuosity of this performance has few, if any, rivals. Of course, Ravel's luxurious orchestral mantle deserves the most opulent recorded sound, and its absence must bring a degree of reservation. The performance, however, is in a class of its own (some may think it just a shade over-driven, but no conductor of this voltage fails to sound high-powered) and this transfer is an improvement on the earlier stereo transcription: it is smoother and in better focus.

A brilliant account under Pritchard, in which the personality of the orchestra comes over strongly, the players obviously enjoying themselves and their own virtuosity. The very clear, dry recording makes every detail of the orchestration glitter, even if it lacks atmosphere, and the conductor's characterization of each picture is equally positive. The building of the *Great Gate of Kiev* finale is vividly exciting. This recording has recently been remastered and recoupled, and its sharpness of detail is now even more striking, both on disc and on tape (which approaches demonstration standard).

Pictures at an Exhibition (original piano version, ed. Horowitz).
*** RCA (m) VH 017. Horowitz – BRAHMS: *Violin sonata No. 3* etc.*(*)
(*) RCA (m) VH 010. Horowitz – HAYDN: *Piano sonata No. 52.*(*)

Playing of this calibre invites a stunned silence rather than any attempt to describe its impact, except perhaps to say that it is the pianistic equivalent of Toscanini's famous record of the orchestral transcription. Horowitz's technique is, of course, transcendental, and the excitement he generates in the studio version made in 1947 (which is offered on VH 017) has rarely been surpassed on record, even by Richter. The piano quality calls for some degree of tolerance, but its shallowness is soon forgotten as the playing unfolds.

Baba-Yaga is even more dazzling, perhaps, in the later 'live performance' (VH 010), which derives from a Carnegie Hall recital of 1951. Not content with the work's challenges, Horowitz rewrites the end of *Gnomes* as well as parts of *Limoges, Catacombs*, and *The Great Gate of Kiev*, and he adds octaves here and there. Yet it is not all barnstorming virtuosity; there is great delicacy of articulation in the *Ballet of the chicks*. The quality of the sound here is even more primitive and clangorous: hence the qualified star rating, but the playing is extraordinary. Indeed, whichever version you choose, Horowitz's *Pictures at an Exhibition* is like any phenomenon of nature – quite miraculous.

The Marriage (opera).
   (*) Everest Olympic (m) 9105. Agroff, Desmazures, Mollien, Popovitsky, Paris PO, Liebowitz.

Just what processing has been used to produce the curious sound here is hard to imagine. The recording was originally made many years ago, and presumably the jangling bottled quality with copious distortion stems from an attempt to open up boxy sound. Despite the sound barrier the magnificence of some of the singing in Mussorgsky's charming comedy about an old bachelor comes over well, notably the dark bass of Nicolas Agroff in the central role of Podkolesine. The text (with one or two misprints) is printed on the back of the sleeve, and though the measure of music is short (only thirty-two minutes) it is good to be reminded of an attractive one-act piece otherwise unavailable on record.

Nielsen, Carl (1865–1931)

Symphony No. 4 (Inextinguishable), Op. 29; En Sagadrøm (tone poem), *Op. 39.*
   **(*) DG Heliodor 2548 240. Royal Danish Orch., Markevitch.

In some ways this must be accounted the best version of the *Fourth Symphony* now on the market. It is a wartime work, begun in 1914 and finished two years later, and it strikes a darker, more northerly note than any of its predecessors. The smiling Danish countryside of the *Espansiva* gives way to an altogether wilder and more violent landscape. Markevitch's recording, made in the mid-1960s for the Danish Fona label, has the measure of its power, and conveys something of its sweep and majesty. The moments of repose are well handled too. The Royal Danish Orchestra play capably for their distinguished guest, and respond in *Sagadrøm* with playing of cool sensitivity and atmosphere. Unfortunately, the Heliodor transfer is made at a much lower level than the Danish original, and accordingly there is some loss of impact and presence, unless the level setting is high (and surface noise thus increased). Were that not the case, this would be a three-star recommendation. It offers far better value than Mehta's full-price Decca recording in having a fill-up, and it poses a stiff challenge to Ole Schmidt's LSO record on Unicorn, also bereft of any companion. Given the enormous saving, Markevitch will probably be many collectors' first choice.

As we go to press, RCA have reissued André Previn's LSO recording of the *First Symphony*, and this is likely to remain unchallenged at medium price. It is coupled with the *Prelude to Act 2* from *Saul and David* on GL 42872 [GK]. Unicorn have also announced medium-priced reissues of the Schmidt recordings with the LSO: *Symphony No. 1* KPM 7001; *Symphony No. 2* KPM 7002; *Symphony No. 3* KPM 7003.

Orff, Carl
(born 1895)

Carmina Burana (cantiones profanae).
(*) C.f.P. CFP 40311 [TC-CFP]. Soloists, Houston Chorale and Youth Symphony Boys' Choir, Houston SO, Stokowski.
(*) Pye GSGC 15001 [ZCCCB]. Soloists, Salzburg Mozarteum Choir and Orch., Prestel.
** DG Heliodor 2548 194 [3348 194]. Soloists, Leipzig Radio and Children's Choirs and Radio SO, Kegel.

Rhythmic relentlessness is a quality much in demand in Orff's cantata, and though Stokowski brings to this unexpected repertory his usual flair and individuality, he does not have the bite one really needs for such music to have its full impact. The recording, originally from Capitol, is not as bright as some from that source, but at the price this is a more than acceptable record on which to get to know a work that has defied

the pundits in remaining genuinely popular. Moreover, any doubts about the rather recessed effect of the Capitol recording on disc (which appears to come from the original masters) is dispelled on tape, which offers quite different sound, brilliant at the top, with incisively vivid projection for the chorus.

There is an excellent case, too, for Kurt Prestel's version (a favourite of I.M.'s). This is amiably earthy and direct, in a reading which favours rather slow speeds but does not lose forward momentum. By the standards of more expensive versions the imprecisions of ensemble may irritate some ears, but there is a vitality about the performance that matches Orff's prose well. The cassette is of outstanding quality, with fine sparkle and edge.

On Herbert Kegel's earlier DG recording, reissued on Heliodor, he directs a literal, largely unpointed reading which conveys little of the fun of the extrovert numbers or the tenderness of the first spring chorus. The ensemble of the magnificent Leipzig Choir is superb, sounding relatively small in a very clean acoustic. The recording is nicely balanced and immediate.

Palestrina, Giovanni da
(c. 1525–94)

Missa Papae Marcelli.
(*) C.f.P. CFP 40339 [TC-CFP]. Tallis Scholars, Phillips – ALLEGRI: *Miserere*; MUNDY: *Vox Patris caelestis.****

Palestrina's *Missa Papae Marcelli* has a famous historical reputation for its influence on decisions made at the Council of Trent. The Catholic hierarchy had become concerned that the elaborate counterpoint of much church music, and the interpolation of non-liturgical texts, was obscuring the ritual purpose of the mass itself. Palestrina's work, with its syllabic style and clear text, supposedly demonstrated that great music need not cover the religious message and so influenced the decision not to ban polyphony altogether. If the story is apocryphal, there is no doubt that Palestrina's settings satisfied the authorities, while the quality of his music, and the memorability of the *Missa Papae Marcelli* in particular, are equally certain. With its apparent simplicity of line and serene beauty, which disguises an underlying fervour, it is not a work which lends itself readily to performers with an Anglican background. This account is certainly the finest at present available on record, catching the music's cool dignity and much of its expressive richness. The singing has purity of tone, a refined control of dynamics and beauty of phrasing. It is splendidly recorded within the admirably reverberant acoustic of Merton College, Oxford.

Pergolesi, Giovanni (1710–36)

Oboe concerto (arr. Barbirolli).
*** Pye GSGC 15034. Rothwell, Hallé Orch., Barbirolli – HAYDN and CORELLI; *Concertos.****

Evelyn Rothwell's neat, feminine style suits this work to perfection. This is a Barbirolli arrangement using tunes from sonatas, a song and the *Stabat Mater*; but the whole is so felicitously put together that no one could guess it was not conceived in this form. The predominant mood is pastoral, with a slow opening leading to a gracious *Allegro*

and an *Andantino* intervening before the gentle finale. The performance characterizes the music perfectly.

Praetorius, Michael (1571–1621)

Dances from Terpsichore.
***C.f.P. CFP 40335 [TC-CFP].
Praetorius Consort, Ball – HOLBORNE:*Airs*; LAMBRANZI: *Dances.****

Terpsichore is a huge collection of some three hundred dance tunes used by the French court dance bands of Henry IV. They were enthusiastically assembled by the German composer Michael Praetorius, who also harmonized them and arranged them in four to six parts. Moreover he left plenty of advice as to their manner of performance, although he would not have expected any set instrumentation – this would depend on the availability of musicians. Any selection is therefore as arbitrary in the choice of items as it is conjectural in the matter of their orchestration. Christopher Ball has arranged the present suite skilfully, although the consort he uses tends to be marginally too recorder-dominated. The playing is alive and spontaneous and has a real sense of fun. The ready tunefulness of the music is most engaging. At times the ear might wish for rather more use of viols, although variety is provided by employing lute and crumhorns etc. to vary the colouring. The C.f.P. recording is crisp and clean, and the couplings are imaginative. The tape is of demonstration quality – there is no discernible difference between the disc and cassette. Highly recommended.

Prokofiev, Serge
(1891–1953)

Cinderella (ballet) *Op. 87:* excerpts.
** Everest 3016. NY Stadium
Orch., Stokowski – VILLA-
LOBOS: *Bachianas Brasileiras
No. 1* etc.**

Stokowski made up his own suite from
the *Cinderella* ballet to follow the story
sequentially, whereas Prokofiev's own
suites both depart radically from the
ballet sequence. It is well played and
brilliantly recorded.

'Favourite composer': (i–iii) *Piano
concerto No. 3 in C major, Op. 26;*
(iv) *Lieutenant Kijé: Suite, Op. 60;*
(v) *The Love of Three Oranges:
March; Scherzo;* (vi; ii; vii) *Peter
and the Wolf, Op. 67;* (ii; viii)
*Romeo and Juliet, Op. 64; extended
suite;* (ii, vii) *Symphony No. 1 in D
major (Classical), Op. 25.*
⊛*** Decca DPA 617/8 [KDPC].
(i) Katchen; (ii) LSO; (iii)
Kertesz; (iv) Paris Cons. Orch.,
Boult; (v) Suisse Rom. Orch.,
Ansermet; (vi) Richardson
(narrator); (vii) Sargent; (viii)
Abbado.

A truly outstanding set which would
make an admirable basis for any collection of Prokofiev's music. The performances are all highly recommendable. Sir
Malcolm Sargent's account of the
Classical symphony may not be the most
brilliant available, but it is full of character and the recording is remarkably
vivid. All the tempi, except perhaps the
finale, are slow, but Sir Malcolm's self-
assurance carries its own spontaneity,
and this is one of the richest gramophone
offerings he gave us.

Sir Ralph Richardson's version of
Peter and the Wolf is also superbly
recorded in the very best Decca manner,
sumptuous and colourful. Sir Malcolm's
direction of the orchestral contribution
shows his professionalism at its very
best, with very finely prepared orchestral
playing, and many imaginative little
touches of detail brought to one's attention, yet with the forward momentum of
the action perfectly sustained. Sir Ralph
brings an actor's feeling for words to the
narrative. He dwells lovingly on their
sound as well as their meaning, and this
preoccupation with the manner in which
the story is told matches Sargent's feeling exactly. There are some delicious
moments when that sonorous voice
delights in its own coloration, none more
taking than Grandfather's very reasonable moral: 'and if Peter had not caught
the wolf . . . what then?' But of course
he did, and in this account it was surely
inevitable.

Katchen's performance of the *Third
Concerto* is first-class in every way and
no less welcome is Sir Adrian Boult's
witty and atmospheric account of *Lieutenant Kijé,* the recording hardly showing its age (1958) except for the inclusion
of rather more background noise than
usual. The surprise bonus is Abbado's
selection from *Romeo and Juliet,* which
includes some of the most delightful
numbers that are normally omitted from
the suites, such as the *Dance with man-
dolins,* the *Aubade* and so on. Despite
a slight want of intensity and fire, there
is an admirable lightness and delicacy of
touch here that are most captivating.
The recording – warm and rather soft-
grained – has a beautifully balanced
overall perspective and suits the style of
the music-making. With demonstration-
worthy cassette transfers to match the
discs closely, this set can be strongly
recommended in either format.

Peter and the Wolf, Op. 67.

** C.f.P. CFP 185 [TC-CFP]. Richard Baker, N. Philharmonia Orch., Leppard – BRITTEN: *Young Person's Guide.* **

Richard Baker, balanced well forward in a different acoustic from the orchestra, provides an extra introductory paragraph which might become tedious on repetition. But he enters into the spirit of the story well enough and is only occasionally too coy. Leppard provides an excellent account of the orchestral score and the recording is vivid. But in the last analysis one's reaction to this record depends on how one takes to the narration, and there will be mixed views on this. The disc is excellent value, and so is the cassette, which is admirably clear.

Romeo and Juliet (ballet), *Op. 64:* excerpts.
* C.f.P. CFP 40266. LPO, Pritchard.

This compilation is no match for earlier anthologies from *Romeo and Juliet.* It is not as well recorded as Efrem Kurtz's Philharmonia account of the mid-1960s nor as well played as the Ančerl version with the Czech Philharmonic, both of which have been on the Classics for Pleasure label at one time or another. The recording is a little bottom-heavy, and though the LPO respond sensitively to Pritchard, there is none of the sense of atmosphere or the dramatic fire that are essential to the score. The Abbado version with the LSO (see above) is a little cool but it has no want of sensitivity and is beautifully recorded. The LPO version is really not quite distinguished enough to make the grade.

Symphony No. 1 in D major (Classical), Op. 25.
*(**) RCA Camden CCV 5025

[**(*) c4]. LSO, Previn – *Concert.* *(**)
** RCA Victrola (m) AT 122. NBC SO, Toscanini – KODÁLY: *Háry János*; SIBELIUS: *Finlandia.* **
*(*) C.f.P. CFP 40319 [TC-CFP]. LPO, Davison– MUSSORGSKY: *Pictures.* **

A neatly turned account of this delightful symphony from Previn and the LSO is included in a potentially attractive RCA Camden showcase concert. The snag is the recording, which has been artificially brightened and offers unattractively edgy string tone. One can achieve more smoothness with the controls, but this clumsy remastering has also robbed the recording of much of its bloom. A similar (apparently artificial) quality also detracts from Davison's modern LPO recording. The brightness here is even less appropriate because the performance is basically genial and relaxed (not unlike Sargent's version – see above). But when the piccolo joins the violins the shrillness is piercing, and the sound is much the same on both disc and cassette.

Toscanini's reading is elegant and nicely pointed, with tempi never rushed. The slow movement is given a measured reading and the finale is sparkling in its clarity. This is well coupled with other works that show an unexpected side to the conductor, though they are poorly recorded.

Symphony No. 5 in B flat major, Op. 100; Romeo and Juliet, Op. 64: excerpts.
⊛*** RCA Victrola (m) VL 12021. Boston SO, Koussevitzky.

Under Serge Koussevitzky the Boston Symphony achieved heights it has never quite equalled since, and this remarkable set offers evidence of it at its most inspired. This record was made in 1945, shortly after the *Fifth Symphony*'s American première, and not even the Berlin Philharmonic and Karajan surpass its virtuosity and brilliance. The strings of the Boston orchestra sing with magnificent eloquence, and their account of the slow movement has a lyrical intensity unequalled on record. The scherzo has terrific rhythmic bite. The *Romeo* excerpts have incisive attack, a superb dramatic fire and excitement, and the recording (made in the same year) is breathtakingly vivid for its age. An astonishing and thrilling record.

Puccini, Giacomo (1858–1924)

La Bohème (opera): complete.
  ** RCA Victrola (m) AT 203 (2 discs). Albanese, Peerce, Valentino, McKnight, Moscona, Cehanovsky, NBC SO and Chorus, Toscanini.

La Bohème was the first Italian opera that Toscanini conducted for NBC in New York, and his joy in returning to the piece he helped to bring into the world in the 1890s is very clear all through. There is some stiffness and the very occasional breathlessness, but in general this is one of the most warm-hearted performances that Toscanini ever put on record, with the maestro delightedly joining in with vocal contributions during such climaxes as Rodolofo's *Che gelida manina*. Despite flaws Jan Peerce and Licia Albanese make an appealing pair of lovers, though always it is the conducting rather than the singing which commands first attention, a performance of unparalleled drive which knits the structure tautly together.

The recording is typically dry and unatmospheric.

Those wanting a modern stereo version can turn to the medium-priced Decca set. Tebaldi and Bergonzi head a strong cast, with Bastiani and Siepi both first-rate as Marcello and Colline. The recording sounds slightly dated now (the orchestral strings lack body and richness) but the voices come over without loss of bloom: Decca D 5 D 2 [K 5 K 22]. Similarly the Decca catalogue provides an outstanding medium-priced version of *La Fanciulla del West*, an opera that has recently very much come back into favour. Tebaldi here gives one of her most warm-hearted and understanding performances on record: Ace of Diamonds GOS 594/6. No less famous is Tebaldi's recording of *Madama Butterfly*; the characterization is not dramatically subtle, but her singing is consistently rich and beautiful. She is well supported by Bergonzi and Cossotto, and Serafin conducts expansively: Decca D 4 D 3. Also in the medium price-range is the Victoria de los Angeles HMV set of the same opera, recorded in Rome under Santini. The 1960 recording displays her art at its most endearing, her range of golden tone-colour lovingly exploited. Opposite her, Jussi Bjoerling was making one of his very last recordings, and though he shows few special insights, he produced a flow of rich tone to compare with that of the heroine. The rest of the cast is less distinctive. The sound has plenty of body and clarity as well as bloom both on disc and tape: SLS 5128 [TC-SLS].

For *Manon Lescaut* one turns back even further to the mid-fifties, when Tebaldi was at the height of her career. While her characterization of the heroine hardly suggests the little woman of Puccini's dreams, she produces a consistent flow of gorgeous rich tone. As in *Fanciulla* her tenor partner is Mario del Monaco, whose coarseness as Des

PUCCINI

Grieux mars the set, but this is exciting red-blooded singing and he does not overwhelm Tebaldi in the duet sequences. With warmly intense direction from Molinari-Pradelli and remarkably good sound, this remains fully competitive at Ace of Diamonds price: Decca GOS 607/8.

There has never been a finer recording of *Tosca* than Callas's first, with Victor de Sabata conducting and Tito Gobbi as Scarpia. Giuseppe di Stefano as the hero, Cavaradossi, was also at his finest. The conducting of Victor de Sabata is spaciously lyrical as well as sharply dramatic, and although the recording (originally mono, here stereo transcription) is obviously limited, it is superbly balanced in Walter Legge's fine production: HMV SLS 825 [TC-SLS]. For those wanting the full advantage of stereo in this most atmospheric of operas, Karajan's Decca set, with Leontyne Price assuming the title role, can also be strongly recommended. Price is at the peak of her form and di Stefano as Cavaradossi sings most sensitively. Giuseppe Taddei as Scarpia displays a marvellously wide range of tone-colour, and although he cannot quite match the Gobbi snarl, he has almost every other weapon in his armoury. The Vienna Philharmonic Orchestra sounds splendidly vivid and opulent, and Karajan's direction deserves equal credit with the singers: Decca 5BB 123/4 [K 59 K 22].

'*Favourite composer*': Arias, duets and ensembles: (i–v) *La Bohème: Che gelida manina; Sì, mi chiamano Mimì; O soave fanciulla; La commedia è stupenda; Quando men vo; In un coupé; O Mimì, tu più non torni;* (i–ii; v–vi) *Madama Butterfly: Love duet; Flower duet; Humming chorus:* (i; vii–viii; ix) *Tosca: Sante ampolle; Recondita armonia; Te Deum; Vissi d'arte; E lucevan le stelle;* (i; vii; ix) *Manon Lescaut; In quelle trine morbide; Oh, sarò la più bella; Tu, tu amore;* (i; vii; x–xi) *Turandot: Signore, ascolta; Non piangere, Liù; Ah! per l'ultima volta; In questa reggia; Nessun dorma; Tu che di gel sei cinta;* (xii–xiii; xi) *La Fanciulla del West: Ch'ella mi creda;* (i; xiii–xiv) *Gianni Schicchi: O mio babbino caro.*
*** Decca DPA 533/4 [KDPC]. (i–xi) Chorus and Orch. of St Cecilia Academy, Rome; (i) Tebaldi; (ii) Bergonzi; (iii) d'Angelo; (iv) Bastianini; (v) Serafin; (vi) Cossotto; (vii) del Monaco; (viii) London; (ix) Molinari-Pradelli; (x) Borkh; (xi) Erede; (xii) Bjoerling; (xiii) Orch. of Maggio Musicale Fiorentino; (xiv) Gardelli.

This two-disc (or tape) anthology was compiled from Decca's first generation of stereo recordings (Tebaldi had, of course, previously recorded *Bohème, Butterfly* and *Tosca* in mono). For those not investing in the complete sets (discussed above) it is especially valuable in reminding us how high the overall standards, both of artistry and recording, were and in particular the superb contribution made by Tebaldi, one of the richest voices of our time, or indeed any other time. The selection is made and edited with characteristic Decca skill and provides an enriching experience, containing as it does some of the greatest lyric opera ever written. The tape transfers are consistently well done to match the discs closely.

Purcell, Henry
(1658–95)

Abdelazer: Suite. Chacony in G minor. Come, ye sons of art: Overture. The Indian Queen: Trumpet overture. (Trio) *Sonata No. 9 in F major (Golden).*
** C.f.P. CFP 40208. Virt. of England, Davison.

Arthur Davison presents this music in his usual lively way, verging on briskness, but not without style. The recording is extremely bright, so that the sound of the trumpet in the opening piece is extremely brilliant, and the strings want something in body. The recording in fact sounds more like an older disc refurbished than one made in 1974/5. The suite from *Abdelazer* is the most successful item here: it includes the tune Britten made famous in his *Young Person's Guide to the Orchestra*, although here it is given a dotted rhythm which is infectious. On the whole an enjoyable collection, if not a distinctive one.

Turning to Purcell's vocal music, it is worth remembering that Oiseau-Lyre offer two outstanding recordings of stage works at medium price. Their set of *King Arthur*, conducted by Anthony Lewis, dates from the earliest days of stereo but sounds as fresh as the day it was made, with outstanding contributions from singers of the calibre of Elsie Morison, Heather Harper, John Whitworth, Wilfred Brown, John Cameron and Hervey Alan: SOL 60008/9. Janet Baker's first (1962) recording of *Dido and Aeneas* was also conducted by Lewis, and although the supporting cast is somewhat uneven, Baker's is a truly great performance. Like *King Arthur* the record is beautifully engineered: SOL 60047.

Rachmaninov, Sergei
(1873–1943)

(i) *Piano concerto No. 1 in F sharp minor, Op. 1;* (ii) *Rhapsody on a theme of Paganini, Op. 43.*
⊛*** C.f.P. CFP 40267 [TC-CFP].
(i) Binns, LPO, Gibson; (ii) Wayenberg, Philharmonia Orch., Dohnányi.

This record and tape are extraordinary in presenting two separate occasions when everything in the recording studio went right. Malcolm Binns is shown on the evidence here to be an uncommonly fine player. He gives a youthfully fresh performance of Rachmaninov's *First Concerto* that captures the listener from the first note to the last. His affinity for the Rachmaninov phraseology is such that the tunes blossom naturally and the structure knits convincingly together. Gibson is hardly less sympathetic; the LPO playing is splendidly alert and sparkling and yet relaxes tenderly for the presentation of the memorable lyrical tune of the finale. The recording is superb. There is no version of any Rachmaninov concerto balanced more naturally, with a vivid and truthful piano image perfectly set within the orchestral tapestry. The record was originally made for World Records and it is perhaps not surprising to find that the balance engineer was Anthony Griffith.

When one turns over for the *Rhapsody* it is to find another performance and recording hardly less vivid and with the same feeling of a live occasion that distinguishes the *Concerto*. Each variation is grippingly and spontaneously characterized, and Christoph von Dohnányi brings out every detail of the orchestration. The famous *Eighteenth* has striking poetic fervour, and the closing pages generate great excitement. The recording is sparklingly clear, yet has no want of substance or depth, while the piano image is crisp in just the right way. The cassette transfer is of demonstration quality; there is little perceptible difference between the two media. Perhaps if anything the orchestral strings are more firmly focused on tape than on disc. An outstanding recommendation.

Piano concerto No. 2 in C minor, Op. 18.
* RCA Camden CCV 5037 [c4]. Brailowsky, San Francisco SO, Jorda– MENDELSSOHN:*Piano music.**(*)
Piano concerto No. 2; Preludes: in D major, Op. 23/4; in G major, Op. 32/5; in G sharp minor, Op. 32/12.
**(*) C.f.P. CFP 167 [TC-CFP]. Lympany, RPO, Sargent.

Moura Lympany's Classics for Pleasure performance has not quite the temperament of her earlier, mono account, in which she was partnered by Malko; but this is a good, straightforward reading, helped by superb recording, with full, rich piano tone and excellent balance. There are many little touches of phrasing and dynamic shading to distinguish the orchestral playing, and the slow movement is notably beautiful. Just occasionally there is the feeling that the tension is *too much* under control, but this is only momentary, for clearly both conductor and soloist are in great sympathy with Rachmaninov's melodic inspiration. The three *Preludes* are admirably chosen and are very effective indeed. The tape transfer is of excellent quality, matching the disc closely.

Alexander Brailowsky's reading is indulgently romantic, the very epitome of the grand manner. The opening chords are played deliberately and melodramatically; then the orchestra rather disconcertingly sets off into a briskly

paced allegro. The first movement's climax is effective, and the slow movement is played expressively, the closing pages warmly intense. The finale has plenty of impulse but its effect is reduced by the pianist's slipping technique, so that an intention of incisive brilliance is somewhat blunted. Nevertheless the playing has an overall spontaneity that commands a response from the listener in spite of the undistinguished recording, reverberant and unrefined in detail.

'Favourite composer': (i; ii) *Piano concerto No. 2 in C minor, Op. 18;* (ii–iv) *Rhapsody on a theme of Paganini, Op. 43;* (v) *Symphony No. 2 in E minor, Op. 27;* (iii) *Prelude No. 1 in C sharp minor, Op. 3/2;* (vi) *Vocalise, Op. 34/14.*
** Decca DPA 565/6 [KDPC]. (i) Katchen, Solti; (ii) LSO; (iii) Vered (piano); (iv) Vonk; (v) LPO, Boult; (vi) Söderström; Ashkenazy (piano).

Katchen's performance of the *Second Concerto* is a brilliant one (see below) and it is a pity that Decca did not stay with this artist instead of choosing Ilana Vered's less successful recording of the *Rhapsody*. Boult's performance of the *Second Symphony* has come up with surprising freshness here, but taken as a whole this is not one of Decca's finest *Favourite composer* anthologies, although the recording is generally excellent. However, the sound on the first tape (with the *Concerto* and the *Rhapsody*) is not as clean in the treble as is usual with Decca. The symphony emerges freshly.

(i) *Piano concerto No. 2 in C minor, Op. 18;* (ii) *Rhapsody on a theme of Paganini, Op. 43.*
*** Decca SPA 505 [KCSP].

Katchen, with (i) LSO, Solti; (ii) LPO, Boult.

Julius Katchen gives a dramatic and exciting account of the *C minor Concerto* such as we would expect from this pianist. He had a fabulous technique and was always at pains to demonstrate it at its most spectacular. Generally in this recording it leads to the highest pitch of excitement, but there are a number of passages – notably the big climax as well as the coda of the first movement – where he plays almost too fast. Miraculously he gets round the notes somehow but the result inevitably seems breathless, however exciting it is. The stereo recording is in Decca's best manner and manages to be brilliant and well co-ordinated at the same time. The *Rhapsody* is even more successful, superbly shaped and notable not only for its romantic flair and excitement but also for the diversity and wit displayed in the earlier variations. There is no question of anti-climax after the *Eighteenth*, for the forward impetus of the playing has tremendous power and excitement. The recording is vivid and full-blooded. The transfer to tape of both works is first-class, bold and clear and with strikingly rich and firm piano timbre. This issue is in the lower-middle price-range but its bargain quality seems unarguable with so much music included.

Piano concerto No. 3 in D minor, Op. 30.
  **(*) RCA Victrola (m) VH 004. Horowitz, RCA Victor SO, Reiner.
  ** C.f.P. CFP 40257. Sheppard, LPO, Pritchard.
  *(*) RCA Camden CCV 5043 [c4]. Janis, Boston SO, Munch.

Each of Horowitz's three recordings of Rachmaninov's *Third Piano concerto* is different and each sheds some new light on this familiar and much loved score. Rachmaninov himself much admired Horowitz's earlier version, made with Albert Coates in 1930, as well he might, for Horowitz is the only pianist on record whose readings can be put alongside the composer's own. This version comes from 1951 and combines delicacy and power alongside the fire and tension which characterize all Horowitz's performances. Both of his earlier recordings observe the traditional cuts (as did Rachmaninov himself in his indispensable recording) and use the 'easier' cadenza rather than the more flamboyant one printed above it in the miniature score (and favoured by Ashkenazy, Berman and others). If the playing is dazzling, the recorded sound calls for some tolerance, though it is far from unacceptable. The balance focuses attention on the soloist, who is very forward and masks some orchestral detail, and less than full justice is done to Horowitz's own tone. Horowitz buffs will have to have all three versions (his 1978 account with Ormandy is at full price and is discussed in its cassette form in the *Penguin Cassette Guide*), but the 1930 account does better justice to his featherlike pianissimo tone, and one soon forgets its primitive recording. We only hope that RCA will reissue it in due course, for it possesses marvellous spontaneity. Here Fritz Reiner produces warm playing from the RCA Victor Orchestra, and the reservation about a full three-star grading is attributable to the limited sound.

Craig Sheppard has made a considerable name for himself in the concert hall since he attracted attention at Leeds in 1972, but he has given us few commercial records. He is an artist to be taken seriously, and though this performance may not have the glamour and charisma of Berman's or Gavrilov's (not to mention Ashkenazy and Horowitz) it is purposeful and eloquent. Sheppard may not always be as commanding as some of his rivals (for example, in the first-movement cadenza, where he opts for the now fashionable alternative) but he is unfailingly musical and often perceptive. It is a pity that he makes a small cut in the finale. The recording is not quite in the first bracket though it is well balanced and sounds natural. Pritchard provides a sympathetic accompaniment.

Byron Janis recorded this concerto in the early days of stereo with the L S O and Dorati, but the Boston version is earlier still. He is a big pianist, well equipped to cope with the formidable demands of this wonderful score; everything is full-blooded and commanding yet there is no want of poetry when it is required. The piano tone, however, is shallow and the orchestral sound is not as refined as was Mercury's for Dorati. Munch gives good support, and if the recording were less coarse in climaxes and wider in range, this would carry a strong recommendation.

Rhapsody on a theme of Paganini, Op. 43.
   ** D G Heliodor 2548 287 [3348 287]. Cornil, R T B S O, Hoffman – M O Z A R T : *Piano concerto No. 21.***

Dominique Cornil's recording was made in 1975 during the Concours Musical International Reine Elisabeth in Brussels. The recording balance is less than perfect, with the piano very forward. But for the most part the orchestral detail comes through well enough, although the strings are somewhat masked at the opening of their big tune in the *Eighteenth variation*. But the overall effect is vivid to match a performance of considerable power, yet not lacking romantic feeling. This makes a thoroughly acceptable (if curious) coupling for Mozart's K.467 *Concerto* (which is a better-balanced studio recording).

The sound is equally good on disc and cassette, and the piano is certainly vividly projected.

Symphony No. 2 in E minor, Op. 27.
   **(*) C.f.P. CFP 40065. Hallé Orch., Loughran.

Loughran's account makes an excellent recommendation. Although the performance takes a little while to warm up, the intensity develops. The slow movement is particularly fine, and the orchestral playing throughout is excellent. The recording too is vivid and refined in detail. The cassette version, which was unsuccessful, has been withdrawn. Loughran plays the work uncut.

Ravel, Maurice (1875–1937)

'Favourite composer': (i) *Alborada del gracioso; Boléro; Daphnis et Chloé: Suite No. 2; Ma Mère l'Oye: suite; Pavane pour une infante défunte; Rapsodie espagnole; La Valse;* (ii) *Introduction and allegro for harp, flute, clarinet and string quartet.*
   ** Decca DPA 561/2 [KDPC]. (i) Suisse Rom. Orch., Ansermet; (ii) Osian Ellis (harp), Melos Ens.

This Decca collection is based on the recordings of Ernest Ansermet. The *Daphnis* suite is not as well played nor as sensuous as one might ideally ask (the latter being partly the fault of the clinical sound balance). *Ma Mère l'Oye* is serviceable; the playing lacks the last ounce of polish and refinement, but the recording is excellent. The *Alborada* is vivid enough, and both the *Pavane* and the *Rapsodie espagnole* are played with character. The indispensable Melos version of the *Introduction and allegro* is also available on an attractive single disc (and tape) anthology at lower middle price, well worth investigating: '*The world of Ravel*', Decca SPA 392 [KCSP]. The '*Favourite composer*' set makes a useful anthology, but one remembers how much more attractive were Cluytens's Classics for Pleasure collections of Ravel orchestral music (CFP 40036 and 40093), which have been withdrawn. C.f.P. intend to reissue this material in 1981, adding an extra item to each collection. The two groups are planned as follows: *Alborada del gracioso, Boléro, Pavane pour une infante défunte, Rapsodie espagnole* and *La Valse*; and *Une Barque sur l'océan* (from *Miroirs*), the *Suite No. 2* from *Daphnis et Chloé*, the *Menuet antique*, *Le Tombeau de Couperin* and the *Valses nobles et sentimentales*. This will make two exceptionally generous compilations; Cluytens is recorded with consistent vividness and the performances are first-class, some of them still arguably the best on record

Boléro; La Valse.
   ** HMV 45 r.p.m. HMV 4. N. Philharmonia Orch., Maazel.
   *(*) RCA Camden CCV 5031 [c4]. Boston SO, Munch – DUKAS: *L'Apprenti sorcier*; IBERT: *Escales*.**

Maazel's speeds are fast: *Boléro* takes two seconds under thirteen minutes; *La Valse* just twelve. Both are brilliant, extrovert performances of characteristic flair and intensity; both have rhythmically mannered climaxes. The orchestral playing is excellent and the spectacular recording – artificial in balance – is undoubtedly given great presence and impact in this 45 r.p.m. format.

The Munch versions with the Boston Symphony Orchestra emanate from the early 1960s, and neither the *Boléro* nor *La Valse* is in the first class now. But this issue is worth its price for the buyer who (with good reason) seeks a recording of Ibert's *Escales*. The remastered cassette sounds remarkably clear, but the dynamic range is relatively restricted: the side-drum which opens *Boléro* is much too loud in relation to the final climax.

Daphnis et Chloé (ballet): complete.
   **(*) C.f.P. CFP 40323. Duclos Choir, Paris Cons. Orch., Cluytens.

Cluytens's set of Ravel's orchestral music was one of the best to appear in the 1960s, and it sounds astonishingly vivid even now. His *Daphnis et Chloé* is poetically conceived and has much to recommend it, even though the Paris Conservatoire Orchestra is not in the very first flight. Some will find the wide horn vibrato a little off-putting, but apart from this, there is a great deal of pleasure to be had from this finely recorded performance. Taken on its own merits it is thoroughly recommendable; but excellence is the enemy of the good, and Monteux's medium-priced LSO account (Decca Jubilee JB 69 [KJBC]), no less well recorded and rather better played, is well worth the extra money. Even more ecstatic in its sense of rapture and poetry is Martinon's set, which HMV plan to reissue on the Concert Classics label. This is better recorded than either, and Martinon's dedication to this marvellous score seems more ardent than Monteux's. This is the most intoxicating account to appear since the Munch version of the mid-1950s, and it is sumptuously recorded.

(i) *Daphnis et Chloé: Suites Nos. 1*

and 2. *Ma Mère L'Oye (Mother Goose;* ballet): complete.
> *** Turnabout TVS 34603 [KTVC].
> Minnesota Orch., Skrowaczewski, (i) with St Olaf Choir.

The first *Daphnis suite* is absolutely magical in Skrowaczewski's hands, and in terms of sheer atmosphere and imaginative vitality these performances can compare with any of their more prestigious rivals. The Minnesota Orchestra may not be a superlative ensemble, but there is nothing second-rate about its playing, and the recording is beautifully balanced and wide-ranging. Skrowaczewski conveys every subtlety of texture and colour, and he shapes phrases not merely with good taste and fine musical judgement but also with a genuine feel for the sensuous, sumptuous qualities of these scores. His *Ma Mère l'Oye* is complete, and can stand comparison with the finest performances on record. This coupling (in the lower-medium price-range) must rate very highly indeed among the available issues of Ravel's music, especially as the recording is so good. The tape transfer is sophisticated, smooth and clear, with a richness and depth of string tone that are quite unexpected on a recording from a Turnabout source.

Daphnis et Chloé: Suite No. 2.
> **(*) RCA (m) AT 107. NBC SO, Toscanini – MUSSORGSKY: *Pictures.* **(*)

A classic account of the second suite from Toscanini, and it offers playing of the very highest order of virtuosity. Its sonic limitations tell a little, and the texture does not glow radiantly in quite the same way as in Karajan's version from the mid-1960s, which will surely be reissued soon on DG's medium price label. Toscanini's reading is, however, enormously exciting, and the *Danse*

générale is particularly thrilling. No admirers of Toscanini should miss this issue, and if the coupling is what you want, and the highest-fi is not a priority, you will be well rewarded. These are performances of great stature.

Ma Mère l'Oye: suite.
> **(*) C.f.P. CFP 40086 [TC-CFP]. Scottish Nat. Orch., Gibson – SAINT-SAËNS: *Carnival* ⊛ ***; BIZET: *Jeux d'enfants.* ***

Gibson is highly persuasive here, shaping the music with obvious affection and a feeling for both the spirit and the texture of Ravel's beautiful score. The orchestral playing is excellent, the recording very good but wanting a little in atmosphere. But with its well-chosen couplings this is a fine bargain; the quality on cassette is first-rate too.

Rapsodie espagnole.
> *(*) RCA Camden CCV 5039 [c4]. Boston SO, Munch – DEBUSSY: *La Mer.* *(*)

Munch secures highly polished playing from the Boston Symphony Orchestra and is well enough recorded. His reading could perhaps be both more sensitive and more sensuous, particularly in the outer movements: here Fritz Reiner and the Chicago Orchestra, also recorded in the late 1950s, scored over the Bostonians, and had the advantage of a more spacious recorded sound. The orchestral playing here is finer than Ansermet's, though the recording is by no means as satisfactory; but Munch's performance does not in any way challenge Giulini, who is well worth the extra outlay at medium price. His couplings are the *Alborada*, the second *Daphnis et Chloé suite* and the *Pavane*: HMV SXLP 30198.

Introduction and allegro for harp, flute, clarinet and string quartet.
(*) DG Heliodor 2548 281 [3348 281]. Zabaleta, Paul Kuentz CO – HANDEL: *Harp concerto**; MOZART: *Flute and harp concerto.***(*)

Nicanor Zabaleta is marvellous in Ravel's magical *Introduction and allegro* and this is overall a highly sensitive performance, well recorded on both disc and tape. However, the music's beauty and subtlety are even more memorably caught in the famous Melos performance, which is available in Decca's *'Favourite composer'* compilation (see above) or in a Decca anthology called *'The world of Ravel'*. But many readers will wish to seek the original mid-priced Oiseau-Lyre disc from which it is taken (SOL 60048), where it is coupled to music by Debussy, Roussel and Roparts.

Respighi, Ottorino
(1879–1936)

The Fountains of Rome; The Pines of Rome (symphonic poems).
⊛*** RCA Victrola (m) AT 100. NBC SO, Toscanini – BERLIOZ: *Carnaval romain.****

We have always revelled in these lush and gorgeous scores, which have held the allegiance of audiences for many decades (and survived the sneers of superior critics). In the hands of a second-rate conductor they seem merely picturesque, but artists of the order of Toscanini and Reiner uncover a vein of genuine feeling as well as tremendous atmosphere. Although he does not have the advantage of modern stereo, Toscanini conveys more colour than most maestros who do. The last of the four sections, *La fontana di Villa Medici al tramonte*, has an intense nostalgia and that suggests that this music meant a very great deal to Toscanini. Not even Reiner's beautifully controlled and no less evocative version with the Chicago Symphony, recorded in the early 1960s, or Karajan's recent version with the Berlin Philharmonic comes closer to the spirit of this score. *The Pines* flourish equally well and come vividly to life in a virtuoso performance which exhilarates, electrifies and also, in the moments of repose, touches the listener. The RCA engineers have improved the sound image very considerably, and there is admirable definition and detail. In any event the inevitable sonic limitations do not detract from the impact of these stunning performances.

The Pines of Rome.
*** DG Heliodor 2548 267 [3348 267]. Berlin PO, Maazel – RIMSKY-KORSAKOV: *Capriccio espagnol****; MUSSORGSKY: *Night on the Bare Mountain.***(*)

It is good to see this outstanding Berlin Philharmonic compilation of the very early sixties restored to the catalogue. It was this issue, together with Maazel's coupling of Stravinsky's *Firebird suite* and *Chant du rossignol*, which endorsed this conductor's international reputation. The Berlin Philharmonic plays here with breathtaking virtuosity in *The pines of the Villa Borghese*, balanced by wonderfully tender playing in the two middle movements. Then comes the gripping and tautly built crescendo to the exultant climax of the triumphant procession along the Appian Way. The brass is magnificent here, and the atmospheric stereo throughout, which made it one of DG's finest early issues in this medium, is still riveting on both disc and tape.

Rimsky-Korsakov, Nikolas (1844–1908)

Capriccio espagnol, Op. 34.
  *** DG Heliodor 2548 267 [3348 267]. Berlin PO, Maazel – MUSSORGSKY: *Night on the Bare Mountain**(*);* RESPIGHI: *Pines of Rome.****
  ** HMV 45 r.p.m. HMV 8. Orchestre de Paris, Rozhdestvensky – BORODIN: *Polovtsian dances.***

The restoration of Maazel's performance to the catalogue is very welcome. This Heliodor disc offers the original couplings, including a memorable account of Respighi's *Pines of Rome.* The playing in the *Capriccio espagnol* is almost equally fine, and the relaxed virtuosity in the *Scena e canto gitano,* coupled to stereo of almost demonstration quality, is a delight to the ear after the gorgeous strings and horns in the earlier variations. No less impressive is the breathtaking virtuosity of the closing pages, with every note in its place. The cassette transfer is clear but has rather less richness and amplitude than the LP.

Rozhdestvensky's 45 r.p.m. 12-inch disc makes an obvious coupling, but the performance of the *Capriccio,* although affectionately detailed, is a little underpowered, and the orchestral playing lacks a compensating voluptuousness. The recording too is brilliant rather than sumptuous; but this seems good value for money.

Scheherazade (symphonic suite), *Op. 35.*
  *** C.f.P. CFP 40341 [TC-CFP]. Philharmonia Orch., Kletzki –

TCHAIKOVSKY: *Capriccio italien.***(*)
  *** RCA Camden CCV5010[c4]. Chicago SO, Reiner.
  *(*) C.f.P. CFP 174. RPO, Kempe.

Kletzki's famous recording of Rimsky-Korsakov's orchestral showpiece was a best-seller on HMV's Concert Classics label for over fifteen years. The recording has an attractively spacious acoustic, and the Philharmonia solo playing is superb, with highly distinguished violin solos from Hugh Bean. Kletzki's reading is broad in the first movement, and he makes the second glow and sparkle (the famous brass interchanges having the most vivid projection). The richness of the string playing in the third movement is matched by the exhilaration of the finale. The recording has been brightened in the new transfer and now sounds remarkably clear, though lacking something in sumptuousness, especially in the first movement. The second remains as demonstration-worthy as ever. The finale has rather more weight, but generally the sound balance is enhanced by a slight treble cut and comparable bass boost. The tape transfer is first-class.

Reiner's account is a dramatic one, the first movement having a strong forward impulse, and the finale equally brilliant and exciting. The two central movements are beguilingly played, but the readings are individual, and some may not care for the conductor's romantic nudgings here and there. However, Reiner always sounds spontaneous: there are many delightful touches, and the third movement is wonderfully languorous. The recording is vivid, with the strong character of the Chicago Hall adding its own special ambience. Returning to this record, one is surprised to find how effective it is, spacious, and making up in colour and atmosphere for any lack of internal clarity. The cassette too is exceptionally successful, one of the very best from this source. The wide dynamic range is impressively caught (the bass drum in the finale is somewhat explosive, but no matter), and the orchestral textures are rich and full-blooded. There is surprisingly little background noise, considering the age of the master tape.

Scheherazade is not a score that easily yields to the German romantic tradition, and the music does not really suit Kempe. He is broad in the first movement, and at his best in the slow movement; but elsewhere the performance, although beautifully played and warmly recorded, lacks vitality.

Mozart and Salieri (opera): complete.
(*) Everest Olympic (m) 9106. Linsolas, Mollien, Jacobs, Paris Chorus and PO, Leibowitz.

The only commendable thing about the appalling recording quality here is that the French words come over astonishingly clearly, and that is just as well in a rare piece which depends heavily on its plot. The legend that Mozart was poisoned by Salieri inspired Rimsky-Korsakov to a delightfully pointed one-acter, though here the charm is undermined; the solo strings sound very raw as they rehearse *Batti, batti* from *Don Giovanni*. Leibowitz's conducting is strong and stylish, the singing clean and direct. At the price it is worth investigating this rarity.

Rodrigo, Joaquín
(born 1902)

Concierto de Aranjuez (for guitar and orchestra).

** C.f.P. CFP 40012 [TC-CFP]. Zaradin, Philomusica, Barbier – *Recital.***
* Pye GSGC 15030 [ZCCCB]. Cubedo, Barcelona SO, Ferrer – BACARISSE: *Concertino.*
Concierto de Aranjuez; Fantasia para un gentilhombre (for guitar and orchestra).
* RCA Camden CCV 5004 [c4]. De la Maza, Falla Orch. of Madrid, Halffter.

John Zaradin's performance is bright-eyed and straightforward, with a crisp, immediate recording. The orchestral outline is clear-cut in the somewhat dry manner favoured by John Boyden, who produced many of the Classics for Pleasure original recordings. This is coupled with a recital of solo guitar pieces, discussed below in our Recitals section. Although the dynamic range of the recording of the concerto is limited by the close balance of the solo guitar, the recording conveys an attractive intimacy, and there is plenty of bloom on the sound. There is little to choose in quality between disc and cassette.

Neither Manuel Cubedo nor Regino Saint de la Maza gives a particularly distinguished account of the concerto, and both suffer from an unrealistically forward balance. In both performances there is a lack of vitality in the outer movements, and although the famous *Adagio* is not without atmosphere there is nothing really memorable about either solo contribution. The Pye recording has rather more presence and personality, but the RCA Camden coupling is the more attractive, and the performance of the *Fantasia* has greater personality. However, in the pressing we tried the reverberant RCA sound picture produced the occasional patch of roughness in the upper range. The Pye sound is cleaner, although still somewhat overblown, but the cassette has passages of severe distortion in the slow movement. The C.f.P. issue is in every way more sophisticated, and for those who want the coupling with *Gentilhombre* there is an outstanding Decca record and tape in the lower-middle price-range, by Narciso Yepes with the Spanish National Orchestra conducted by Argenta or Frühbeck de Burgos. This can be recommended without reservation: SPA 233 [KCSP].

Rossini, Gioacchino (1792–1868)

Overtures: *Il Barbiere di Siviglia; La Cenerentola; La Gazza ladra; La Scala di seta; Il Signor Bruschino; William Tell.*
    *** RCA Camden CCV 5020 [C4]. Chicago SO, Reiner.

Reiner offers sparkling, vivacious performances. One would have liked the opening bars of *La Scala di seta* neater – they are too lavishly presented here – and there is a hint of coolness at the opening of *William Tell*. But generally this is a very fine set, and *La Cenerentola* offers superb orchestral bravura. The record has a very wide dynamic range, and the reverberation of Chicago's Symphony Hall is well controlled by the recording. The blaze of brass tone at the beginning of the *William Tell* galop reminds us that the Chicago orchestra was always famous in this department.

Overtures: *Il Barbiere di Siviglia; La Cenerentola; La Gazza ladra; Semiramide; Il Signor Bruschino; William Tell.*
    *(*) RCA Victrola (m) AT 108. NBC SO, Toscanini.

These recordings date from different sessions in New York between 1945 and 1953. Unfortunately most come from the earlier date, and the sound is depressingly dry, not helping performances that are in any case somewhat relentless. Toscanini had the reputation of being a sparkling Rossinian, and in the crispness and precision and the sharpness of tension here one can understand that; but Rossini without charm is a limited joy.

Overtures: *La Gazza ladra; L'Italiana in Algeri; Semiramide; Il Signor Bruschino; William Tell.*
    *** C.f.P. CFP 40077 [TC-CFP]. RPO, Colin Davis.

A first-rate bargain collection from Colin Davis. These performances are admirably stylish, with an excellent sense of nuance. The orchestral playing is splendid, and the new C.f.P. pressing of a very good EMI recording is natural and full-blooded, though there seems marginally more sparkle on side two than side one, which contains *William Tell* and *La Gazza ladra*. *Semiramide*, which opens side two, is a superb performance, wonderfully crisp and vivid. In *Il Signor Bruschino*, which comes next, it sounds as if the bow-tapping device is done by the leader only. The cassette version has been successfully remastered and now has a wide dynamic range and a proper sense of spectacle, although there are moments when the refinement of focus slips just a little because of the resonance and high-level transfer.

Saint-Saëns, Camille (1835–1921)

Carnival of the Animals.
    ⊕*** C.f.P. CFP 40086 [TC-CFP].

Katin, Fowke, Scottish Nat. Orch., Gibson – RAVEL: *Ma Mère l'Oye***(*); BIZET: *Jeux d'enfants.****

An outstanding performance in every way, not bettered in the present catalogue at any price. The two pianists, Peter Katin and Philip Fowke, enter into the spirit of the occasion splendidly (their own portrait has plenty of gusto), and Gibson accompanies with affectionate, unforced humour. The gentler lyrical items (*The aviary, The cuckoo in the woods*) are delicately evocative, and *Fossils* is wittily abrasive, all the quotations nicely brought out. The recording is excellent and the tape transfer demonstration-worthy. In short, with its imaginative couplings this is very attractive indeed.

Satie, Erik (1866–1925)

Parade (ballet); *En habit de cheval; Trois petites pièces montées;* (i) *Socrate*, Part 3: *La Mort de Socrate.*
** Everest 3234. French Nat. Radio and TV Orch., Rosenthal, (i) with Denise Monteil.

None of these pieces is otherwise available at bargain price, so this issue is valuable. The performance of *Parade* is not ideally sophisticated or (considering its provenance) particularly idiomatic, although the special-effects department is on top form. This is such delightful music that its representation on disc at such a reasonable price is welcome. The *Trois petites pièces montées* are very characterful and combine Satie's taste for circus music with moments of quiet gravity. *Socrate*, which many of Satie's admirers (including

Constant Lambert), have considered his masterpiece, has never been well served by the gramophone. Its final section is vividly recorded here and well sung by Denise Monteil. Neither these performances nor the recording is in the highest bracket, but the music-making readily communicates and the disc must be given a warm welcome.

Piano music: *Chapitres tournés en tous sens; Croquis et agaceries d'un gros bonhomme en bois; Gnossiennes Nos. 2 and 4; 3 Gymnopédies; Heures séculaires et instantanées; Nocturnes Nos. 2 and 4; Nouvelles pièces froides; Passacaille; Le Piège de Méduse; Prélude No. 2 (Le fils des étoiles); Sonatine bureaucratique.*
** C.f.P. CFP 40329 [TC-CFP]. Lawson.

Satie's deceptively simple piano writing poses problems for the interpreter; it has to be played with great sensitivity and subtlety if justice is to be done to its special qualities of melancholy and irony. Peter Lawson is very well recorded both on disc and on tape (there is little difference between them, except for the virtually silent background of the cassette). The recital opens with the famous *Gymnopédies*, played coolly but not ineffectively. The highlight is a perceptive and articulate characterization of *Le Piège de Méduse*, seven epigrammatic *morceaux de concert*, originally written as incidental music for a comedy in which Satie himself took the lead. Elsewhere Peter Lawson's playing is fresh and clean but lacking in individuality. His way is quietly tasteful, and though he catches something of Satie's gentle and wayward poetry he is less successful in revealing the underlying sense of fantasy. There are more distinguished and memorable recordings available at full price; but the present issue is a good

SCHUBERT

deal more than serviceable for those with limited budgets.

Schubert, Franz
(1797–1828)

'*Favourite composer*': (i; ii) *Rosamunde: Overture (Die Zauberharfe, D.644); incidental music: Entr'acte in B flat major; Ballet music Nos. 1 and 2, D.797:* (i; iii) *Symphony No. 8 in B minor (Unfinished), D.759.* (iv) *Piano quintet in A major (Trout), D.667.* (v) (Piano) *Impromptu on B flat major, D. 935/3; Moment musical in F minor, D.780/3.* (vi) *An Sylvia;* (vii) *Die Forelle; Heidenröslein;* (viii) *Ständchen.*
   ** Decca DPA 545/6. (i) Vienna PO; (ii) Monteux; (iii) Schuricht; (iv) Curzon, members of Vienna Octet; (v) Backhaus; (vi) Prey, Engel; (vii) Price, Lockhart; (viii) Krause, Gage.

This makes a satisfactory anthology, including a good version of the *Unfinished*. Schuricht's performance dates from 1957 and was admired in its day. It is an affectionate reading, warmly played, with a strong forward impulse but some lack of drama. This latter aspect is emphasized by the stereo, which, while pleasing and naturally balanced, has a limited dynamic range. Monteux's *Rosamunde* excerpts are distinctive, with striking characterization and good playing and recording. The highlight of the set is the classic performance of the *Trout quintet* by Clifford Curzon with splendidly stylish support from the Vienna players. The recording sounds a little dated now in the matter of string tone (this is more noticeable

on tape than disc), but the piano recording is firm and clear. The songs are well chosen and delightfully sung, and Backhaus's contribution is worthwhile too, if characteristically rather gruff.

Symphony No. 5 in B flat major, D.485.
   * RCA Victrola (m) AT 123. NBC SO, Toscanini – MENDELSSOHN: *Symphony No. 5.* **(*)

In this warmly lyrical work Toscanini sounds too ruthless, totally missing the lightness and charm and with speeds generally too hectic. The record can nonetheless be recommended for the fine Mendelssohn on the reverse. The reader is reminded that Beecham's mid-price coupling of Symphonies Nos. 3 and 5 on HMV Concert Classics (SXLP 30204 [TC-SXLP]) is one of the most magical Schubert records ever made: sunny, smiling performances with beautifully alive rhythms and luminous textures.

Symphonies Nos. 5 in B flat major; D.485; 8 in B minor (Unfinished), D.759.
   *** C.f.P. CFP 40245. LPO, Pritchard.
   **(*) RCA Camden CCV 5001 [c4]. Chicago SO, Reiner.

Pritchard's performances are superbly refreshing. His reading of the *Unfinished* is unusually direct, establishing the first movement as a genuine symphonic allegro but with no feeling of breathlessness, even in the melting lyricism of the incomparable second subject. The high dramatic contrasts – as in the development – are fearlessly presented, with fine intensity, and the second movement too brings purity and freshness. In the *Fifth Symphony* Pritchard's directness allows for nudging delicacy, for example at the very start, and the playing of the LPO is again superbly refined. With glowing recording to match, this disc in no way falls short of full-price rivals.

Reiner's too is a most attractive disc, warmly if not always clearly recorded. The reading of No. 5 is essentially sunny, but with a strongly vigorous finale following a third movement where Reiner indulges the trio with an affectionate *rallentando*. The *Unfinished* has a superbly dramatic and impulsive first movement and a richly lyrical *Andante*, with a beautiful opening and a no less poetic coda. The remastered tape transfer is most successful. The *Fifth* sounds particularly fresh and vivid; the *Unfinished* is less clear but suitably atmospheric.

Symphony No. 8 in B minor (Unfinished), D.759.
*(*) RCA Victrola (m) AT 101. NBC SO, Toscanini – MENDELSSOHN: *Symphony No. 4.**(*)

Toscanini takes a characteristically fierce view of the *Unfinished*, presenting the first movement more clearly than usual as a symphonic allegro. It is not a reading that one would want to hear always, and the studio sound is poor, but the compulsion and concentration are undeniable.

Symphony No. 9 in C major (Great), D.944.
⊛*** Decca SPA 467. LSO, Josef Krips.
*** C.f.P. CFP 40233. LPO, Pritchard.
**(*) RCA Camden CCV 5054. Boston SO, Munch.
*(*) RCA Victrola (m) AT 102. NBC SO, Toscanini.

As in Symphonies Nos. 5 and 8, John Pritchard gives a superbly vital and fresh performance of the *Great C major*. As in the *Unfinished* the tempi are on the fast side and the manner direct, but the results are never breathless. It is always a significant sign when one welcomes repeats observed in this already long symphony, and Pritchard observes more than anyone else on record, even Boult. Only the exposition repeat in the finale is omitted, which is a pity when the repeat in the first movement adds so effectively to the scale of the argument. The very opening brings a slightly square account of the introductory horn theme, but after that the resilience of the LPO's playing excels even that under Boult in the HMV full-priced version with the same orchestra, although here the players are challenged even more keenly by the fast tempi.

Yet splendid as this Classics for Pleasure disc is, it must take second place to the outstanding Decca Krips version, which costs a pound more but is well worth every new penny. Josef Krips never made a finer record than this, and in the current reissue the sound is outstanding too, with a glowing bloom cast over the entire orchestra. The performance itself has a direct, unforced spontaneity which shows Krips's natural feeling for Schubertian lyricism at its most engaging. The playing is polished yet flexible, strong without ever sounding aggressive. In the two final movements Krips finds an airy exhilaration which makes one wonder however other conductors can keep the music earthbound as they do. The pointing of the trio in the scherzo is delectable, and the feathery lightness of the triplets in the finale makes one positively welcome every single one of its many repetitions. As a whole this reading represents the Viennese tradition at its very finest, and this record is not surpassed in the present catalogue either on grounds of sound or as a performance. Unfortunately the cassette [KCSP 467] is transferred at

101

marginally too high a level, which produces some roughness at peaks in the outer movements.

Munch gives a magnificent performance. In sheer dramatic tension he even outshines Toscanini. This is very much the Toscanini approach – the introduction and allegro of the first movement even faster than his – but one must emphasize that it is far from being an unsympathetic rough-riding account of the kind we sometimes get from the other side of the Atlantic. True there is more excitement than repose, and at the big climax of the slow movement Munch reinforces the dissonances with an *accelerando*. Yet throughout he and his players show an implicit sympathy: indeed in the hushed slow-movement passage immediately after the climax the rubato is controlled in an exact and precise manner, yet somehow is spontaneous-sounding still. The recording is sharp-edged and though it has plenty of atmosphere, it is not without some of the acoustic throwback which is a feature of the Boston recordings. It makes a splendid bargain issue just the same.

When Toscanini's reading of the *Great C major Symphony* was first heard its directness was refreshing, for he questioned many of the performing convenions that grew up during the years. It remains fiercely dramatic, but there is little of Schubertian love here – least of all in the clipped and square slow movement – and no warmth. The sound is dry in the characteristic N B C manner.

Piano quintet in A major (Trout), D.667.
**(*) C.f.P. CFP 40085 [TC-CFP]. Lympany, principals of the LSO.
** D G Heliodor 2548 122 [3348 122]. Demus, Schubert Qt –
MOZART: *Divertimento for wind.***

(**) RCA Camden CCV 5046 [c4]. Augmented Festival Qt.

Moura Lympany's performance sets off in a brisk manner, the playing lively and fresh. In the second movement the interpretation relaxes, and the variations are attractively done. The matter-of-fact approach is balanced by the overall spontaneity of the music-making. The balance favours the piano and the first violin seems backward – in his decorations of the 'Trout' theme he is too distant, with less body to his tone, as recorded, than the lower strings. But in most respects this is a lively and enjoyable account, not wanting in perception. The cassette transfer offers excellent quality, though it is a little light in the bass.

An excellent reading on Heliodor, with Demus dominating, partly because the piano recording and balance are bold and forward and the string tone is thinner. There is – as befits the name of the string group – a real feeling for Schubert, and the performance has spontaneity and style. The first movement is especially arresting, and the *Theme and variations* are well shaped. The sound is good; the cassette transfer is clear, though tending to emphasize the thinness of the strings. The coupling on cassette is different: instead of Mozart we are offered Schubert's *Violin sonatina* (D.385), played by Wolfgang Schneiderhan and Walter Klien.

The performance by the so-called Festival Quartet (with Stuart Sankey, double-bass, but the pianist remaining anonymous) is an attractive one, with plenty of impulse and spontaneity throughout and no lack of imagination in the variations. Unfortunately the recording (especially on side one) is poorly focused, with distortion in the upper range. It seems likely that this is a fault in the current pressings and that a new master could produce a much more acceptable sound. The cassette too has been transferred at marginally too high a level, and there is congestion on side one; side two is more acceptable.

Piano sonata No. 21 in B flat major, D.960.
* RCA Victrola (m) VH 016. Horowitz – SCHUMANN: *Kinderscenen.**(*)

The Schubert *B flat Sonata* is not otherwise represented on bargain label (perhaps DG will one day reissue the Kempff recording on Heliodor). Horowitz's version comes from 1950 and the shallowness of the recording diminishes its appeal. Despite masterly pianism, it finds Horowitz ill at ease and matter-of-fact. Schubert's depth and spirituality elude him, and neither as a performance nor as a recording does this give more than sporadic musical satisfaction. The coupling is more successful.

VOCAL MUSIC

Lieder: Volume 1 (Lieder composed from 1817 to 1828).
*** DG 2720 006 (12 discs). Fischer-Dieskau, Moore.

With over 200 songs on twenty-four sides, there would be danger of indigestion for even the most dedicated Schubertian were it not for the endless imagination of both these artists. In their Berlin recording sessions they adopted a special technique of study, rehearsal and recording most apt for such a project. The sense of spontaneity and new discovery is unfailing, since each take was in fact a performance. On a later occasion both artists might have taken a different view, but, used intelligently for sampling, this collection stands as a unique contribution to Lieder on record. The songs in this volume are presented broadly in chronological order, from *An*

die Musik of 1817 onwards. Clean, well-balanced recording.

Lieder: Volume 2 (Lieder composed from 1811 to 1817).
*** DG 2720 022 (13 discs). Fischer-Dieskau, Moore.

Volume 2 of this great project presents an essential supplement to the collection of mature songs in the first volume. Already in 1811, as a boy in his early teens, Schubert was writing with astonishing originality, as is shown in the long Schiller setting, a *Funereal fantasy*, the very first item here, with its rough, clashing intervals of a second and amazing harmonic pointers to the future. Performances and recording are just as compelling as in Volume 1.

'*Favourite Lieder*': (i; x) *An die Musik;* (ii; x) *Auf dem Wasser zu singen;* (iii, x) *Erlkönig;* (iv; xi) *Die Forelle;* (v; xii) *Frühlingsglaube;* (ii; x) *Heidenröslein;* (iv; xi) *Im Abendrot;* (vi; x) *Lachen und weinen;* (i; x) *Litanei auf das Fest aller Seelen;* (vii; xiii) *Der Musensohn;* (i; xiv) *Nacht und Träume;* (ii; x) *Nähe des Geliebten;* (viii; xv) *Die schöne Müllerin: Das Wandern; Ungeduld;* (vi; x) *Seligkeit;* (vii; xiii) *Wanderers Nachtlied;* (ii; x) *Wiegenlied;* (ix, x) *Die Winterreise: Der Lindenbaum.*
*** DG Heliodor 2548 268 [3348 268]. (i) Bumbry; (ii) Streich; (iii) Borg; (iv) Wunderlich; (v) Ludwig; (vi) Seefried; (vii) Fischer-Dieskau; (viii) Haefliger; (ix) Hotter; pianists: (x) Werba; (xi) Giesen; (xii) Bohle; (xiii) Demus; (xiv) Peschko; (xv) Bonneau.

A fascinating recital, generous in

offering eighteen songs and a most distinguished roster of artists. Rita Streich makes a particularly charming contribution, and her sweetness of timbre (which over the span of a whole disc or tape might become too soft-centred) here effectively contrasts with other, more robust voices. Kim Borg is memorably dramatic in *Erlkönig*; Fischer-Dieskau is inspirational in *Wanderers Nachtlied* (a most moving performance); and Irmgard Seefried shows an impressive control of colour in *Seligkeit*. Ernst Haefliger is a little stiff in *Das Wandern*, but unwinds for the famous *Ungeduld*, and if Grace Bumbry is a little heavyweight in *An die Musik*, Miss Streich is at her most delightful in the *Wiegenlied* (D.468), which touchingly ends side one. Hans Hotter's *Der Lindenbaum* too is nobly sung. The recording is generally kind to the voices, although the balance tends to vary from item to item. A most rewarding issue and excellent value.

Schumann, Robert
(1810–56)

Piano concerto in A minor, Op. 54.
*** C.f.P. cfp 40255 [tc-cfp]. Solomon, Philharmonia Orch., Menges– GRIEG: *Concerto*.***
(*) Pye [zccob 656]. Cherkassky, LPO, Boult– GRIEG: *Concerto*.(*)
(**) Everest (m) 3434. Gieseking, Berlin PO, Furtwängler – GRIEG: *Concerto*.(**)

Solomon's coupling is given full, natural sound in the C.f.P. reissue. The warmth and freshness of the performance give much pleasure; Solomon plays very beautifully, with the most delicate fingerwork, and the famous duet between piano and principal clarinet in the central section of the first movement is caressed lovingly. As in the Grieg, Menges does not emerge as a strong personality, but he is always sympathetic and his comparative reticence does not mar the performance. In fact there is much that is memorable; this is a reading which grows on the listener with familiarity. The cassette transfer is of outstanding quality, well detailed yet with a striking overall bloom on orchestra and piano alike.

The partnership between Cherkassky and Boult also provides one of the most satisfying accounts of this elusive concerto available on any label at any price. It is at present not available on disc in any form. Unfortunately the Pye transfer has been made at a very ambitious level and – as can be heard in the opening flourish – it is fractionally too high; the quality of the tuttis lacks freshness. But this concerto is lightly scored and for nearly all the time the sound is very pleasing, and the piano image is clear and truthful. The balance remains good. The reading strikes a near-perfect balance between romantic boldness – the masculine element – and feminine waywardness and charm. The pastel shades of the opening pages are realized with delicacy, while the first-movement dialogues between the solo piano and the orchestral woodwind are most sensitively managed. Later the interplay with the strings in the *Andante* has an appealing simplicity. Cherkassky's contribution is not without the occasional idiosyncrasy, but the spontaneity of the performance means that the listener's attention is always held.

Gieseking's performance is wonderfully warm and poetic, and Furtwängler brings to it a great sense of line and humanity. Gieseking's ideas will be of interest to everyone, not just pianists; but the recording, made under wartime conditions (and presumably taken off the air), calls for *considerable* tolerance.

This does not displace Solomon for normal listening purposes.

'Favourite composer': (i; ii) *Piano concerto in A minor, Op. 54;* (iii) *Symphony No. 1 in B flat major (Spring), Op. 38.* (Piano) (i) *Carnaval, Op. 9;* (iv) *Kinderscenen, Op. 15: Träumerei;* (v) *Romance in F sharp major, Op. 28/2.* (vi) *Frauenliebe und Leben, Op. 42.*

*(*) Decca DPA 623/4 [KDPC]. (i) Katchen; (ii) Israel PO, Kertesz; (iii) LSO, Josef Krips; (iv) Vered; (v) Cooper; (vi) Ferrier, Newmark.

Katchen's is essentially a virtuoso reading of the *Concerto* and it will not be to all tastes; but his wilfulness does not exclude moments of romanticism, and there is a pervading freshness. The opening movement has a number of tempo changes and sounds more boldly rhapsodical than usual. In the spirited finale, however, the fast main tempo hardly relaxes for the bumpy little second subject. The recording is clear and brilliant on disc but disappointingly shallow in the tape transfer, which also displays a brittle piano image. Krips gives a lightweight performance of the *Spring symphony*, but his view is undoubtedly persuasive, with sympathetic playing from the LSO. The recording shows its age a little but is well balanced. Katchen's account of *Carnaval* has a mono source and this also produces rather shallow piano tone, although the playing has plenty of character, while Kathleen Ferrier's *Frauenliebe und Leben* offers recording which must be regarded as 'historic'. The piano pieces played by Ilana Vered and Joseph Cooper sound altogether more congenial.

Kinderscenen (Scenes from Childhood), Op. 15.

*(*) RCA (m) VH 016. Horowitz – SCHUBERT: *Piano sonata No. 21.* *

This performance comes from a Carnegie Hall recording made in 1953 and the sound calls for much tolerance: it is thin and brittle. Horowitz's account of *Kinderscenen* is at times overdriven (the *Knight of the Hobbyhorse* is an example), but there are plenty of poetic touches and in the finale, *The poet speaks*, an authentic kind of inward feeling. As always, the sheer keyboard mastery is commanding, and if only the sound and the coupling, an unidiomatic Schubert *B flat Sonata*, were more successful, this would be attractive.

Scriabin, Alexander (1872–1915)

Preludes, Op. 11, Nos. 1 in C major; 3 in G major; 9 in E major; 10 in C sharp minor; 13 in G flat major; 14 in E flat minor; 16 in B flat minor; Op. 13, No. 6 in B minor; Op. 15, No. 2 in F sharp minor; Op. 16, Nos. 1 in B major; 4 in E flat minor; Op. 27, No. 1 in G minor; Op. 48, No. 3 in D flat major; Op. 51, No. 2 in A minor; Op. 59, No. 2; Op. 67, No. 1. Piano sonata No. 3 in F sharp minor, Op. 23.

**(*) RCA (m) VH 005. Horowitz.

Horowitz has confessed a strong sympathy for Scriabin, and it is difficult to imagine these performances being surpassed. They appeared for the first time in the mid-1950s and find Horowitz as much at home in the passionate rhetoric of the *Third Sonata* as in the mysterious later pieces on the reverse side or in the demonic *Ninth* (see VH 014 in the Recitals section below). Although the performances are of the utmost authority, the quality of the recording calls for tolerance, and some of the preludes suffer from a trace of wow. Nonetheless, these are indispensable accounts for collectors who care about the piano.

Shostakovich, Dmitri (1906–75)

Symphonies Nos. (i) *1, 4, 6, 8–9, 11;* (i–ii) *2–3;* (iii–iv) *5;* (iii; v) *7 and 10;* (vi) *12;* (i–ii; vii) *13;* (viii) *14;* (ix; iv) *15;* (x; iv) *The Age of Gold* (ballet): *suite, Op. 22;* (x–xi; iv) *The Bolt* (ballet): *suite, Op. 27a;* (xii; i) *The Sun Shines over our Motherland* (cantata), *Op. 90.*

*** HMV SLS 5025 (13 discs). (i) Moscow PO, Kondrashin; (ii) RSFSR Academic Choir; (iii) USSR SO; (iv) Maxim Shostakovich; (v) Svetlanov; (vi) Leningrad PO, Mravinsky; (vii) Bisen; (viii) Marishnikova, Vladimirov, Moscow CO, Barshai; (ix) Moscow Radio SO; (x) Bolshoi Theatre Orch.; (xi) Zhukovsky Military Air Academy Band; (xii) Russian Republican Chorus, Moscow Choir School Boys' Choir.

Even though this box represents a considerable outlay, it is still a good bargain at £2·50 per LP. The discs are sensibly laid out with the symphonies in chronological order, though this means that Nos. 4, 5 and 8 straddle separate discs. Kondrashin is the conductor most

generously represented; the composer's son Maxim takes the baton in Nos. 5 and 15, Svetlanov in Nos. 7 and 10, and Mravinsky and Rudolf Barshai in Nos. 12 and 14 respectively. It is a pity that Kondrashin's account of the *Sixth* was chosen, rather than Mravinsky's more searching reading with the Leningrad Philharmonic. Nevertheless, there are many triumphs here: Maxim Shostakovich's *Fifth* is an extremely fine reading and splendidly recorded, and much the same can be said for the *Fifteenth*, of which he gave the first performance. Kondrashin's versions of Nos. 4, 9 and 13 more than compensate for his less than intense reading of No. 8, and Svetlanov's record of the *Tenth* has the measure of its brooding despair. The voices in No. 14 are somewhat forwardly balanced, but the performance is also conducted authoritatively; Barshai directed its very first performance. Even in the less distinguished performances (Kondrashin's account of Nos. 1 and 6) there are no grounds for serious criticism, and throughout the set the recordings are more than acceptable; the quality is often very good indeed, particularly in Nos. 5 and 15. Most of the symphonies are not available on bargain label (and No. 3 is not otherwise available at all), and there is at present no more economical way of acquiring them than in this package. Considering the artistic satisfaction that the set offers (Svetlanov's *Tenth* is only a shade less impressive than Karajan's), this is a tempting proposition.

Symphony No. 5 in D minor, Op. 47.

**(*) Everest 3010. NY Stadium Orch., Stokowski.

**(*) C.f.P. CFP 40330. Bournemouth SO, Berglund.

* RCA Camden CCV 5045 [c4]. Nat. SO of America, Mitchell.

Berglund's recording (originally HMV) dates from as recently as 1976. It is reissued in its original quadraphonic format, and whether it is played on quad or ordinary stereo equipment the quality is superb, full-bodied, rich and atmospheric. But as a performance it must yield first place to Stokowski's Everest disc. It was Stokowski who gave us the first recording of this symphony in the 78 era and it was one of the very finest of his many outstanding achievements with the Philadelphia Orchestra. The Stadium Symphony Orchestra of New York is neither as flexible nor as virtuoso an ensemble as the superb instrument he created in Philadelphia during the first decade of electric recording, but the Stokowski electricity is here as intense as ever and it makes his stereo LP an unforgettable experience. His feel for tempi is so much more natural than Berglund's, and any idiosyncrasies (the slight broadening at the climax of the first movement, for instance) only add to the compulsion of the performance. There is less subtlety in the individual wind solos than in the old 78 set, but the strings again create that intense 'drenched' radiance of texture in the upper register which Stokowski made his own, and which makes the lyrical climax of the third movement so memorable, while its closing pages have an equally magical translucence. The finale has tremendous energy. This is a thrilling performance, and although the recording needs a strong treble cut-back (which has the advantage of also reducing the high background noise of the master recording, made on 35 mm film) it can be made to sound well.

Berglund's performance is altogether more measured, even sober, but it is undeniably eloquent, and the slow movement is given with genuine nobility, though with less spontaneity than in Stokowski's version. Those for whom sound quality is of paramount importance will value this silent-surfaced C.f.P.

disc, which yields altogether superior results to the imported Everest pressings of the Stokowski version.

The version made by the (Washington) National Symphony Orchestra is a workaday performance, moderately well recorded, it is true, but in no way the equal of either the Stokowski or the Berglund recordings.

Symphony No. 10 in E minor, Op. 93.
**(*) C.f.P. cfp 40216. LPO, Andrew Davis.

Shostakovich's finest symphony draws from Andrew Davis a fresh and direct reading, with the LPO in excellent form. It lacks a little in individuality but is still compelling, both in the long paragraphs of the first and third movements and in the pointedly rhythmic second and fourth. The recording quality is excellent.

Sibelius, Jean
(1865–1957)

(i) *Violin concerto in D minor, Op. 47. Tapiola* (symphonic poem), *Op. 112.*
** Everest 3045. LSO, Hannikainen, (i) with Spivakovsky.

Spivakovsky's opening, with its gleaming tone and poised beauty of phrase, is immediately compelling, and throughout the work his technical security and lyrical eloquence are impressive. One suspects that the (forwardly balanced) solo image is small, but the recording allows the soloist to dominate the proceedings without obscuring the orchestral detail. Hannikainen's accompaniment is idiomatic and powerful, and although the orchestral recording is not very sumptuous, the playing itself has plenty of energy. In *Tapiola* this is reserved for the final climax; at the opening the tension is more slackly held, and the score is laid out rather didactically. This effect is emphasized by the rather spare recorded textures.

'*Favourite composer*': (i; ii) *Violin concerto in D minor, Op. 47;* (iii) *Finlandia, Op. 26;* (ii; iv) *Karelia suite, Op. 11;* (iii) *Kuolema: Valse triste, Op. 44; Legend: The Swan of Tuonela, Op. 22/2;* (ii; v) *Symphony No. 2 in D major, Op. 43.*

**(*) Decca DPA 531/2 [KDPC].
(i) Ricci, cond. Fjeldstad; (ii) LSO; (iii) Hungarian State SO, Jalas; (iv) Gibson; (v) Monteux.

Ricci's account of the *Violin concerto* has the clean, clear-cut and effortless technique that is a prime necessity for this work, and he makes light of its many difficulties. The reading is straightforward, with no lack of dash or intensity. A great contribution to the success of the performance is made by Fjeldstad and the orchestra, and this is well projected in spite of the forward balance of the soloist. About Monteux's exciting account of the *Second Symphony* there can be few reservations. This is a strong and agreeably unmannered reading, well played and brilliantly recorded. It is a pity that Maazel's version of the *Karelia suite* was not chosen instead of the relatively flabby account under Gibson, but *The Swan of Tuonela* seems to sound more atmospheric here than on its parent LP. The cassettes are well transferred, the sound rather brighter than the equivalent LPs.

Symphonic poems: *Finlandia, Op. 26; En Saga, Op. 9. Karelia suite,*

Op. 11. Legends: The Swan of Tuonela, Op. 22/2.
**(*) C.f.P. CFP 40247 [TC-CFP].
Vienna PO, Sargent.

Sargent's collection is highly successful. Without being especially idiomatic, each performance has conviction and character, and the four pieces complement each other to make a thoroughly enjoyable programme. The Vienna Philharmonic Orchestra bring a distinct freshness to their playing of music which must have been fairly unfamiliar to them, and Sir Malcolm imparts his usual confidence. The brass is especially full-blooded in *En Saga*, and even *Finlandia* sounds unhackneyed. Perhaps Sir Malcolm's tempi for *Karelia* are on the brisk side, but the music projects vividly and the orchestral playing is excellent. In the new C.f.P. pressing, however, the sound seems drier and rather less refined than on the original HMV issue. The vivid cassette transfer has been remastered since its first issue and now has a wide dynamic range. The sound is not always quite as clean as the disc, but the difference is not great and overall the orchestra has plenty of body and impact.

Finlandia, Op. 26.
** RCA Victrola (m) AT 122. NBC SO, Toscanini – KODÁLY: *Háry János*; PROKOFIEV: *Symphony No. 1.***

Toscanini conducts a searing performance of Sibelius's most hackneyed symphonic poem, one which with its conviction makes one forget the near-vulgarity. Such a performance deserves more brilliant recording than this limited mono.

Finlandia, Op. 26. Karelia suite, Op. 11: Alla marcia. Kuolema: Valse triste, Op. 44. Scènes historiques, Op. 25: Festivo.

** HMV 45 r.p.m. HMV 6. Bournemouth SO, Berglund.

This is a curious compilation. A much better coupling would have backed *Finlandia* plus the *Valse triste* with the complete *Karelia suite*. However, *Finlandia* certainly sounds brilliant, with the most telling percussion effects at the close. Berglund is rather too easy-going in the *Alla marcia* from *Karelia*, but elsewhere he is always sympathetic and the recording is consistently good, if over-bright.

Symphonic poems: *Finlandia, Op. 26; Night Ride and Sunrise, Op. 55; The Oceanides, Op. 73; Pohjola's Daughter, Op. 49; Tapiola, Op. 112.*
* Pye GSGC 305 (2 discs). LPO, Boult.

Sir Adrian has always been an eloquent and persuasive Sibelian, and he was the first to record *The Oceanides* and *Night Ride and Sunrise* in pre-war days. These performances were committed to disc in the mid-1950s in mono, and the present two-record set is a stereo transcription. The playing of the LPO in *The Oceanides* is not as impressive as that of the BBC Orchestra in the 1930s; and generally speaking their performances are not in the very highest flight. It is of course good to have Sir Adrian's thoughts on these masterly scores, but given the rather subfusc sound quality, these records cannot be given a strong general recommendation.

Symphony No. 2 in D major, Op. 43.
** RCA Camden CCV 5029 [c4]. Stockholm PO, Dorati.
*(*) C.f.P. CFP 40315 [TC-CFP]. Sinfonia of London, Hannikainen.

It is perhaps surprising that, apart from the *Second*, there are no satisfactory bargain-priced issues of the Sibelius symphonies in the current catalogue. At medium price Maazel and Bernstein both offer complete cycles (with each record available separately), and among these Maazel's Vienna PO Decca Jubilee versions of Nos. 1 (JB 42 [KJBC], with the *Karelia suite*), 2 (JB 43 [KJBC]), 4 (JB 45 [KJBC], with *Tapiola*) and 7 (JB 46 [KJBC]) can be recommended with few or no reservations on grounds of either performance or recording. Maazel's *Seventh*, however, is joined to a controversially hard-driven performance of the *Fifth*, and for that work one turns either to Karajan's magnificent DG Accolade issue (2542 109 [3342 109], with *Finlandia* and *Valse triste*) or Bernstein's splendidly played NYPO disc (CBS 61808, with *Pohjola's Daughter*). Maazel's coupling of Nos. 3 and 6 (JB 44 [KJBC]) is only partly successful; Bernstein's pairing of Nos. 6 and 7 (CBS 61806) is much better managed, although the recording is no match for the Decca series.

Ever since the days of Kajanus and Schnéevoigt (whose recordings from the thirties are admirably represented in superb LP transfers on World Records), there has been much interest in Finnish interpreters of Sibelius. Indeed there has been something of a mystique about them, and judging from the evidence of the records made by Berglund, Kamu and Hannikainen, there is no reason to believe that the Finns offer special truths denied to Beecham, Koussevitzky, Karajan, Barbirolli and others. Hannikainen's version of the *Second Symphony*, made in the early sixties and still sounding astonishingly vivid (on both disc and cassette) as reissued by C.f.P., enjoyed great acclaim in its day, in spite of the off-beat timpani in the closing bars, and indeed perhaps it was overrated. The Sinfonia of London plays well and the performance is well shaped; but in the last analysis, Hannikainen's view, though thoroughly idiomatic, lacks real personality and intensity.

Dorati's version with the Stockholm Philharmonic is marginally cheaper, and the recording is more modern (it dates from the late 1960s). The sound is remarkably good on both disc and tape. In his autobiography Dorati spoke of his early dislike for Sibelius, which he said persisted for the rest of his life. Listening to this reading one would never guess any antipathy. On the contrary, it is well-shaped and finely proportioned, and it falls short of distinction largely on the score of the orchestral playing. The Stockholm orchestra is a good one but it cannot match the N Y P O, and there are none of the impulsive yet compelling touches that make Bernstein's medium-priced account (on CBS 61805) so memorable. Nor do the performance and the recording equal the other medium-priced recordings by Barbirolli (RCA GL 25011) or Szell (Philips Festivo 6570 084 [7310 084]). To that number Karajan's name must also be added, for his 1961 recording with the Philharmonia (HMV SXLP 30414 and on an excellent tape [TC-SXLP]) is a very strong contender. The Philharmonia plays for Karajan with greater finesse than the Sinfonia for Hannikainen, and the reading has a feeling of leonine power. It is preferable to Maazel's Decca account, which is more traditionally lush and leans more to a romantic view of the work, stressing the Tchaikovskian inheritance. The Decca Jubilee cassette, however, is technically the finest available version on tape.

Smetana, Bedřich (1824–84)

Má Vlast: complete.
  * Decca D P A 575/6 [K D P C 2 7044].
    Vienna PO, Kubelik.

This Decca set must be virtually discounted on grounds of recording. The strings are thin and papery, the high treble peaky, and there is a feeling of congestion at climaxes. The Vienna Philharmonic are on good form, but Kubelik's readings are somewhat lacking in purpose and colour. The tape is no more satisfactory than the discs.

Má Vlast: Vltava. The Bartered Bride: Overture; Polka; Dance of the comedians.
  **(*) C.f.P. CFP 40290. Hallé
    Orch., Loughran – DVOŘÁK:
    Slavonic dances. **(*)

Vigorous, strongly characterized performances: the dances from *The Bartered Bride* are notably vivacious, and the brilliant modern recording projects them vividly. In *Vltava* a less forward balance would have produced a greater degree of subtlety (and more bloom on the massed string timbre). Every detail of Smetana's descriptive river journey registers, but occasionally the ear craves more of a feeling of atmosphere, although the 'moonlight' sequence is beautifully done.

Stainer, John (1840–1901)

The Crucifixion.
  *** C.f.P. CFP 40067. Hughes,
    Lawrenson, Guildford Cath-

edral Choir, Barry Rose; Williams (organ).

The music of Stainer's famous *Crucifixion* (written in 1887) is central to the tradition of nineteenth-century English oratorio and owes not a little to the Mendelssohn of *Elijah*. It is not melodically distinguished and includes such harmonic clichés as the cadence at the climax of *Fling wide the gates, the Saviour waits* (but one cannot be surprised at that, since the couplet is not the happiest choice of rhyme). There are five hymns in which the congregation is invited to join: the C.f.P. version omits one of these. But the recording is of fine quality, forward, with clear projection of the words. John Lawrenson makes a movingly eloquent contribution to the performance, and the Guildford Cathedral Choir sings with feeling and taste.

Strauss, Johann, Snr (1804–49)
Strauss, Johann, Jnr (1825–99)
Strauss, Josef (1827–70)
Strauss, Eduard (1835–1916)

(All music listed is by Johann Strauss Jnr unless otherwise stated)

'*A Strauss Gala*': Marches: *Egyptian, Op. 335; Napoleon, Op. 156; Persian, Op. 289.* Overtures: *Die Fledermaus; Der Zigeunerbaron. Perpetuum mobile, Op. 257.* Polkas: *Annen, Op. 117; Auf der Jagd, Op. 373; Banditen galop, Op. 378;*

Champagne, Op. 211; Eljen a Magyar, Op. 332; Explosionen, Op. 43; Leichtes Blut, Op. 319; Neue Pizzicato, Op. 449; Pizzicato (with Josef); *Tritsch-Tratsch, Op. 214; Unter Donner und Blitz (Thunder and Lightning), Op. 324.* Waltzes: *Accelerationen, Op. 234; An der schönen blauen Donau (Blue Danube), Op. 314; Frühlingsstimmen (Voices of Spring), Op. 410; Geschichten aus dem Wiener Wald (Tales from the Vienna Woods), Op. 325; Kaiser (Emperor), Op. 437; Künstlerleben (Artist's Life), Op. 316; Morgenblätter (Morning Papers), Op. 279; Rosen aus dem Süden (Roses from the South), Op. 388; 1001 Nacht, Op. 346; Wein, Weib und Gesang (Wine, Women and Song), Op. 333; Wiener Blut (Vienna Blood), Op. 354; Wiener Bonbons, Op. 307; Wo die Zitronen blühn (Where the Lemon Trees Bloom), Op. 364.* STRAUSS, Eduard: *Bahn frei polka galop, Op. 45.* STRAUSS, Johann, Snr: *Radetzky march, Op. 228.* STRAUSS, Josef: Polkas: *Eingesendet, Op. 240; Feuerfest, Op. 269; Jockey, Op. 278; Plappermäulchen, Op. 245.* Waltzes: *Mein Lebenslauf ist Lieb und Lust, Op. 263; Sphärenklänge (Music of the Spheres), Op. 235.*
*** Decca D 145 D 4 (4 discs) [K 145 K 44]. Vienna PO, Willi Boskovsky.

Following a succession begun in the days of mono LPs with Clemens Krauss, Decca have over the years issued a series of incomparable stereo issues collecting the music of the Strauss family and directed with almost unfailing sparkle by Willi Boskovsky. The VPO has a tradition of New Year Strauss concerts, and it has become a happy idea at Decca to link the new issues with each year's turn. This four-disc compilation, like the two more selective double albums below, uses material from recordings made during the sixties. It is remarkably comprehensive and very reasonably priced. The rearrangement of items is most successful, with a judicious selective order, so that polka and waltz alternate engagingly. The first group, opening with a particularly vivacious account of the *Die Fledermaus* overture, gets the set off to an excellent start, and there are very few disappointments among the performances generally. The inclusion of four polkas by Josef Strauss, together with two of his finest waltzes, is particularly welcome. The recording seldom sounds really dated and is often very good; the cassette transfers are remarkably consistent too, generally full, bright and well focused.

'*Favourite composer*': Overtures: *Die Fledermaus; Der Zigeunerbaron. Egyptian march, Op. 335. Perpetuum mobile, Op. 257.* Polkas: *Auf der Jagd, Op. 373; Explosionen, Op. 43; Neue Pizzicato, Op. 449; Pizzicato* (with Josef); *Unter Donner und Blitz, Op. 324.* Waltzes: *An der schönen blauen Donau, Op. 314; Du und Du (Fledermaus waltz), Op. 367; Frühlingsstimmen, Op. 410; Geschichten aus dem Wiener Wald, Op. 325; Kaiser, Op. 437; Künstlerleben, Op. 316; Rosen aus dem Süden, Op. 388; 1001 Nacht, Op. 346; Wein, Weib und Gesang, Op. 333; Wiener Blut, Op. 354.*
*** Decca DPA 549/50 [KDPC].
Vienna PO, Boskovsky.

An attractive shorter compilation from the earlier records in the Boskovsky Decca series. The recordings are perhaps not so uniformly natural and rich as the current full-priced ones, but from the beginning Decca set a high technical standard, and if the sound of the strings sometimes slightly dates the source of individual items, the overall ambient glow is consistent throughout. The playing is reliably idiomatic and usually has fine spontaneity, and the selection includes many top favourites. The variation of recorded quality is slightly more noticeable on cassette than on disc, but both can be given a strong recommendation.

'*Favourite waltzes*': *An der schönen blauen Donau, Op. 314; Du und Du, Op. 367; Frühlingsstimmen, Op. 410; Geschichten aus dem Wiener Wald, Op. 325; Kaiser, Op. 437; Künstlerleben, Op. 316; Rosen aus dem Süden, Op. 388; 1001 Nacht, Op. 346; Wein, Weib und Gesang, Op. 333; Wiener Blut, Op. 354; Wiener Bonbons, Op. 307.*
*** Decca DPA 513/4 [KDPC].
Vienna PO, Boskovsky.

One might think that a succession of Strauss waltzes spread over two discs might produce a degree of listening monotony, but that is never the case here, such is the composer's resource in the matter of melody and orchestration. There are some splendid performances here, even if one or two of the more famous waltzes (the *Blue Danube* and the *Emperor*, for instance) have been recorded elsewhere with greater distinction. But no orchestra can articulate Strauss with quite the same natural rhythmic impulse as the Vienna Philharmonic; and the sound is admirably smooth and vivid. There is little difference between discs and tapes, although perhaps the former have slightly more sparkle.

Waltz: *An der schönen blauen*

Donau, Op. 314. Champagne polka, Op. 211. STRAUSS, Johann, Snr: *Radetzky march, Op. 228.*
** HMV 45 r.p.m. HMV 5. Johann Strauss Orch. of Vienna, Boskovsky – SUPPÉ: *Light Cavalry.***

These recordings were made during Boskovsky's EMI recording period in the early seventies. The opening *Radetzky march* has almost a demonstration impact (although it cannot match Boskovsky's later marvellous digital recording for Decca: D 147 D 2 [KSXC 2 7062]). Boskovsky is a little bland in the *Blue Danube* but the playing has both lilt and warmth. The recording is full-blooded but fractionally too resonant for complete clarity of focus.

Waltzes: *An der schönen blauen Donau, Op. 314; Frühlingsstimmen, Op. 410; Geschichten aus dem Wiener Wald, Op. 325; Kaiser, Op. 437; Rosen aus dem Süden, Op. 388; Wein, Weib und Gesang, Op. 333.*
** RCA Camden CCV 5027 [c4]. Oslo PO, Fjeldstad.

Fjeldstad's performances are essentially more vigorous than Guschlbauer's (see below), and he shows a nice flexibility of phrasing and rubato. Moreover he offers six waltzes as against only four on the C.f.P. issue. But the Oslo orchestra fails to produce the body and richness of the string tone of the LPO, although the age of the recording (1965) makes its contribution to this. The cassette offers high-level, lively transfers. There is a degree of shrillness in the upper range, but this responds quite well to the controls.

Waltzes: *An der schönen blauen Donau, Op. 314; Kaiser, Op. 437;*

Künstlerleben, Op. 316; Wein, Weib und Gesang, Op. 333.
**(*) C.f.P. CFP 165 [TC-CFP]. LPO, Guschlbauer.

Theodor Guschlbauer readily conveys his affection in these Viennese-style performances, and he makes the London Philharmonic play almost as if they were Vienna-born. The shaping of the opening of each waltz is very nicely done, and the orchestra are obviously enjoying themselves, even though the tension is held on comparatively slack reins. The recording, made in a reverberant acoustic, has warmth and bloom, and the percussion comes over well. The cassette has been successfully remastered and now matches the disc fairly closely, except that, because of the reverberation, the upper range (the side-drum, for instance) is rather less cleanly focused.

'Viennese night': *Egyptian march, Op. 335;* Polkas: *Banditen, Op. 378; Im Krapfenwald'l, Op. 336; Pizzicato* (with Josef). Waltzes: *Geschichten aus dem Wiener Wald, Op. 325; Morgenblätter, Op. 279; Rosen aus dem Süden, Op. 388. Der Zigeunerbaron: march.* STRAUSS, Eduard: *Bahn frei polka galop, Op. 45.* STRAUSS, Josef: *Eingesendet polka, Op. 240.*
*(*) C.f.P. 40256 [**TC-CFP]. Hallé Orch., Loughran.

This is a case where the more recently issued cassette is greatly preferable to the disc, which is disappointingly lacking in bloom and lustre and has thin upper strings and an exaggerated treble. On tape the sound has plenty of life at the top but much more emphasis on the middle frequencies. The result is to add a greater feeling of warmth to the music-making. Loughran has not yet inherited Barbirolli's mantle in this music, though

113

he is good in the polkas and gives an exhilarating presentation of Eduard Strauss's delightful 'railway' galop, *Bahn frei*. The waltzes are less successful, sounding too cosy and relaxed, although there is genuine magic in the delicate opening of *Tales from the Vienna Woods*.

OPERETTA

Die Fledermaus: complete.
> ** Everest s 463/2. Lipp, Holm, Schock, Nicolai, Berry, Curzi, Steiner, Vienna State Opera Chorus, Vienna SO, Stolz.
> (***) Decca DPA 585/6. Gueden, Lipp, Dermota, Patzak, Vienna State Opera Chorus, Vienna PO, Krauss.

Robert Stolz, himself a distinguished operetta composer, directs a sparkling performance of *Fledermaus*, bright and atmospheric if not as subtle in expression as, say, Karajan's. The jollity of the *Woe is me* trio (*O je, o je*) emerges in each stanza just a little too soon, for example. The cast represents a good sample of Viennese singers, but Wilma Lipp at the very end of her career is disappointingly shrill as Rosalinde, and not well contrasted with the charming Adèle of Renate Holm. The recording is vivid and immediate, the production excellent, and in spite of the reservations this makes much more congenial listening than the far superior performance on Decca.

This offers the classic version conducted by Clemens Krauss, one of the first major successes of the LP era. With an authentic Viennese cast and a conductor who in the years after the war understood the Viennese tradition more deeply than any, this could hardly be more persuasive as an interpretation. The pity is that the recorded sound is not just limited in range; it has a distressing thinness and edge on the string

tone. In this transfer it is a sound hard to get used to. There ought to be some way of rescuing such a scintillating early recording, perhaps by going back to the original mono masters.

One must remember that the superb 1955 Karajan set of *Die Fledermaus* has been successfully reissued on HMV at medium price. Although this is a mono recording – given a brighter edge in the new pressings – its freshness and clarity are most appealing, and the singing is endlessly delightful. Schwarzkopf makes an enchanting Rosalinde, and Rita Streich as Adèle produces her most dazzling coloratura. Gedda and Krebs are beautifully contrasted in their tenor tone, and Erich Kunz gives a vintage performance as Falke. With an excellent cassette equivalent, slightly smoother than the discs, this will be first choice for many: RLS 728 [TC-RLS]. The companion set of *Der Zigeunerbaron* recorded under Ackermann in 1958 is another vintage production from Walter Legge and enjoys a similar degree of success; Schwarzkopf is a radiant gipsy princess, and Gedda and Kunz are both on top form: HMV SXDW 3046 [TC2-SXDW].

Wiener Blut (Vienna Blood): complete.
> **(*) Everest s 472/2. Schock, Schramm, Gueden, Lipp, Kusche, Kunz, Vienna State Opera Chorus, Vienna SO, Stolz.

This scintillating performance under the direction of Robert Stolz, with a first-rate singing cast headed by Rudolf Schock, Hilde Gueden and Erich Kunz, can be strongly recommended. Though the voices are balanced forward the production (with sound effects) is very atmospheric, making this Strauss confection – drawn from various earlier numbers with the blessing of the composer – a fizzing Viennese entertainment. It is a delight to have the famous *Morning Papers* waltz, for example, turned into a song for Gabriele in Act 1; and here Gueden sings it charmingly, though hardly with the finesse of Schwarzkopf, whose performance in Walter Legge's medium-priced mono set of the mid-fifties is, of course, incomparable. Schwarzkopf is matched by the regular team of Gedda and Kunz, with Emmy Loose and Erika Köth in the secondary soprano roles. The original mono recording was beautifully balanced, and the facelift provided by the stereo transcription is tactfully achieved; the tape transfer is no less successful: HMV sxdws 3042 [тc2-sxdws].

Strauss, Richard (1864–1949)

An Alpine symphony, Op. 64.
** DG Heliodor (m) 2548 175 [3348 175]. Dresden (Saxon) State Orch., Boehm.

While a pictorial work like the *Alpine symphony* obviously calls for all the resources of modern stereo, the success of the Boehm mono recording of 1957 is remarkable. The performance is both gripping and evocative, and it shows Boehm in extrovert form, revelling in every detail of Strauss's complex orchestration. The orchestral playing is first-class in every way and has great vitality. The *Sunrise* section comes off splendidly, and even without stereo the recessed horns make a good effect. On LP the upper strings are given plenty of life but lack amplitude by the standards of a modern recording, and the brass fortissimos are clear rather than expansive; the cassette, which has marginally less upper range, tends to give more

body and warmth to the sound. But both are fully acceptable and project the music with considerable impact.

Also sprach Zarathustra (symphonic poem), *Op. 30.*
*** RCA Camden ccv 5040 [c4]. Chicago SO, Reiner.
Also sprach Zarathustra; Salome: Dance of the Seven Veils.
**(*) C.f.P. cfp 40289 [tc-cfp]. LPO, Del Mar.

Fritz Reiner was one of the very finest Straussians of his time, and in the fifties, when this recording was made, he had at his command an orchestra which then as now was among the greatest in the world. He was also treated to recording quality which, if not ideally clear, has a richness and depth that stand the test of time and make this RCA Camden disc an excellent recommendation, not so clean in sound as the C.f.P. version but more passionately convincing. The forward thrust is tremendous and the final climax superbly exciting, with a poetic closing section.

Norman Del Mar's performance lacks something of this thrust and warmth, but it is a refined reading, which shows how perceptive an interpreter of Strauss he is. There is no hint of vulgarity here, and playing and recording (late-seventies vintage) are excellent. On cassette the treble needs cutting back if the upper strings are not to lack body, but the powerful opening is well caught, and the sinuous performance of *Salome's Dance* sounds especially vivid.

Symphonic poems: *Also sprach Zarathustra, Op. 30; Don Juan, Op. 20; Till Eulenspiegels lustige Streiche, Op. 28.*
*** Decca Jubilee jb 27 [kjbc]. Vienna PO, Karajan.
'Favourite composer': (i) *Also*

sprach Zarathustra; (ii) *Don Juan;* (i) *Till Eulenspiegels lustige Streiche;* (ii) *Der Rosenkavalier: 1st Waltz sequence;* (i) *Salome: Dance of the Seven Veils.*
> **(*)** Decca DPA 543/4 [KDPC]. Vienna PO, (i) Karajan, (ii) Maazel.

With superlative performances of Strauss's three most popular symphonic poems squeezed on to a single disc, the Jubilee issue is an outstanding bargain even at medium price. In Strauss no one can quite match Karajan in the flair and point of his conducting, and these Vienna performances of the early sixties make up in warmth what they may slightly lack in polish compared with Karajan's later Berlin versions for DG. The sound, though not as full as the DG recordings, is extremely good for its period. There seems little reason to prefer the two-disc package in Decca's 'Favourite composer' series. Karajan's reading of *Don Juan* is in any case preferable to Maazel's, good though that is, and as makeweight for the second disc there is only *Salome's Dance* and the *Rosenkavalier Waltzes.* However, on cassette the transfer of *Also sprach Zarathustra* is more secure at the opening here than on the Jubilee tape, which is otherwise well managed.

(i) *Burleske in D minor for piano and orchestra. Don Juan, Op. 20; Der Rosenkavalier: Waltz sequence.*
> *** RCA Camden ccv 5051 [c4]. Chicago SO, Reiner, (i) with Janis.

The *Burleske* is not mentioned on the front of the sleeve of this LP (as if the distributors thought it might put people off!). In fact the work is a comparative rarity, a product of the composer's early twenties, when his brilliance almost outshone his inventiveness. The brilliance is well brought out by Byron Janis, and the hard American recording of the piano helps to ensure that Strauss's writing does not sound too sweet. But most will buy this issue for Reiner's marvellous performance of *Don Juan*, with its superbly thrilling climax where (in spite of muddy recording) the great leaping horn theme rings out unforgettably. The *Rosenkavalier Waltzes* are nicely done too. In the cassette transfer the *Burleske* sounds exceptionally well, and it is a pity that the transfer level in *Don Juan* has been slightly misjudged, bringing some congestion in the climaxes. Obviously a few less decibels would have given excellent results.

Death and Transfiguration (Tod und Verklärung), Op. 24; Don Juan, Op. 20; Till Eulenspiegels lustige Streiche, Op. 28.
> (**) RCA Victrola (m) AT 105. NBC SO, Toscanini.

Toscanini's readings of Strauss have been much praised for their sharpness of characterization, and certainly all these performances are purposeful, with *Death and Transfiguration* built up to a superb climax. But quite apart from the sadly limited recording quality it is absurd to have a break in *Till Eulenspiegel* after only four minutes, when it could easily be accommodated on a single side with *Don Juan.*

Don Juan, Op. 20; Festival prelude, Op. 61; Till Eulenspiegels lustige Streiche, Op. 28; Salome: Dance of the Seven Veils.
> **(*)** Everest 3023. NY Stadium Orch., Stokowski.

Not surprisingly with the old magician Stokowski in charge, Salome is made to languish more unashamedly than ever before, and even Till in his posthumous epilogue has a languishing mood on him, although the execution scene is splendidly dramatic. Surprisingly, on the great unison horn call of *Don Juan* Stokowski holds back a little, with less than spacious phrasing. But as ever he is nothing if not convincing, and those looking for really ripe versions of these pieces need not hesitate. The recording is not of the most modern, basically spacious and atmospheric but with a little fuzz on the strings at climaxes. However, with a slight treble reduction (which also serves to moderate the background noise) it can be made to sound both brilliant and exciting.

Don Juan, Op. 20; Till Eulenspiegels lustige Streiche, Op. 28.
 ** C.f.P. CFP 40307. LPO, Mackerras – TCHAIKOVSKY: *Romeo and Juliet.***

These are good, serviceable accounts of two popular symphonic poems, recorded with admirable detail and perspective. Now reissued in a coupling with a comparable performance of Tchaikovsky's *Romeo and Juliet*, directed by John Pritchard, they are good value; but it would be idle to pretend that there are not more distinctive versions available at a comparable cost.

Ein Heldenleben, Op. 40.
 **(*) C.f.P. CFP 40325. LSO, Barbirolli.

Sir John Barbirolli's account of Strauss's *Ein Heldenleben*, made right at the end of his life, lacks something in dramatic urgency, but the ripeness of the sound is wonderfully matched by the conductor's expansiveness. The fulfilment theme at the end has rarely sounded so noble, and even if – at slow speeds – the conflict is minimized, making the Critics quite nice chaps and the Battle rather jolly, it presents an

excellent alternative version. The beauty of the 1970 recording, its richness almost never masking inner clarity, is a joy in itself.

Waltzes: *München (Memorial waltz); Schlagobers, Op. 70. Feuersnot* (opera): *Love scene. Der Rosenkavalier* (opera): *Act 1: Introduction; Act 2: Letter scene and Waltz; Act 3: Introduction and Waltzes (Supper scene).*
 *** C.f.P. CFP 40327. LPO, Del Mar.

With Beecham overtones, Norman Del Mar and the LPO give ripely persuasive performances of a series of Strauss lollipops. The pot-pourris from *Rosenkavalier* are well coupled with three rarities, none of them great or even memorable Strauss, but worth having as musical whipped cream – the *Waltz* from the ballet *Schlagobers*, the *Love scene* from *Feuersnot* and the *Munich Waltz.*

Der Rosenkavalier (opera): complete.
 **(*) Decca 4BB 115/8. Reining, Jurinac, Gueden, Dermota, Weber, Poell, Vienna State Opera Chorus, Vienna PO, Erich Kleiber.

Erich Kleiber's set of *Rosenkavalier* was one of the classic recordings of the early LP era, and his persuasive way with the music makes this bargain issue well worth investigating, particularly when so many of the singers give comparably magical performances – Jurinac and Weber among them. Gueden as Sophie is good too, but the big blot is the Marschallin of Maria Reining, ill-focused and tentative enough to make one wonder at her high reputation on stage in this role. The playing of the

Vienna Philharmonic is not immaculate, and the recording is not really full enough for so rich a score, but at its price it should not be missed.

For those who (understandably) resist mono recording in Strauss's richly opulent score, the classic Karajan set can be enthusiastically suggested at medium price. It's one of the greatest of all the opera recordings produced by Walter Legge, and the cast includes Schwarzkopf at the peak of her career. Christa Ludwig is a ravishing Octavian, and she is marvellously partnered by Teresa Stich-Randall: this is self-recommending (HMV SLS 810 [TC-SLS]). On Decca Jubilee there is a splendid single disc (or tape) of excerpts. Régine Crespin has rarely, if ever, made a better record, and if her singing of the Marschallin does not outshine Schwarzkopf, it is still very moving, and she is beautifully supported by Elisabeth Söderström and Hilde Gueden. Silvio Varviso conducts the Vienna Philharmonic seductively and the recording is both rich and sparkling in Decca's best manner. The selection is most generous and well chosen with a substantial excerpt from Act 1, the presentation of the silver rose and duet (*Mir ist die Ehre*) from Act 2, and the Trio and final duet from Act 2. The tape matches the disc closely (although the transfer level is higher on side two): Decca JB 57 [KJBC].

Stravinsky, Igor
(1882–1971)

(i) *The Firebird* (ballet): *suite* (1919 score). (ii) *Petrushka* (ballet): complete (1911 score).
  *** Decca SPA 152. Paris Cons. Orch., Monteux.
  **(*) RCA Camden CCV 5034

[c4]. (i) as above; (ii) Boston SO, Monteux.

The Decca record, which is in the medium price-range, restores to the catalogue a coupling originally issued on RCA in the earliest days of stereo. The actual recording was made by Decca and this has now been greatly enhanced. The closing pages of *Petrushka* are of demonstration quality, and the sound throughout has richness and lustre; the natural bloom more than compensates for a certain lack of refinement in the orchestral playing. Julius Katchen, no less, was recruited for the piano part in *Petrushka*. The style of the French wind-playing is noticeable in *The Firebird*, where the Paris brass bring a characteristic bray to the finale. But with any reservations these are still fine performances, vividly recorded.

The Camden reissue, which is considerably cheaper than the Decca, uses a different version of *Petrushka*, made in Boston. It is an extremely lively performance and offers finer orchestral playing than the Paris version. There is a particularly exciting account here of the final scene, all the bustle of the Shrovetide carnival brilliantly conveyed. The snag is the Boston acoustic, which adds a touch of harshness to the sound. However, whichever recording is chosen, many collectors will be glad to have an account of the score under the conductor who directed its première, a reading which is strongly conscious of the dance, its rhythms and colours, and less emotionally involved with the underlying pathos of the story.

(i) *The Firebird: suite* (1919 score); (ii) *The Song of the Nightingale* (*Le Chant du rossignol*; symphonic poem).
  ⊛*** DG Heliodor 2548 145 [3348 145]. Berlin PO, Maazel.
  **(*) C.f.P. CFP 40328. Philhar-

monia Orch., (i) Josef Krips, (ii) Silvestri.

The attractive Heliodor issue restores to the catalogue a much-praised coupling dating from the earliest days of LP. *Le Rossignol* is an underrated Stravinsky opera; its derivative opening, with overtones of *Nuages*, and its Rimskian flavour have led to its virtues being undervalued. Among them is its extraordinarily rich fantasy and vividness of colouring; and the symphonic poem that Stravinsky made from the material of this work deserves a more established place in the concert repertoire. The exotic effects and glittering colours are superbly caught here; the Berlin Philharmonic offers the utmost refinement. Maazel's reading of the *Firebird suite* too has an enjoyable *éclat*, and he has the advantage of the most beautiful woodwind playing, notably the oboe in the *Princesses' dance* and the bassoon in the *Berceuse*. The recording of both works was notable for its splendid atmosphere, and only the massed upper strings hint at its early date. A first-rate record, and a very good cassette too.

The Classics for Pleasure issue has the considerable advantage of much more modern recorded sound. Silvestri's *Song of the Nightingale* dates from 1961 and the orchestra is given more body and breadth. His approach is more romantic than Maazel's, but not excessively so; and he too secures first-class orchestral playing. Krips, recorded in 1965, has an even greater advantage, but his account of the *Firebird suite* lacks the flair and panache of Maazel's, especially in the score's lyrical moments. Yet the extra richness of the EMI recording undoubtedly tells, notably in the finale.

The Rite of Spring (*Le Sacre du Printemps*; ballet): complete.
*** C.f.P. CFP 129. Philharmonia Orch., Markevitch.

On its original issue this Markevitch version became rather submerged, partly because there were several other outstanding records available. But at bargain price, and with the stereo recording sounding remarkably vivid and modern, it is very highly recommendable indeed. The Philharmonia playing is superbly exciting (one of the highlights of this performance is the spectacular use of the tamtam) and at all times equal to Markevitch's vitality and ruthless forward momentum.

Sullivan, Arthur (1842–1900)

Pineapple Poll (ballet, arr. Mackerras): extended suite.
(*) C.f.P. CFP 40293. LPO, Mackerras – VERDI: *Lady and the Fool.*(*)

This is a very generous suite from *Pineapple Poll*, and it is brilliantly played by the LPO under its arranger, Charles Mackerras. The recording too is sparkling and vivid, though it lacks something in amplitude; the brass has plenty of bite, but the massed strings could ideally do with more richness. This is still very entertaining, but Mackerras's complete recording on HMV Greensleeve (ESD 7028 [TC-ESD]) has a bloom and sumptuousness that are not so much in evidence here.

OPERA

The Gondoliers: complete, without dialogue.
*(*) Decca DPA 3075/6. Green, Watson, Halman, Harding, Mitchell, Osborn, Styler,

D'Oyly Carte Opera Co., Godfrey.

Like *The Mikado* (see below) the first D'Oyly Carte L P set of *The Gondoliers* dates from the very beginning of the fifties, and the recording shows signs of wear. Curiously this includes serious end-of-side distortion, which was present also on the 1963 Ace of Clubs mono discs (A C L 1151/2), together with vocal edginess and moments of blasting. If anything these stereo transcription pressings sound better than that reissue of the sixties. Provided the top is cut well back the solo voices retain their presence and colour, and the upper range is crisper than others in the current D P A series. Savoyards will undoubtedly be willing to put up with this to remember several very fine performances. This was one of Ella Halman's very best sets; the insecurity of intonation that mars some of her other recordings is not apparent here, and her duets with Martyn Green are a joy. Muriel Harding (as Gianetta) sings with real charm, and Richard Watson is a splendid Grand Inquisitor: both of his principal solos are treasurable. The chorus is below par, and the ensembles are not always secure in intonation, so that the opening scene of Act 1 is not the place to sample. But Isidore Godfrey displays his affection for this score (his later full-priced stereo set is quite outstanding), and the freshness and spontaneity of the music-making are never in doubt. Act 2, which depends a great deal on the principals, is first-class, and the *Cachucha* (which is so limp in Sargent's H M V set: S X D W 3027 [T C2-S X D W]) is superbly spirited here.

Iolanthe: complete, without dialogue.
  *(*) Decca D P A 3055/6. Green, Osborn, Morgan, Thornton, Styler, Mitchell, Halman,

Drummond-Grant, D'Oyly Carte Opera Co., Godfrey.

The joy of this set is of course Martyn Green's Lord Chancellor, made the more effective when heard against Ella Halman's ripe characterization of the Fairy Queen. Margaret Mitchell (Phyllis) and Alan Styler (Strephon) sing with plenty of character if not always impeccable intonation. Ann Drummond-Grant is a rather colourless Iolanthe. The stereo transcription adds a curious hollow resonance and blunts the edge of the sound without improving the anaemic string tone. Act 2 tends to sound better than Act 1, and the close of the opera is vivaciously managed. However, Sargent's medium-priced H M V stereo set is worth the extra cost, though it has its drawbacks. John Cameron's Strephon is rather dark-timbred and George Baker's *Nightmare song* is no match for Martyn Green's version. But with Monica Sinclair a splendid Fairy Queen and Ian Wallace, Owen Brannigan, Alexander Young and Elsie Morison, this cast is far stronger than the one on Decca, and the H M V recording is infinitely more realistic: H M V S X D W 3047 [T C2-S X D W].

The Mikado: complete, without dialogue.
  (***) Decca D P A 3049/50. Fancourt, Green, Osborn, Watson, Mitchell, Halman, D'Oyly Carte Opera Co., Godfrey.

This 1950 version of *The Mikado* was among Decca's first L P releases and in its day the recording showed a startling clarity and detail, making every word easily audible, yet with an attractive resonance and bloom on the voices. True there was occasionally excessive sibilance (notably in Martyn Green's *Little list* song), but the choral sound had striking immediacy and depth, and even the rather thin orchestral strings were acceptable because of the overall feeling of presence. In this stereo transcription much of that presence is masked, yet the orchestral strings sound unattractively thin and fizzy. Apart from the overture (which is best left unplayed) the sound is still tolerable, the words generally clear, although the focus of the ensembles has lost its crispness. The performance remains a classic account of the most popular of the Savoy operas. Darrell Fancourt was in superb form, and his Mikado's edict that the punishment should fit the crime has an irresistible authority. Martyn Green's Ko-Ko is equally delectable. Leonard Osborn was past his best, but *A wandering minstrel* shows what a strong contribution he could make, especially in the boisterous middle sections. Ella Halman could no longer sing her lyrical aria perfectly in tune, but she is incomparably magisterial elsewhere. With Richard Watson a splendid Pooh-Bah, and the three little maids (Margaret Mitchell, Joan Gillingham and Joyce Wright) pertly characterized, there is still much to enjoy once the ear adjusts to the sound.

Patience: complete, without dialogue.
** Decca DPA 3063/4. Mitchell, Fancourt, Pratt, Green, Stylcr, Griffiths, Halman, Drummond-Grant, Mitchell, D'Oyly Carte Opera Co., Godfrey.

Patience was one of the last of the earlier Decca D'Oyly Carte series, and the recording here has more body and substance than most of the others (although the upper range is curiously veiled and the orchestral strings are singularly unrealistic). It is a vintage performance. Margaret Mitchell is too precious in the name role, but her sophistication is not entirely out of character. Peter Pratt ably represents the

new generation and Neville Griffiths too makes an attractive début, as the Duke of Dunstable. Darrell Fancourt, Martyn Green (an irresistible Bunthorne), and Ella Halman remind us of past glories. Godfrey conducts throughout with zest and obvious affection, and the performance undoubtedly has spontaneity, particularly in Act 2. But *Patience* was one of the very best of Sargent's series for HMV, and his set (with Elsie Morison, Alexander Young, George Baker, and John Cameron) is the finest available in the present catalogue at any price. Moreover it costs only about a pound more than the historic Decca reissue: SXDW 3031 [TC2-SXDW].

The Pirates of Penzance: complete, without dialogue.
**(*) Decca (m) DPA 3051/2. Green, Fancourt, Watson, Harding, Osborn, Halman, D'Oyly Carte Opera Co., Godfrey.

More than any of the other reissues of these vintage recordings from the early fifties *The Pirates of Penzance* preserves the qualities that made them so popular. For some reason best known to themselves the Decca engineers have left the sound untampered with: we are offered mono pressings. They are far from perfect; the upper range is not always clean and there are background rustles, but the original balance, bloom and clarity are preserved and the strings are not consistently tiresome. There is a feeling of stage atmosphere and presence. And the performance is indispensable. Martyn Green is on top form; not only is his famous Major-General's song superbly thrown off (the little coughs and asides are a delight), but the set is worth having alone for his inimitable rendering of *I'm telling a terrible story, which doesn't diminish my glory* . . . There are almost no weaknesses among the principals.

Darrell Fancourt's Pirate King has splendid charisma and Ella Halman was surely born to portray Ruth, so that the *Paradox* number in Act 2 is specially telling. Richard Watson is a gloriously genial (and knowing) Police Sergeant, and the choral interchanges between police and pirates are great fun, with the slight lack of polish in the choral singing enhancing rather than detracting from the characterization. Muriel Harding is a delightful Mabel, and if Leonard Osborn as Frederic is a little husky in the delightfully sentimental duet (*Leave me not to pine alone*), they still bring it off very nicely. The close of the opera, with Darrell Fancourt expressing his loyalty, is perfectly judged, the satirical element nicely buffered by the sheer warmth of the loyal tribute. Even if you invest in Sargent's splendid set on mid-priced HMV, with Owen Brannigan as Sergeant of the Police and modern stereo sound (sxdw3041[tc2-sxdw]), this first LP version is well worth exploring.

Ruddigore: complete, without dialogue.
> *(*) Decca DPA 3061/2. Green, Mitchell, Osborn, Fancourt, Halman, D'Oyly Carte Opera Co., Godfrey.

Although seriously flawed by a bad tape-join in the finale to Act 1 which causes an uncomfortable change of pitch, this set has a number of good things to recommend it for dedicated G. and S. enthusiasts. Godfrey conducts throughout with characteristic zest, and the feeling of a live performance persists, in spite of the close microphones and absence of dialogue. The overture, with its exaggerated top and whistly strings, is best left alone, but the solo voices are clear and immediate, even if Margaret Mitchell's high notes, like those of the sopranos in the chorus, are made to peak

by the over-modulation in the grooves. All this may well seem damning, but one soon comes under the spell of the strong personalities in the cast. Martyn Green is memorable as Robin and finds an engagingly warm tone for his Schubertian duet with Rose Maybud in Act 1. If Margaret Mitchell hardly conveys the charm of the heroine with her book of etiquette, she projects well. Leonard Osborn is a superbly boisterous Richard, and Ann Drummond-Grant, although too sober in Mad Margaret's Act 1 solo, partners Sir Despard splendidly in their Act 2 duet. Darrell Fancourt's classic account of the ghost song is part of an effectively atmospheric scene in Act 2, although the primitive sound-effects detract from the impact of the solo voice. Godfrey's one miscalculation is his tempo for the patter trio, *If my eyes were fully open*, which leaves the participants breathless. Ella Halman is on top form in her Act 1 solo, but both she and Fancourt are less reliable when they finally get together at the end of Act 2. In many ways this set has more character than the later stereo remake, but the general reader's attention must be directed to HMV's medium-priced reissue of the Sargent set, which is superb in every way and offers first-class stereo on both disc and tape: sxdw 3029 [tc2-sxdw].

The Sorcerer: complete, without dialogue.
> **(*) Decca DPA 3057/8. Pratt, Griffiths, Morgan, Harding, Drummond-Grant, Adams, Skitch, D'Oyly Carte Opera Co., Godfrey.

The D'Oyly Carte Company of the fifties was at its peak at the time of this recording. New blood had been infiltrated and was by now well absorbed into the system. Ann Drummond-Grant, in particular, had assumed Ella

Halman's mantle with considerable authority, and she sings superbly here as Lady Sangazure. Neville Griffiths makes an attractive Alexis, and Donald Adams, who was to develop as a worthy successor for Darrell Fancourt, is an excellent Notary. But the Sorcerer *is* John Wellington Wells, and this predominantly lyrical score needs an unforgettable performance of the title role if it is to succeed away from the theatre. Peter Pratt gives such a performance, and indeed the whole spell scene is memorable. Godfrey too is on top form, and conducts throughout with stylish affection. The orchestra is an ad hoc group (only much later in the stereo era was Decca to provide the RPO), but its playing is polished, even elegant, and the chorus is excellent. As a performance this is quite the equal of the later stereo version made in 1967, and it is very well recorded for its date. The stereo transcription, it is true, adds an artificial hollow resonance and tends to blunt the choral sound (basically clear and incisive), but orchestra and solo voices are not too badly affected. It is to be hoped that Decca will one day reissue the original mono pressings.

'*Highlights*' from *The Gondoliers; HMS Pinafore; Iolanthe; The Mikado; The Pirates of Penzance; The Yeomen of the Guard.*
*** C.f.P. CFP 40238 [TC-CFP]. Richard Lewis, Monica Sinclair, Geraint Evans, John Cameron, George Baker, Elsie Morison, Marjorie Thomas, Owen Brannigan, Glyndebourne Festival Chorus, PA Orch., Sargent.

An attractive selection of highlights, generously offering samples of six of Sir Malcolm Sargent's HMV recordings. There is some distinguished solo singing and if the atmosphere is sometimes a little cosy (the *Cachucha* from *The Gondoliers* sounds slower than ever when heard out of the context of the complete performance), there is a very great deal to enjoy. The recording has transferred well, and the cassette is first-class too.

'*Highlights*', *Vol. 2*, from *The Gondoliers; Iolanthe; The Mikado; Patience; The Pirates of Penzance; Trial by Jury.*
** C.f.P. CFP 40260 [TC-CFP]. Artists as on above, Sargent.

This is generally a less appealing compilation than the earlier one (above). Of course there are some good things here, notably Owen Brannigan's *Sentry song* from *Iolanthe* and the items from *The Pirates of Penzance*. But generally these excerpts show Sargent's broad manner and occasional lack of sparkle, and this is reflected especially in the numbers from *The Mikado* and *The Gondoliers*. The recording is good on both disc and cassette.

'*Highlights*', *Vol. 3*, from *The Gondoliers; HMS Pinafore; The Mikado; Patience; Ruddigore; The Yeoman of the Guard.*
⊛*** C.f.P. CFP 40282 [TC-CFP]. Artists as on above two issues, Sargent.

This is easily the most attractive of the collections of highlights from the Sargent recordings. The selection could not have been better made. Each of the six generous groups is beautifully balanced to match lyricism with fun, and the standard of singing is stunningly high. One especially remembers George Baker's *Flowers that bloom* and *Tit Willow* (from *The Mikado*) and his performance of Sir Joseph Porter's autobiographical monologue from *Pinafore*. The selection from *Patience* is enchanting: *Prithee, pretty maiden, A*

123

magnet hung, If Saphir I chose to marry – with a deliciously pointed accompaniment – and *When I go out of door* follow one another in rollicking inspirational profusion. The lyrical numbers from *Yeomen* provide ballast on side one. The recording is first-rate throughout and the tape has only fractionally less freshness and range than the disc (and that only noticeable on an A/B comparison). Very highly recommended.

'Highlights', Vol. 4, from The Gondoliers; Iolanthe; The Mikado; The Pirates of Penzance; Ruddigore; Trial by Jury.
  ** C.f.P. CFP 40338 [TC-CFP]. Artists as on above three issues, Sargent.

The collection here is enjoyable enough, but selected and arranged with no special perception. Owen Brannigan demonstrates that he was indeed a more humane Mikado than most, and though his words in the famous song are articulated with superb clarity, the characterization is too soft-centred. The attractive excerpts from *Trial by Jury* are spoiled by fades: it would have been better to offer one continuous excerpt. The *Ruddigore* items come off well, especially the patter trio – so much more polished here than in Godfrey's complete set (see above) – and the other distinctive group is from *The Pirates of Penzance*, although this ends side two and the closing number could have been more cleverly chosen to make a good finale. The recording is excellent on disc; the cassette matches it closely.

Suppé, Franz von (1819–95)

Overture: *Light Cavalry.*
  ** HMV 45 r.p.m. HMV 5. Johann Strauss Orch. of Vienna, Willi Boskovsky – J. STRAUSS: *An der schönen blauen Donau* etc.**

The brassy ebullience of *Light Cavalry* is effectively presented by the 45 r.p.m. format, and the performance is lively, though the reprise of the fanfare theme at the end is not completely convincingly done.

Tallis, Thomas (c. 1505–1585)

Ecce tempus idoneum; Gaude gloriosa Dei Mater; Hear the voice and prayer; If ye love me; Lamentations I; Loquebantur variis linguis; O nata lux; Spem in alium.
  ** C.f.P. CFP 40069. Clerkes of Oxenford, Wulstan.

A useful issue, giving us a bargain-label version of the magnificent forty-part motet *Spem in alium*. At the same time its value is diminished by the somewhat brisk tempi David Wulstan chooses, which leave the music wanting in its proper dignity. There is also some sense of strain among the women, though their tone is clean and well-focused. Reservations notwithstanding, there are fine things on this disc and it can be recommended.

Tartini, Giuseppe
(1692–1770)

Violin sonata in G minor (*The Devil's Trill*; arr. Kreisler).
*** RCA Camden CCV 5015 [c4].
Szeryng, Reiner – TCHAIKOV-
SKY: *Violin concerto.* ***

This is a generous fill-up for an out-standing bargain performance of the Tchaikovsky *Violin concerto*. Szeryng's style is not so romantic that he is hampered in his treatment of a classical work, and Charles Reiner's contribution is stylish, even though he uses a piano rather than a harpsichord. The high-level tape transfer is marginally less refined than the disc, but is still acceptable.

Tchaikovsky, Peter
(1840–93)

Capriccio italien, Op. 45.
**(*) C.f.P. CFP 40341 [TC-CFP].
Philharmonia Orch., Kletzki –
RIMSKY-KORSAKOV: *Scheheraz-ade.* ***

Kletzki's performance, is very enjoyable. It is superbly played and very well recorded, making a good bonus for a highly recommendable version of *Scheherazade*.

Capriccio italien, Op. 45; (i) *1812 overture, Op. 49.*
** HMV 45 r.p.m. HMV 2.
Bournemouth SO, Silvestri, (i) with Band of Royal Marines.

This is an obvious coupling for HMV's twelve-inch 45 r.p.m. format,

and both recordings are extremely brilliant and clear, with very little end-of-side fall-off. Indeed *1812* with its ferocious cannonade is remarkably clean, yet the feeling of spectacle is well conveyed. The sound balance is improved by a treble cut and bass boost; otherwise the opening of the *Capriccio italien* is too fierce. The performances are not strong in forward thrust, but the detail is good, and Silvestri works up plenty of excitement towards the end of each piece.

Capriccio italien, Op. 45; Marche slave, Op. 31; Nutcracker suite, Op. 71a.
**(*) DG Heliodor 2548 275
[3348 275]. Berlin PO, Leitner.

Ferdinand Leitner's collection dates from the early sixties but the sound has been successfully refurbished, and the quality is remarkably fresh. The *Capriccio italien* is not especially Italianate, but it is played with style and creates plenty of excitement without being frenzied. The *Marche slave* has dignity, and the *Nutcracker suite* is rather gently played, with considerable effect. An excellent bargain, both on disc and on tape (which is freshly transferred).

Piano concerto No. 1 in B flat minor, Op. 23.
⊛*** RCA Victrola (m) AT 113.
Horowitz, NBC SO, Toscanini.
** RCA Camden CCV 5016 [c4].
Gilels, Chicago SO, Reiner.
(**) RCA (m) VH 015. Horowitz NBC SO, Toscanini.
*(*) C.f.P. CFP 115 [TC-CFP].
Katin, LPO, Pritchard –
LITOLFF: *Scherzo.* ***

The partnership of Horowitz and Toscanini in Tchaikovsky's *B flat minor*

125

Concerto has been legendary since the war years, when the 1941 recording (on AT 113) was available in 78 r.p.m. form. It still sounds astonishingly well: the piano timbre is somewhat clattery, but one soon adjusts, and the orchestral sound has plenty of brilliance and life. For once Tchaikovsky's conception of a 'battle' between soloist and orchestra is played out by equal adversaries, as the opening immediately shows, with its sweeping strings and bold, striding piano chords. The breathtaking bravura of the first-movement climax is matched by Horowitz's cadenza, where he sounds as if he had four hands instead of two. No less impressive is the scintillating scherzando playing at the centre of the slow movement, and the final climax of the last movement with its thundering octaves is electrifying. The alternative version by the same artists (on VH 015) was also recorded in Carnegie Hall, but at a live concert in 1943, and the recording is muffled in the first movement and shrill in the finale. Here, however, Horowitz's climactic octaves are even more riveting, but the performance is marred not only by the variable sound but also by some awkward woodwind playing near the opening of the slow movement. Both records are affected by a low-pitched bass rumble, especially noticeable near the end of the first movement on AT 113. However, this is a recorded performance that earns a place in every collection.

For those wanting stereo, Gilels's RCA recording should serve, although it is somewhat over-reverberant and there is an element of coarseness. But this too is an exciting, full-blooded performance, including a beautifully gentle account of the outer sections of the slow movement and a vivid dance-like projection of energy in the finale.

Katin's Classics for Pleasure version is given a brilliant, modern recording and is basically quite a strong, musical reading. But somehow there is a lack of drama, and the absence of extrovert bravura from the soloist (especially in the middle section of the slow movement) produces an impression of facelessness. But no one could fault this issue on grounds of taste, and it has an excellent filler. The cassette transfer is good, full-blooded and clear.

'Favourite composer': (i–iii) *Piano concerto No. 1 in B flat minor, Op. 23;* (ii; iv) *1812 overture, Op. 49;* (v) *The Nutcracker, Op. 71; Trepak; Dance of the Sugar Plum Fairy; Waltz of the Flowers; Swan Lake, Op. 20: Waltz; Scene; Dance of the Little Swans; Czardas;* (vi) *Symphony No. 6 in B minor (Pathétique), Op. 74.*
*(*) Decca DPA 547/8 [KDPC]. (i) Katin; (ii) LSO; (iii) Kundell; (iv) Alwyn, with Band of Grenadier Guards; (v) Suisse Rom. Orch., Ansermet; (vi) RPO, Henry Lewis.

Katin's performance of the *Piano concerto* is a strong one, and the recording sounds as vivid here as ever. Unfortunately the set is let down by the performance of the *Pathétique*, by no means outstanding and marred by a very dry acoustic. The other works are well done, although it is a pity that room was not found for the full *Nutcracker suite*. The cassettes are of generally good if somewhat uneven quality, though the *Concerto* offers first-class sound.

Piano concerto No. 2 in G major, Op. 44 (arr. Siloti).
** DG Heliodor (m) 2548 298 [3348 298]. Cherkassky, Berlin PO, Kraus.

This famous recording now reappears in excellent mono sound. Relatively few allowances have to be made for it, though it dates from 1955. DG are to be congratulated for not trying to transcribe it for stereo, since the overall effect is perfectly acceptable, though one could wish for a richer, fresher string sound. Cherkassky's playing is superb throughout, and although it is a drawback that he uses the truncated Siloti edition, his flair and poetry more than compensate. The cassette is slightly less smooth than the disc, but readers should not allow minor reservations to put them off this classic account.

Violin concerto in D major, Op. 35.
*** RCA Camden CCV 5015 [C4]. Szeryng, Boston SO, Munch – TARTINI: *Devil's Trill sonata.****

When it first appeared at full price (without a coupling), Szeryng's early RCA performance was widely accounted to provide the ideal combination of brilliance, warmth and subtlety. In the bargain Camden reissue that enthusiasm must be reinforced. The purity of Szeryng's playing is remarkable when the technical problems are so demanding, and quite apart from his effortless sense of bravura, he is able to bring all the lyrical sweetness and slavonic yearning needed for Tchaikovsky's big melodies. First-rate playing by the Boston orchestra and a wide stereo spread. The cassette transfer is made at a high level, which brings a slight loss of refinement in the orchestral fortissimos. But otherwise the sound is clear and clean.

1812 overture, Op. 49 (see also above under *Capriccio italien*).
** C.f.P. CFP 101 [TC-CFP]. LPO, Welsh Guards Band, Mackerras – *Concert.* **

1812 overture; Marche slave, Op. 31; Romeo and Juliet (fantasy overture).

** Pickwick Contour CN 2021. N Philharmonia Orch., Del Mar.

Mackerras gives a characteristically lively performance of *1812*, apparently using mortar-fire at the end. The recording is bright and vivid and has transferred successfully to cassette, without the usual distortion. It is part of a good though not distinctive LPO concert of Russian music (see below).

Del Mar's disc is very well recorded indeed and the engineers handle the end of *1812* with spectacular yet thoroughly musical results. The orchestral playing too is excellent, but the performances, although offering plenty of detail, are lacking in a compelling emotional thrust. *Marche slave* comes off the most effectively, its colourful orchestration well realized by performers and recording alike. This disc is excellent value.

Francesca da Rimini (fantasy), *Op. 32; Hamlet* (fantasy overture), *Op. 67a.*
⊛ *** Everest 3011. NY Stadium Orch., Stokowski.

One had always tended to think of *Hamlet* as one of Tchaikovsky's near-misses, but here it emerges as a superb piece of writing, and Stokowski plays the central string tune so convincingly that, if it has not quite the romantic panache of *Romeo and Juliet*, it has instead the proper sombre passion suitable to the altogether different atmosphere of Shakespeare's *Hamlet*. It is the dignity of the music and its close identification with the play that come over so strikingly. And, fascinatingly, Stokowski shows us how intensely Russian the music is: this is Shakespeare played in the vernacular of that great country, with its national feeling for epic drama; the funeral march at the end is extremely moving. *Francesca* is hardly less exciting. Surely the opening whirlwinds have seldom roared at such tornado speeds before, and the skilful way Stokowski builds up the climax out of the fragmentation of Tchaikovsky's score is thrilling indeed. The central section is played with the beguiling care for detail and balance for which this conductor is famous. When the great polyphonic climax comes, and the themes for the lovers' passion intertwine with music to suggest they are discovered, the tension is tremendous. The recording throughout is astonishingly vivid when one considers that it was made more than two decades ago: this is an outstanding issue in every way.

Francesca da Rimini (fantasy), *Op. 32; Romeo and Juliet* (fantasy overture).
** RCA Camden ccv 5013 [c4]. Boston SO, Munch.

Munch's performances are hard-driven and exciting, with Dante's Inferno most convincingly evoked. *Francesca* is the more successful of the two works; *Romeo and Juliet*, although passionate, lacks the romantic nobility of a great performance. The recording is clear and vivid, a little lacking in inner warmth and – in the central section of *Francesca* – without much glow for the woodwind soloists.

(i) *Marche slave, Op. 31; Suite No. 4 (Mozartiana), Op. 61;* (ii) *Romeo and Juliet* (fantasy overture).
** Everest 3463. (i) Vienna SO, Perlea; (ii) NY Stadium Orch., Stokowski.

Stokowski's later recording of *Romeo and Juliet* for Decca had a truncated ending, so this earlier complete version is most welcome. It is a spaciously romantic reading; even the duel sequences are strong and bold rather than frenetic, and the great love theme is warmly and tenderly shaped, balanc-

ing rapture with nobility. Clearly Stokowski saw a link with the *Hamlet* fantasy overture, of which he made an inspirational recording with this same orchestra (see above). The present version of *Romeo and Juliet* does not match that in intensity but it has a comparable elegiac quality in the coda. The recording is full-blooded, though lacking the last degree of refinement. The other two performances are by the Vienna Symphony Orchestra under Jonel Perlea and the playing is altogether more homely. But a bargain-priced version of *Mozartiana* is welcome, and Perlea's account is stylishly conceived, making up in spontaneity for what it lacks in finesse and polish. The recording is acceptable although there is a curious low-pitched background noise.

The Nutcracker (ballet), *Op. 71:* complete.
⊛*** Decca DPA 569/70 [KDPC 2 7043]. Suisse Rom. Orch. (with chorus), Ansermet.

Ansermet's complete *Nutcracker* has been attractively reissued in a double sleeve, and there is also an excellent tape transfer on a single cassette. The performance is undoubtedly one of Ansermet's finest, and the Decca recording still sounds remarkably rich and vivid, with a freshness and sparkle to match the conductor's approach. Ansermet's feeling for orchestral colour and detail tells throughout, and the short dances of Act 2 have much piquancy of characterization. The whole of the opening scene of Act 1 has a bright-eyed quality that catches the listener's full attention and the *Transformation scene* and the *Waltz of the Snowflakes* have a frisson-making enchantment throughout. This is a real desert-island set.

The Nutcracker, Op. 71: excerpts.

** C.f.P. CFP 40272. Sinfonia of London, Hollingsworth.
** RCA Camden CCV 5022 [c4]. Boston Pops Orch., Fiedler.

These two selections are broadly similar, though Hollingsworth includes rather more of the party scene in Act 1. Both records include the *Transformation scene* but Fiedler scores by also offering the delightful *Waltz of the Snowflakes*. The London recording (originally issued by World Record Club) has rather more bloom and atmosphere than Fiedler's Boston record but less range and brilliance. Similarly while the London woodwind solo playing has greater individuality, Fiedler's overall direction has more vitality and sparkle (although Hollingsworth finds more lilt in the *Waltz of the Flowers*). The Camden cassette transfer is vivid if not too clean at the top. But it is made at high level and with a fairly strong cut-back of treble the sound can be smoothed yet retain its life.

Nutcracker suite, Op. 71a; Romeo and Juliet (fantasy overture).
** RCA Victrola (III) AT 119. NBC SO, Toscanini.

Toscanini's *Nutcracker suite* is surprisingly well recorded; indeed no one could complain about this on sonic grounds. Moreover the performance has splendid life and detail, and the *Waltz of the Flowers* is played with an attractive expressive lilt. It has a curious ending, however, with four extra bars which are not in the score of the suite. *Romeo and Juliet* is less successful as a recording, with a tendency to shrillness, but the adrenalin of the performance is undeniable. A good disc to show the maestro's versatility.

Nutcracker suite, Op. 71a; Swan Lake, Op. 20: suite.

*(*) C.f.P. CFP 40002. Philharmonia Orch., Sawallisch.

This recording dates from the very earliest days of stereo. The playing is brilliant if somewhat literal in the *Nutcracker suite*, which lacks charm. But *Swan Lake* comes off very well; the violin and cello duet in the *Dance of the Queen of the Swans* is beautifully done. The sound too is more expansive here, although the brightly lit treble persists. In the *Scene* from Act 4 (No. 28), where Tchaikovsky gives his big, romantic tune to the four horns in unison, they tend to be too far back, but otherwise the natural balance is effective. The disc is worth its cost for there is no doubt of the excellence of the Philharmonia at the time of this recording.

Romeo and Juliet (fantasy overture).
** DG Heliodor 2548 226. Dresden State Orch., Sanderling – BORODIN: *In the Steppes* etc.**
** C.f.P. CFP 40307. LPO, Pritchard – R. STRAUSS: *Don Juan* etc.**

In considering bargain recordings of *Romeo and Juliet* we must remember Stokowski's spaciously romantic version on Everest (see above) and Karajan's dramatic and exciting account, which is linked on a mid-priced Decca Jubilee disc and cassette (JB 71 [KJBC]) to a fine account of Dvořák's *Eighth Symphony*, an exceptionally generous coupling. Sanderling's performance too is distinguished; it has genuine romantic flair and is played with exciting spontaneity. The recording is not a new one, but it emerges with striking freshness. Pritchard's account has plenty of surface excitement, but emotionally it is rather reserved and it lacks panache. The C.f.P. recording is brilliant but somewhat dry, underlining Pritchard's conception.

129

Serenade for strings in C major, Op. 48.

** D G Heliodor 2548 121 [3348 121]. Dresden State Orch., Suitner – DVOŘÁK: *Serenade.* **

Serenade for strings; Suite No. 3 in G major, Op. 55: Theme and variations.

*(*) C.f.P. CFP 40300. LPO, Del Mar.

Suitner uses a full orchestral string complement (the composer asked for 'as many strings as possible'), and the playing of the Dresden State Orchestra has splendid bloom and warmth. It is a fine performance in every way, well shaped, spontaneous and played with vigour and feeling as well as polish. The recording is good on disc, less well focused on tape.

Norman Del Mar too uses the full LPO string section, which provides alert playing with plenty of intensity in the outer movements. The second subject of the first is cleanly articulated and nicely pointed. In the *Waltz* Del Mar indulges himself with a tenuto on the sustained notes before the main tune unfolds. The *Elegy* is eloquent and the finale spirited, yet there is a lack of charm and the music rarely smiles. The very brightly lit recording, with a balance favouring the violins, does not help. The performance of the masterly set of variations from the *Third Suite* is disappointingly matter-of-fact. The conductor is impeded by the clinical recording, which reveals Tchaikovsky's marvellous changes of orchestral colour in a very literal way, with little added bloom. The gloriously expansive Variation XI (a truly great Tchaikovskian moment) does not fill out as it should, although the brilliant closing *Polacca* is much more effective.

The Sleeping Beauty, Op. 66: suite;

Swan Lake, Op. 20: suite; Eugene Onegin: Polonaise.

*(*) D G Heliodor 2548 125 [3348 125]. Warsaw P O, Rowicki.

Rowicki is sometimes mannered and he chooses some curious tempi; the opening oboe theme of *Swan Lake*, for instance, is surprisingly slow. But this is mostly excellent playing with plenty of life in it, and the Polish woodwind soloists have strong individual personalities. The recording is bright, with a tendency for the brass to blare a little, but this is a reasonable coupling, in spite of dated string tone. The cassette transfer is fairly good.

Swan Lake (ballet), *Op. 20:* slightly abridged recording of the European score.

**(*) Decca DPA 603/4 [KDPC 2 7058]. Suisse Rom. Orch., Ansermet.

Returning to Ansermet's 1959 recording of *Swan Lake* one is amazed by the vigour of the playing and the excellence of the recording. The Drigo version of the score which Ansermet uses dates from 1895. Drigo added orchestrations of his own, taken from Tchaikovsky's piano music (Op. 72), yet left out some sixteen hundred bars of the original score. Ansermet offers the Act 1 Introduction and Nos. 1–2, 4, 7 and 8; Act 2, Nos. 10–13; Act 3, Nos. 15, 17–18 and 20–23, with No. 5 (the *Pas de deux*) then interpolated before Nos. 28 and 29 from Act 4. In spite of the obvious gaps, most of the familiar favourites are included here, and the music-making has such zest and colour that one cannot but revel in every bar. The solo wind-playing is not always as sweet-timbred as in some other versions, but the violin and cello solos are well done, and there is not a dull moment throughout. The cassette transfer is very well managed too, full-blooded and bright, although a little smoothing of the treble improves the timbre of the upper strings. Excellent value.

Swan Lake, Op. 20: highlights.
⊛*** C.f.P. CFP 40296 [TC-CFP].
Menuhin, Philharmonia Orch., Kurtz.

A superb disc – the finest single L P selection from *Swan Lake* in the present catalogue. The Philharmonia are on top form and the woodwind acquit themselves with even more style than usual in Tchaikovsky's solos. The recording (originally HMV) matches the exuberance which Kurtz brings to the music's climaxes with the widest possible dynamic range and a sound balance that underpins surface brilliance with depth and atmosphere. The elegant Philharmonia string playing is beautifully caught. Menuhin finds a surprising amount to play here; besides the famous duet with the cello in the *Danse des cygnes*, which is beautifully done, he includes a ravishing account of the *Danse russe* as a postlude to the main selection. To add a final touch of excellence there is an admirable sleeve-note by Pigeon Crowle, relating each piece to the action it accompanies in the ballet. The cassette transfer (perhaps prudently) has a slightly more limited dynamic range, but otherwise sounds well; when it is heard away from the disc there is no really striking reduction of contrast, but the disc is demonstration-worthy.

Symphonies Nos. (i) *4 in F minor, Op. 36;* (ii) *5 in E minor, Op. 64; 6 in B minor (Pathétique), Op. 74.*
⊛*** DG Heliodor (m) 2700 114 (2 discs). Leningrad PO, (i) Sanderling, (ii) Mravinsky.

These famous performances are not to be confused with the 1961 recordings that Mravinsky made with the same orchestra. The present issues date from 1956, and for many in the West they were an introduction to the Russian Tchaikovsky tradition. The performances electrified listeners with their extraordinary discipline, their magnificently controlled passion and warmth, their vast dynamic range – rarely had one heard such pianissimo string tone – and they made audiences aware that there were facets of this repertoire that Western performers had hitherto failed to illumine. The sheer excitement of their virtuosity, their variety of colour and refinement of dynamic and expressive nuance, was in itself exhilarating; and above all there was an authenticity of feeling that seemed peculiarly Russian. Fine though the stereo remakes were, these mono records retain special qualities, and the sound, which remains untranscribed for stereo, is astonishingly vivid. Put this set against many modern recordings and it survives the test with flying colours. So, too, do the performances: the march in the *Pathétique* is wonderfully exciting; the lyricism that infuses the second group of its first movement is so fresh that it rekindles memories of one's very first encounter with this music, and much the same can be said for the slow movement of the *Fifth*, in spite of the wide vibrato of the Leningrad horn. No phrase in these performances remains untouched by imagination, and no Tchaikovsky collection should neglect them.

Symphony No. 4 in F minor, Op. 36.
*(*) RCA Camden CCV 5036 [c4]. Boston SO, Munch.

In the last analysis this is not really memorable, but (apart from Sanderling's performance within the Heliodor two-disc set above) it currently holds the bargain field alone. With Munch the

131

first-movement *Allegro* begins slowly, but the music moves to a quite impressive climax. There is some fine orchestral playing too in the central movements, and the finale is brilliant enough for anyone. But the recording needs to be richer, and the reader wanting a good modern stereo version would be advised to turn to Szell and the LSO (Decca SPA 206 [KCSP]) or Maazel (Decca Jubilee JB 23 [KJBC]), where fine performances are in each case matched by first-class recording.

Symphony No. 5 in E minor, Op. 64.
  **(*) RCA Camden CCV 5049 [c4]. Boston SO, Monteux.
  * C.f.P. CFP 40317 [TC-CFP]. LPO, Del Mar.

Monteux's recording, which dates from 1959, is vivid, but it lacks something in richness, and the Boston acoustic is without a really expansive bass. However, comparisons using a fairly current pressing, tried on various equipment, have given surprisingly good results. Monteux's reading is straightforward and exciting, among the best available. There are a few eccentricities of tempo – he is rather mannered in the finale – but (unlike Del Mar) he convinces the listener in what he does and there is no doubt that this is fresh, spontaneous and exciting.

Del Mar's C.f.P. version is exciting too and is given a brilliant modern recording (the cassette is marginally less wide in range than the disc but still impressive). There is some splendid wind playing, and the horn solo in the slow movement (played by Nicholas Busch) is beautifully done. But the reading itself is exasperatingly wilful. In all the movements but the *Waltz* (which is graciously straightforward) there are eccentric tempo changes. At bar 108 of the first movement there is an inexplic-

able pulling back; later the preparation of the second subject is spoiled and the exaggerated rubato in the presentation of the theme itself is equally difficult to take. Throughout there are unmarked accelerandos and decelerandos, and pauses too, all of which fail to convince. In the finale Del Mar does not establish his basic tempo at the beginning of the *Allegro vivace* but suddenly quickens as the secondary material arrives. Not recommended.

Symphony No. 6 in B minor (Pathétique), Op. 74.
  *** C.f.P. CFP 40220 [TC-CFP]. Philharmonia Orch., Kletzki.
  ** RCA (m) AT 104. NBC SO, Toscanini.
  *(*) RCA Camden CCV 5024 [c4]. Chicago SO, Reiner.

Kletzki's splendid performance sounds quite different on disc and tape, and for many the cassette will be preferable. It has no lack of range and brilliance, but the strings are richer and warmer, and this gives the first-movement climax more amplitude. On LP the violins are much more brightly lit, and the bass is drier, less resonant; the brass have greater bite and the sound is slightly more open. Whichever medium is chosen this is an outstanding performance which has stood the test of time. The first movement is impetuous but convincing, and Kletzki's broadening of tempo at the reprise of the scherzo march is effective because the orchestral playing has a supporting power and breadth. The deeply felt closing movement makes a powerful impact, although again the cassette produces the fullest string sound.

Toscanini is not a conductor whose name immediately springs to mind in the music of Tchaikovsky (in spite of the famous recording of the *B flat minor Piano concerto* with Horowitz). Yet his version of the *Pathétique* is not without distinction. The first movement suffers from the characteristically dry brilliance of the recorded sound, but it is undoubtedly exciting. The 5/4 movement has its share of elegance, and the third is very much a sparkling scherzo, marvellously alive and pointed. The finale shows a brooding sombre quality in its closing pages which readily projects to the listener in spite of the lack of expansive qualities in the recording.

Reiner is given altogether more full-blooded sound in his early RCA version, but the performance as a whole does not completely convince. It lacks subtlety and yet seldom offers all-out excitement.

Tippett, Michael (born 1905)

Concerto for double string orchestra.
*** C.f.P. CFP 40068. LPO, Handley – VAUGHAN WILLIAMS: *Fantasia on a theme of Tallis.* ***

Tippett's eloquent concerto is well served by this C.f.P. disc, which is well recorded and couples two of the warmest and most memorable string works of the twentieth century in strong, committed performances. No one could here miss the passion behind both the sharp rhythmic inspirations of the outer movement and the glorious lyricism of the central slow movement.

(i) *A Child of our Time* (oratorio); (ii) *The Midsummer Marriage* (opera): *Ritual dances.*
**(*) Argo DPA 571/2. Pritchard, cond. (i) Morison, Bowden, Lewis, Standen, Chorus,

Royal Liverpool PO; (ii) ROHCGO.

In this three-sided format the Pritchard version of *A Child of our Time* competes closely with the full-priced single-disc Philips version from Colin Davis (6500 985), but that does not provide the *Ritual dances* from *A Midsummer Marriage*, which here are a colourful makeweight. Despite the dated (but still fresh) sound there is a clear case for preferring Pritchard to Davis. The ensemble may not be so crisp, but Pritchard's approach is more feeling and sympathetic, and this after all is music which speaks of deep emotion. Elsie Morison (most affecting in *Steal away*) and Richard Lewis both sing beautifully.

Turina, Joaquín (1882–1949)

Danzas fantásticas, Op. 22.
(*) Decca DPA 629/30 [KDPC]. Suisse Rom. Orch., Ansermet – Concert of Spanish music.(*)
** DG Heliodor 2548 284 [3348 284]. Monte Carlo Opera Orch., Frémaux – BRITTEN: *Young Person's Guide**; MILHAUD: *Le Carnaval d'Aix.***(*)

Ansermet constantly draws vivid sounds from his orchestra in these colourful Spanish genre pieces, and there is no want of atmosphere. This is part of an attractive if lightweight concert discussed under 'Spanish music' in our Concerts section below. The Decca recording is brilliant and sophisticated in matters of detail. The Heliodor recording has rather less substance but is still good. Frémaux gives sympathetic performances, though the evocation is as much French as Spanish. However, this is distinctly enjoyable (the opening *Exaltación* comes off especially well) and the Milhaud coupling is well worth having. The tape transfer is smoothly done and matches the disc quite closely.

Vaughan Williams, Ralph (1872–1958)

English folksongs suite (arr. Jacob); *Fantasia on Greensleeves; Fantasia on a theme of Thomas Tallis; Old King Cole* (ballet for orchestra); *The Wasps: Overture.*
  ** Pye GSGC 15019. LPO, Boult.

In 1976 Pye, delving into a twenty-year-old store, came up with two valuable Boult recordings that had never appeared before, a vigorous performance of *The Wasps Overture* and the delightful *Old King Cole* suite taken from a ballet of 1923, the only version in stereo. That with the other proved favourites makes this attractive bargain. The sound, obviously not modern, has been well cleaned up.

Fantasia on a theme of Thomas Tallis.
  *** C.f.P. CFP 40068. LPO, Handley – TIPPETT: *Concerto.***
  *** Lyrita REAM 1. LPO, Boult – ELGAR: *Symphony No. 1.***

Vernon Handley proves a passionately persuasive interpreter of this outstanding masterpiece of English music, aptly coupled with another fine string work. The excellent playing is matched by good, modern recording. Boult's Lyrita record is priced at about a pound higher

but it is generously full and the *Tallis fantasia* is merely a bonus for Sir Adrian's fine reading of Elgar's *First Symphony*. As in the symphony Boult takes a relatively cool and slightly detached view of a masterpiece equally close to his heart, and as in the symphony the degree of understatement is most affecting. First-rate recording of Lyrita's usual high standard.

Job (masque for dancing).
  ** Everest 3019. LPO, Boult.

Vaughan Williams's *Job* was completed in 1930. Dr Geoffrey Keynes, who drew up the scenario from Blake engravings, originally intended it to be used as a ballet for Diaghilev, but the great impresario rejected it as 'too English and too old-fashioned'. He may have been right – from his own point of view – but the score is undeniably one of Vaughan Williams's very greatest compositions. It shows his inspiration at its most deeply characteristic and at its most noble, and the challenge of the music depicting Satan provides a startling contrast to the composer's more usual lyrical style. The performance here under the work's dedicatee is powerful, sensitive and spontaneous. The recording is extremely vivid, but the artificial balance with forward wind and brass is less than ideal. There is an element of stridency and the massed strings lack amplitude. Nevertheless this can be softened with the controls and the impact of the performance is undeniable. Boult has re-recorded the work at full price with the LSO for HMV (ASD 2673) and that recording has exceptional range and truthfulness; but for anyone coming new to the work on a limited budget the Everest issue should readily convey its greatness.

A London symphony (No. 2).

**(*) Pye GSGC 15035. Hallé Orch., Barbirolli.
**(*) C.f.P. CFP 40286 [TC-CFP]. LPO, Handley.

The *London symphony* was the composer's favourite and one can see why. Barbirolli's inspirational recording dates from 1959 but still sounds astonishingly well. Current Pye pressings have good surfaces, and although the sound lacks upper range, and detail tends to be masked at pianissimo levels, the orchestral quality is natural and the strings are full and pleasing. The greatness of the performance emerges at the very opening, which is superbly atmospheric. The intensity in the playing is sublime, both here and in the slow movement with its pensive trumpet and lovely cor anglais and viola solos. The melancholy little march which opens the fourth movement has an affecting elegiac feeling and moves to a superbly expansive climax, while the closing pages of the *Epilogue* have a degree of tension rare in the recording studio.

Vernon Handley's performance on C.f.P. is given a splendid modern recording of striking range. The subtlety of detail, especially at lower dynamic levels, means that many of the composer's orchestral effects are more telling here than on Barbirolli's disc, and the brilliant scherzo gains immeasurably from the sense of spectacle and wide dynamic contrasts. The performance is straightforward and undoubtedly effective. Tempi are well chosen; the slow movement has genuine poetry and its climax, like that of the finale (before the *Epilogue*), has eloquence. The orchestral playing is sensitive throughout (notably in the closing pages of the *Lento*). The cassette has a slightly restricted upper range, compared with the disc (the muted strings in the slow movement are not absolutely clean), but still sounds fully acceptable.

Symphony No. 6 in E minor; Prelude and fugue in C minor.
**(*) C.f.P. CFP 40334. LPO, Handley.

Vaughan Williams's *Sixth Symphony*, written between 1944 and 1947, retains the power to shock the listener with the intensity of its triplet warning figures in the slow movement, and the bleak apocalyptic atmosphere of the finale. Yet it also offers, in the second subject of the ebullient first movement, one of the most heart-warming tunes the composer ever wrote (once famous as a TV signature tune). Handley tends slightly to underplay these strong emotional contrasts; the second movement is chill with stillness, the violence understated, and the opening of the brashly popular scherzo, though well sprung, is not as biting as it might be. Taken as a whole, however, this is a refreshing, clean-cut reading. As the composer's scoring is often so heavy with brass, it is remarkable that Handley is able to clarify textures without making them merely lightweight and without losing intensity. A beautiful performance helped by full yet refined recording, well coupled with an orchestral arrangement of an organ piece (made by the composer for the Three Choirs Festival at Hereford in 1930), never before recorded.

Verdi, Giuseppe (1813–1901)

The Lady and the Fool (ballet, arr. Mackerras): suite.
(*) C.f.P. CFP 40293. LPO, Mackerras – SULLIVAN: *Pineapple Poll.*(*)

Mackerras's score for John Cranko's ballet *The Lady and the Fool* (1954) uses

135

music from the lesser-known Verdi operas in much the same way as he drew upon Sullivan for *Pineapple Poll*. Here too the scoring is as colourful as it is witty, although the selection does not seem quite so inspired as the earlier work. It is very entertaining, but some ears may find there is rather a lot of boisterous music. It is all played with great flair and evident orchestral enjoyment here. The recording too is both vivid and atmospheric, with more bloom and warmth than in the coupling. The suite gives a very generous selection from the complete ballet.

Requiem Mass.
**(*) RCA Victrola (m) AT 201 (2 discs). Nelli, Barbieri, Di Stefano, Siepi, Robert Shaw Chorale, NBC SO, Toscanini.
⊛*** DG Heliodor (m) 2700 113 (2 discs). Stader, Radev, Krebs, Borg, Berlin RIAS Chamber Choir, St Hedwig's Cathedral Choir, Berlin RIAS SO, Fricsay.

The RCA discs (recorded in Carnegie Hall) give far more sense of presence than most of Toscanini's late recordings. One can vividly share in the experience of hearing a searingly intense account of Verdi's choral masterpiece, and at the opening of the *Dies Irae*, with its cataclysmic strokes on the bass drum, the sound has more body than usual with NBC recordings. The chorus is relatively small but superbly disciplined, and the quartet of soloists would be excellent but for the inclusion of the soprano who is a blot on too many Toscanini sets, the negative Herva Nelli. The conductor drills his soloists too rigidly at times, but otherwise this is an incandescent performance to make one forget any flaws.
    Though lacking some of the fire and flair of the unique Toscanini performance, Fricsay's is deeply satisfying in its

clarity and directness, helped by superb choral singing and a very well-matched team of soloists. Maria Stader sings most sweetly, lacking weight only in the dramatic moments of the *Libera me*. Kim Borg has superbly dark tone, and though the mono recording does not allow the singers a true pianissimo, it is surprising how DG's fifties sound still keeps its freshness. In its time it was of demonstration quality, and even now it admirably matches the fresh and dramatic reading of Fricsay, one which is unusually faithful to Verdi's markings. This is in every way satisfying – a real three-star performance – and for many ears it will be preferable to the Toscanini version because of the excellent sound.

Quattro pezzi sacri: Te Deum.
*** RCA Victrola (m) AT 131. Robert Shaw Chorale, NBC SO, Toscanini – BOITO: *Mefistofele: Prologue.****

Verdi's *Te Deum* is the last of the *Quattro pezzi sacri*, written after *Falstaff* in 1895–7. There is only one medium-price alternative (with Leipzig Radio forces under Herbert Kegel) but even if there were many, Toscanini's incandescent performance from 1954 would have special claims on the collector, since it was he who conducted the first performance of the work in 1898! Given its provenance the sound is remarkably good, and the performance is unlikely to be surpassed in terms of authority and intensity.

OPERA

Aïda: complete.
*(*) RCA Victrola (m) AT 302 (3 discs). Nelli, Tucker, Stich-Randall, Valdengo, Robert Shaw Chorale, NBC SO, Toscanini.

Toscanini directs a splendidly precise account of *Aïda*, but there is surprisingly little rhythmic swagger in the great processional scenes of the first two acts, and though the phrasing has much in it that shows the conductor's affection for the music, there is an unwanted tautness too. As for the solo singing, there is much that is disappointing, not least that of the heroine, for Herva Nelli is a negative Aïda, and even Giuseppe Valdengo was below form as Amonasro. Richard Tucker is the shining exception, a ringing Radames; but in general this falls well short of the finest Toscanini recordings of Verdi, and the sound is very boxy.

Un Ballo in maschera: complete.
*(*) RCA Victrola (m) AT 300 (3 discs). Nelli, Peerce, Merrill, Turner, Robert Shaw Chorale, NBC SO, Toscanini.

This was the last operatic performance Toscanini conducted and one of his last ever recordings, made in 1954. It does not have the sparkle of the performance of *Falstaff* which came four years earlier, and much of the solo singing is dull, notably that of the women. But with Toscanini's ability to present a compelling story with unrelenting intensity and with fine contributions from Peerce and Merrill, this is well worth investigating. The recording has the usual NBC faults, but can be made to sound acceptable enough.

Falstaff: complete.
*** RCA Victrola (m) AT 301 (3 discs). Valdengo, Guarrera, Elmo, Nelli, Merriman, Madasi, Stich-Randall, Robert Shaw Chorale, NBC SO, Toscanini.

This was the finest opera set that Toscanini ever recorded, a live perform-ance given in Studio 8 H Radio City in April 1950 and subsequently 'patched' at studio sessions to eliminate one or two flaws. Giuseppe Valdengo is not a characterful Falstaff, but he sings with fine precision and rhythmic gusto, which goes along with Toscanini's own irresist-ible energy. The whole score fizzes and sparkles, and at the end of the final fugue in Act 4 one can readily under-stand the ecstatic eruption of the studio audience. Frank Guarrera is a superb Ford and Cloe Elmo is a vividly char-acterful Mistress Quickly, while Herva Nelli, Nan Merriman and Teresa Stich-Randall make a stronger team of women than Toscanini had in his other opera sets of the period. The recording too is among the best from this source.

Rigoletto: complete.
**(*) Everest s 470/3. Scotto, Bastianini, Kraus, Cossotto, Vinco, Chorus and Orch. of Maggio Musicale Fiorentino, Gavazzeni.

Though at the start the tremulous trumpets sound a little like cornets, the stereo is generally bright and clean to match a vigorous performance. This is a strong team of soloists, with Scotto fresh and girlish, Kraus clean and ringing (as he was in the Solti set of a year or so later) and Bastianini gloriously res-onant. What they all lack – and the recording is in part to blame – is an ability to sing quietly, and at times Scotto is made to sound shrill. But with Gavazzeni directing a beautifully paced and infectiously sprung performance, this is a compelling set, well worth inves-tigating. Ensembles are exceptionally crisp, and no one could fail to appreciate the drama of the piece.

La Traviata: complete.
** RCA Victrola (m) AT 202 (2 discs). Albanese, Peerce,

Merrill, Chorus and NBC SO, Toscanini.

Meeting Toscanini for the first time, Walter Legge was asked by the maestro what he thought of his then recent recording of *Traviata*. Characteristically Legge did not try to disguise his dislike of the fast tempi. The old man respected that, even half-agreeing, and the result of the meeting was ultimately a classic occasion in London when Toscanini conducted Legge's Philharmonia Orchestra. The famous performance, even in improved transfers, remains too taut and unyielding, with variable solo singing from a tremulous Albanese and a lusty Peerce. The Germont *père* of the young Robert Merrill is vocally the finest element in the set, but the playing of the orchestra is consistently electrifying, and the famous preludes, beautifully phrased, have superb intensity to make one accept Toscanini's tempi for the moment.

There is no available bargain-priced version of *Il Trovatore*, but Zubin Mehta's superb RCA set (awarded a rosette in the *Penguin Stereo Record Guide*), with Price, Domingo, Milnes, and an electrifying Azucena from Cossotto, is offered at considerably less than full price: SER 5586/8.

'*Favourite composer*': arias, duets and choruses: *Aïda:* (i) *Se quel guerrier . . . Celeste Aïda; Su! del Nilo . . .;* (ii) *Ritorna vincitor;* (iii) *Triumphal march and ballet music;* (i; iv) *Già i sacerdoti . . . Ah! tu dei. Un Ballo in maschera:* (v) *Morrò, ma prima in grazia. Don Carlo:* (vi) *O don fatale. Falstaff:* (vii) *Ehi! Paggio! La Forza del destino:* (viii) *Overture; Morir! tremenda cosa! . . . Urna fatale. Luisa Miller:* (ii) *Oh! fede negar potessi . . . Quando le sere. Macbeth:* (ix)

Apparition scene. *Nabucco:* (x) *Va, pensiero (Chorus of Hebrew slaves). Otello:* (v) *Willow song; Ave Maria. Rigoletto:* (xi) *Gualtier Maldè . . . Caro nome;* (xii) *La donna è mobile. La Traviata: Prelude to Act 1;* (xi; i) *Brindisi; Un dì felice. Il Trovatore:* (xiii) *Vedi, le fosche (Anvil chorus);* (xiv) *Di quella pira;* (xiv; ii) *Miserere.*

*** Decca DPA 555/6 [KDPC]. (i) Bergonzi; (ii) Tebaldi; (iii) Vienna Singverein, Vienna PO, Karajan; (iv) Simionato; (v) Crespin; (vi) Bumbry; (vii) Evans; (viii) Warren, Santa Cecilia Orch., Previtali; (ix) Fischer-Dieskau, Ambrosian Chorus, LPO, Gardelli; (x) Chorus and Orch. of Santa Cecilia Academy, Rome, Franci; (xi) Sutherland; (xii) Pavarotti; (xiii) Chorus and Orch. of Maggio Musicale Fiorentino, Erede; (xiv) Mario del Monaco.

An outstanding set in every way and cleverly selected. The first record opens with an impressively vibrant account of the *Chorus of Hebrew slaves*, and there are many memorable items, from the electrifying *Macbeth* excerpt to Sutherland's beautiful *Caro nome*, and on the second disc Crespin's *Willow song* and *Ave Maria* from *Otello*, Geraint Evans's scene from *Falstaff* and of course the excerpts from the spectacular Karajan *Aïda*. As should always happen with an anthology of this kind, each item balances with what has gone before and what is to follow. The recording (except perhaps in the *Forza* overture) is of uniformly good quality, and the cassette transfers are admirably vivid.

'*Gala night at La Scala*': *Un Ballo*

in maschera: (i) *Teco io sto. Don Carlo.* (ii) *Ella giammai m'amò;* (iii) *Nel giardin del bello saracin ostello. Rigoletto:* (iv; v) Act 3: finale. *La Traviata:* (vi) *Ah, fors'è lui. Il Trovatore: Gipsy chorus; Soldiers' chorus;* (vi) *Tutto è deserto; Il balen.*
*(*) D G Heliodor 2548 280 [3348 280]. Chorus and Orch. of La Scala, Milan, various conductors, with (i) Stella, Poggi; (ii) Christoff; (iii) Cossotto; (iv) Scotto; (v) Bergonzi, Fischer-Dieskau, Vinco; (vi) Bastinini, Vinco.

The title *Gala night at La Scala* suggests something of an occasion, but a good deal of the content of this LP is rather routine in presentation. The choruses, for instance, somewhat dryly recorded, are not especially exciting. The most distinguished items here are from *Don Carlo,* though Amelia and Richard's duet from *Un Ballo in maschera* is attractively spirited. The disc closes with the finale to *Rigoletto,* and that is movingly done. The tape transfer is generally successful, vivid with just an occasional peak (on a female-voiced climax).

Villa-Lobos, Heitor
(1887–1959)

Bachianas Brasileiras No. 1: excerpt: *Modinha, Uirapurú.*
** Everest 3016, NY Stadium Orch., Stokowski – PROKO-FIEV: *Cinderella.***

Uirapurú, which takes up the greater part of this side, was the first important orchestral work that Villa-Lobos wrote.

The ambitious young composer was determined to rival even the heaviest competition in sheer brilliance of orchestration, using in this programme piece, based on a Brazilian folktale, an amazing range of percussion instruments. It is just the sort of music to inspire the old magician Stokowski, and he responds with a fine performance, beautifully recorded. *Modinha* is well done too, if with Stokowski's habitual layer of emotion. The Prokofiev coupling is not very apt, but attractive enough.

Bachianas Brasileiras No. 2: The Little Train of the Caipira.
** Everest 3041. LSO, Goossens – GINASTERA: *Estancia* etc.**

The Little Train was the result of a journey Villa-Lobos made in Sao Paolo, Brazil, in 1931. The orchestration is imitative, but as in Lumbye's *Copenhagen Steam Railway galop* the descriptive writing has considerable charm. The local colour is provided by the use of Latin percussive effects. Excellent performance and recording, although there is perhaps a shade too much resonance. Readers will appreciate, however, that the short Villa-Lobos piece occupies only a few minutes of a record which is otherwise taken up by two ballet suites by the Argentinian composer Alberto Ginastera.

Vivaldi, Antonio
(1675–1741)

The Four Seasons, Op. 8/1–4 (from *Trial between Harmony and Invention*).
**(*) D G Heliodor 2548 005 [3348 005]. Frasca-Colombier, Kuentz CO, Kuentz.

VIVALDI

**(*) C.f.P. CFP 40016 [TC-CFP].
Sillito, Virt. of England, Davison.

In considering recordings of *The Four Seasons* one must remember that Decca's excellent two-disc '*Favourite composer*' issue (below) includes the Kulka/Münchinger set, which is one of the finest in the catalogue at any price. But for those wanting a single disc the Heliodor is excellent value for money. The soloist, Monique Frasca-Colombier, plays nimbly and is thoroughly musical. The timbre of the solo violin (small-toned but not thin) is bright, and so are the orchestral strings, while the acoustic is warm but not too resonant for the continuo to come through. The playing throughout has plenty of character, and the programmatic detail is well registered. Like the disc, the cassette offers excellent quality, transparent yet with no lack of body.

The version by Arthur Davison and the Virtuosi of England has obviously more modern recording, and is marked by assured and lively solo playing from Kenneth Sillito; but the soloist is balanced rather too far forward and this detracts from gentler expressiveness. Otherwise the sound is strikingly vivid and clear, and the tape transfer matches the disc closely, smooth and firm, with plenty of body, life and detail.

'*Favourite composer*': (i) *The Four Seasons, Op. 8/1–4;* (ii) *L'Estro armonico: Concerto in B minor, Op. 3/10;* (iii) *Flute concerto in G minor (La Notte), Op. 10/2;* (iv; v) *Bassoon concerto in A minor, P.70/RV.498;* (vi) *Concerto for strings in G major (Alla rustica), P.143/RV.151;* (vii; v) *Double trumpet concerto in C major, P.75/RV.537;* (viii) *Gloria in D major.*

*** Decca DPA 609/10 [KDPC].
(i) Stuttgart CO, Münchinger; (ii) Moscow CO, Barshai; (iii) Preston, Academy of Ancient Music, Hogwood; (iv) Gatt; (v) ASMF, Marriner; (vi) Lucerne Fest. Strings, Baumgartner; (vii) Wilbraham, Jones; (viii) Vaughan, Baker, King's College Choir, ASMF, Willcocks.

An outstandingly generous set, which can be cordially recommended on all counts. The *Four Seasons* is Münchinger's latest recording (1974), with a superb soloist, Konstanty Kulka. He is sparkling and expressive in exactly the right way, and his feeling for Vivaldi's line in the *cantilena* melodies is very appealing, the lyrical sensuousness nicely judged. Münchinger has never been more imaginative in the recording studio, and the pictorial detail is splendidly characterized. Yet another major contribution is made by the continuo soloist, Igor Kipnis. He is beautifully balanced, and his stylish playing often adds an extra dimension to the performance: in the opening of *Winter*, for instance, where Münchinger keeps the orchestra at *mezzo-forte* or *piano* to let the keyboard figurations come through, or in the beautiful slow movement of *Autumn*. The recording is superb, with bright, shining upper strings, the bass tellingly resonant without being too sumptuous; and the tape matches the disc closely.

The other performances in this collection are all first-rate, with the bassoon and flute concertos as highlights. The inclusion of the *Gloria* is especially welcome. It uses comparatively small forces and save for the occasional trace of preciosity is very stylish indeed. It has excellent soloists and is very well recorded, both on disc and on tape. Indeed the whole set offers splendidly vivid sound in both media, although on tape there is a slight slipping of refinement in the transfer of the *Concerto for two trumpets.*

Oboe concertos in A minor, P.42; in D minor, P.43.
** C.f.P. CFP 163. Sutcliffe, Virt. of England, Davison – ALBINONI: *Oboe concertos.***

The second half of an attractive coupling with Albinoni, these performances are admirably alive and sensitive to matters of style. Sidney Sutcliffe is an excellent soloist, but Davison's overall direction is characteristically straight. A little more unbending, especially in the slow movements, would have made these performances even more beguiling. However, the sound is crisp and clean and this certainly gives pleasure.

Wagner, Richard (1813–83)

Siegfried idyll. Der fliegende Holländer (The Flying Dutchman): overture. *Die Meistersinger (The Mastersingers): Prelude to Act 3; Dance of the apprentices; Entry of the masters. Rienzi: overture.*
**(*) C.f.P. CFP 40287 [TC-CFP]. LPO, Downes.

Edward Downes was the first British conductor in the post-war period to conduct a *Ring* cycle at Covent Garden. As a Wagnerian he may lack a little in tension and excitement, but here as in the opera house he conducts fresh and direct performances; the selection is generous and well chosen, and it is all warmly and atmospherically recorded in modern stereo. The *Siegfried idyll* is especially successful, and there is some

fine brass playing in the *Prelude to Act 3* of *Die Meistersinger.* In some ways the melodramatic *Rienzi* gains from Downes's slight degree of reticence, yet the opening string tune sounds gloriously ripe. The tape transfer is of outstanding quality, matching the disc closely. It has marginally less upper range, but if anything this is an advantage, smoothing the upper string timbre without robbing the sound of life.

(i) *Lohengrin: Preludes to Acts 1 and 3.* (ii) *Parsifal: Prelude and Good Friday music.* (i) *Tannhäuser: overture.*
*(*) D G Heliodor 2548 221 [3348 221]. Lamoureux Orch., Markevitch; (ii) Bavarian RO, Jochum.

Markevitch's Lamoureux performances are very much Wagner with a French accent, and the recording lacks the full amplitude one needs in this music, notably in *Tannhäuser*, which sounds rather meagre. Jochum's account of the *Parsifal* excerpts is justly famous, and is very much better recorded. Unfortunately the tape transfer loses some of the amplitude of the disc and the brass tends to sound brash. Also at the opening of the *Lohengrin Prelude to Act 1* there is some slight discoloration of the upper partials, while the *Third act Prelude* lacks body and substance.

Lohengrin: Prelude to Act 3. Die Meistersinger: Prelude to Act 1. Tannhäuser: Grand march. Die Walküre: Ride of the Valkyries.
*(*) HMV 45 r.p.m. HMV 10. N Philharmonia Orch. or LPO, Boult.

There is no lack of excitement in the *Lohengrin Prelude* or the *Ride of the Valkyries*; the *Grand march* is mellow, and the *Meistersinger overture* comes off well too, although none of these is a really distinctive performance. The recording balance, however, artificially emphasizes the treble (there is very little bass in the *Ride of the Valkyries*); the cymbals in the *Lohengrin Prelude* are almost explosively brilliant, and the upper strings in the *Overture* are crudely and unnaturally over-lit.

Der Ring des Nibelungen (Das Rheingold; Die Walküre; Siegfried; Götterdämmerung): complete.

*(**) Murray Hill (m) 940477 (11 discs). Flagstad, Hongen, Treptow, Svanholm, Lorenz, Frantz, Pernestorfer, Sattier, Konetzni, Weber, Markwort, Chorus and Orch. of La Scala, Milan (1950), Furtwängler.

(**) HMV (m) RLS 702 (18 discs). Mödl, Frantz, Malaniuk, Windgassen, Patzak, Neidlinger, Suthaus, Chorus and Rome SO, Furtwängler.

No recording of Furtwängler, and certainly not the *Ring* cycle as salvaged by EMI from Rome Radio performances of 1953, can match this 1950 La Scala performance (with Kirsten Flagstad as Brünnhilde) in showing you exactly how exciting this great conductor could be in the opera house. At the climactic moments, notably the close of the Immolation Scene in *Götterdämmerung*, where Furtwängler's electricity takes hold with wildly urgent speeds, there is a feeling of supreme achievement that one only associates with great Wagner performances experienced live. The sound of these records may be dim, but the sense of witnessing a great occasion is inescapable from first to last, and no Wagnerian will regret investigating so historic a performance, even if at times a blanket seems to be dropped in front of it. What matters is the atmosphere,

which makes it easy to listen through the blanket, and Furtwängler will astonish many in the consistent urgency of his reading. And as well as the conductor's volatile genius, the singing of Flagstad as Brünnhilde, massively rich-toned, with astonishing freedom on top, is equally heartwarming. Surely no other soprano has ever sung this music with such a combination of richness and precision, and the achievement is all the more remarkable because the top Cs and upper acrobatics were taken live with no possibility of retake under fresher conditions. Others outstanding in a first-rate cast include Gunther Treptow as Siegmund, Ferdinand Frantz as the Wotan of the first two operas, and Max Lorenz as the *Götterdämmerung* Siegfried. Sides are up to 43 minutes, but the pressings are easy to reproduce, and once the limitations are accepted the sound is more congenial to live with than the harsher, clearer recording of Furtwängler's 1953 *Ring* from Rome, which incidentally costs more than twice as much.

It was, of course, a considerable technical achievement getting this mono recording made for Italian Radio into LP form. The pity is that here the magic of Furtwängler, of which there is ample evidence, is deadened by the matchbox acoustic, so dry that none of the voices is flattered and many are made to sound ugly. Even Windgassen's tenor (in the role of Siegmund) lacks sweetness, and, except in the final Immolation Scene of *Götterdämmerung* (where everyone rises to the challenge), Martha Mödl is unappealing as Brünnhilde. Ferdinand Frantz is a clean-toned Wotan (and Wanderer), but another drawback of the set is the often rough playing of the Rome Symphony Orchestra. The eighteen discs are handsomely packaged. However, for only about ten pounds more one can purchase the complete stereo *Ring* recorded by Karajan for DG (2720 051), with its warm Wagner sound, more mellow and less thrustful than Solti's famous Decca set (D 100 D 19), made under the inspired direction of the late John Culshaw, which currently has a list price of just under sixty pounds.

Arias and duets from *The Ring: Siegfried*: Love duet; *Die Walküre*: Brünnhilde's call; *Die Walküre: Death annunciation Scene; Götterdämmerung*: Immolation Scene. *(**) Everest 3414. Kirsten Flagstad and cast as above, La Scala 1950 recording, Furtwängler.

This is a sampler of well-chosen excerpts from the 1950 complete *Ring* cycle conducted by Furtwängler. The last half-hour of *Siegfried* takes up side one, with Flagstad's voice gloriously established but Set Svanholm's far dimmer. As for the Immolation Scene, it is unforgettable. The transfer is marginally less bright than on the complete set, so that anyone not disconcerted by the obvious limitations can safely investigate further. Alan Blyth's enthusiastic review of the cycle in *Gramophone* (unattributed) makes a tempting sleevenote.

Das Rheingold: Entry of the gods into Valhalla. Tannhäuser: overture and Venusberg music. Tristan und Isolde: Prelude to Act 3. Die Walküre: Ride of the Valkyries.
*** R C A Camden C C V 5005 [c4]. Symphony of the Air and Chorus, with female soloists, Stokowski.

This record makes a fascinating bargain, a truly Stokowskian Wagner record, with the singers totally subservient to the conductor's lusciously rich orchestral conception. That is the only possible description of the string playing

both in the *Tristan Prelude* and in the *Rheingold* extract. This kind of approach – dedicated to sensuous beauty of sound alone – misses the inner quality of the music, and the closing pages of the *Venusberg music*, wonderfully rich as they are, have little feeling of spirituality. But with exciting performances of both the *Tannhäuser overture* (with vivid detail in the middle section) and the *Ride of the Valkyries*, this is highly recommendable, even if the recording itself is not always a model of refinement. The tape too is rough round the edges, but it is excitingly brilliant and responds to a cut-back of treble.

'Favourite composer': (i) *Der fliegende Holländer: Overture;* (ii) *Senta's ballad.* (iii; iv) *Götterdämmerung: Siegfried's Rhine journey.* (v) *Lohengrin: Prelude to Act 1.* (vi) *Die Meistersinger: Prelude to Act 1;* (vii) *Prize song.* (iii; iv; viii) *Parsifal: Ich sah das Kind.* (vi) *Das Rheingold: Entry of the gods into Valhalla.* (ix) *Tannhäuser: Pilgrims' chorus;* (x) *Todesahnung ... O du mein holder Abendstern (O star of eve).* (iii; iv) *Tristan und Isolde: Prelude to Act 1.* (iii; xi) *Die Walküre: Ride of the Valkyries; Magic fire music.*
*(*) Decca D P A 625/6 [K D P C]. (i) R O H C G O, Dorati; (ii) Jones; (iii) Vienna P O; (iv) Knappertsbusch; (v) N Philharmonia Orch., Hurst; (vi) L S O, Stokowski; (vii) King; (viii) Flagstad; (ix) Kingsway Chorus and S O, Camarata; (x) Krause; (xi) Edelmann, various soloists, cond. Solti.

A well-made selection, but hardly an imaginative one, as is underlined by the inclusion of the Camarata/Kingsway version of the *Pilgrims' chorus*, which is sturdily unmemorable. Highlights include Gwyneth Jones's noble account of *Senta's ballad* (vividly transferred) and the brief contributions by Kirsten Flagstad, James King and Tom Krause. George Hurst's account of the *Lohengrin Prelude* has a very forward balance which prevents a real *pianissimo*, although the climax is impressively spacious. Knappertsbusch directs *Siegfried's Rhine journey* eloquently, and Stokowski's *Die Meistersinger Prelude* is also a fine performance, although in neither case is the recorded sound ideal. On tape the sound is patchy, with moments of congestion and variable focus.

Waldteufel, Emil
(1837–1915)

Waltzes: *Estudiantina, Op. 191; España, Op. 236; Les Grenadiers; Mon Rêve, Op. 151; Les Patineurs, Op. 183; Pomone, Op. 155.*
   ***C.f.P. CFP 40305. Philharmonia Orch., Henry Krips.

The opening of *Les Patineurs*, with the late Dennis Brain's beautiful horn playing silkily announcing the melody against a background of shimmering violins, makes one a very receptive listener indeed, and the stereo gives the same evocative atmosphere at the beginning of *Mon Rêve*, where the main tune is in the cellos. Elsewhere the recording, though naturally resonant and excellently balanced, is a little lacking in upper range, but all praise to C.f.P. for not trying to brighten it artificially. It shows what a good record EMI could make in the earliest days of stereo and before the introduction of multi-microphone techniques. The whole orchestra has a pleasing bloom, and the brass sounds excellent at the regal opening of *Les Grenadiers* (listen to the fancy tuba part just a little later on). Henry Krips directs lilting, genial performances, with plenty of vigour when called for. A vintage reissue. (It sounds best played back with a slight bass cut.)

Walton, William
(born 1902)

Belshazzar's Feast (oratorio).
   **(*) C.f.P CFP 40063. Rippon, Hallé Choir and Orch., Loughran.

Loughran's account of *Belshazzar's Feast* is forthright and dramatic, helped by splendid brilliant recording quality. The orchestra is particularly well caught, and so is the excellent soloist, firm and clear in attack. The snag is the work of the chorus, relatively small and placed rather close to the microphones, so that details of imperfect ensemble and intonation tend to be exaggerated. The result is still a fine, convincing account of a gripping masterpiece.

Collections

Concerts of Orchestral and Concertante Music

Academy of St Martin-in-the-Fields, Marriner

'Italian concertos': CORELLI: *Concerti grossi, Op. 6, Nos. 1 in D major; 7 in D major.* TORELLI: *Concerto musicale in D minor, Op. 6/10.* LOCATELLI: *Concerto grosso in D major, Op. 1/9.* VIVALDI: *L'Estro armonico: Quadruple violin concerto in B minor, Op. 3/10. Violoncello concerto in C minor, P.434* (with Kenneth Heath). MANFREDINI: *Concerto in G minor, Op. 3/10.* CHERUBINI: *Étude No. 2 for French horn and strings* (with Tuckwell). GEMINIANI: *Concerto grosso in E minor, Op. 3/3.* BELLINI: *Oboe concerto in E flat major* (with Lord).
*** Oiseau-Lyre DPA 587/8.

This collection of rare and refreshing concertos from the eighteenth and nineteenth centuries is taken from the very first recordings made in the early sixties by the then newly formed St Martin's Academy. They were at once acclaimed: the standard of playing and care for style and detail were to set and maintain a new level of excellence by any international standards. The recording too was of first-class quality and it still sounds excellent in these new transfers. Though not all the music is equally inspired, the music-making is so alive and spirited that it is irresistible. Highlights include the delightful Bellini *Oboe concerto* and the Cherubini horn piece, which must have been almost impossible to play on

the instrument of its day. Barry Tuckwell throws it off with great aplomb. Taken as a whole the concert makes an excellent sampler for anyone wanting music civilized and undemanding.

Ballet

'Favourite ballets' (with (i) ROHCGO; (ii) Lanchbery; (iii) Paris Cons. Orch.; (iv) Martinon; (v) Suisse Rom. Orch., Ansermet; (vii) LSO, Monteux; (viii) Maag; (ix) Israel PO, Solti): excerpts from: (i; ii) HÉROLD: *La Fille mal gardée.* (iii; iv) ADAM: *Giselle.* (v) DELIBES: *Coppélia.* TCHAIKOVSKY: (i; vi) *Swan Lake.* (vii) *The Sleeping Beauty.* (v) *Nutcracker.* (iii; viii) CHOPIN (orch. Douglas): *Les Sylphides.* (ix) ROSSINI (arr. Respighi): *La Boutique fantasque.*
**(*) Decca DPA 515/6 [KDPC].

These sets of excerpts are quite cleverly edited so that they often amount to a miniature suite of highlights. The performances are generally distinguished, though it is a pity that the *Panorama* was chosen for inclusion within Monteux's *Sleeping Beauty* selection: he plays it rather too fast. The recording standard is high on both disc and tape; only the Ansermet *Coppélia* slips a little below the overall quality in the cassette transfer. Otherwise the balance mixes brilliance and warmth very agreeably. Of course the choice of items from the Tchaikovsky ballets is arbitrary, but they sound well in context. The excerpts from *La Fille mal gardée* (including the *Clog dance*) and *Giselle* are particularly enjoyable.

Bolshoi Violin Ens., REYENTOVITCH

'*Russian melodies*': RIMSKY-KOR-SAKOV: *Tsar Saltan: Flight of the bumble bee.* SHOSTAKOVICH: *The Gadfly: Romance.* FIBICH: *Poème.* DVOŘÁK: *Gipsy melody. Serenade for strings in E major, Op. 22.* SVETLANOV: *Aria.* PROKOFIEV: *War and Peace: Waltzes.* RACHMANINOV: *Vocalise, Op. 34/14.* RUBINSTEIN: *Melody in F major, Op. 3/1.*
** D G Heliodor 2548 270 [3348 270].

A fascinating 'old-world' collection recalling the Palm Court days, although the sound this group of excellent string players makes is souped up by the resonance. Do not be put off by the opening *Flight of the bumble bee*, which is not too cleanly focused. After this the recording settles down and is agreeably full-blooded (both on disc and tape). To make the sound even more nostalgic a 'piano continuo' is used; the pianist stays at the keyboard through the Dvořák *String serenade* (played complete) and even makes an effective concertante contribution to the *Larghetto*. But it is for melodies like the *Poème* of Fibich and the Rubinstein *Melody in F* that this collection is memorable, and they are splendidly done – which is not to say that the Dvořák work is not very effectively presented too.

Classical masterpieces

'*Forty classical masterpieces*' (with various artists): works by MASCAGNI; BEETHOVEN; J. STRAUSS

(Snr and Jnr); SAINT-SAËNS; RIMSKY-KORSAKOV; GLIÈRE; DEBUSSY; MOZART; TCHAIKOVSKY; SCHUMANN; BENJAMIN; KHACHATURIAN; BRAHMS; ELGAR; HAYDN; RUBINSTEIN; WALTON; HANDEL; MASSENET; BINGE; MENDELSSOHN; BIZET; BORODIN; HUMMEL; CZIBULKA; DINICU.
Pickwick PLD 8007 (2 discs).

With a roster of artists which includes the L S O and conductors such as Vilem Tausky, Robert Stolz and John Hollingsworth, such a collection would appear to have at least some merit, particularly as the records are cleanly pressed and silent-surfaced, and the recording is always acceptable and sometimes good. But the editing is cavalier in the extreme and shows neither taste nor any feeling for the production of a compilation of this kind. Many of the excerpts are snippets, and even when a work is complete it is sometimes faded out during the penultimate few bars, making nonsense of the composer's climactic intention. On occasion the fade comes in midstream, as it were, as in Mozart's *Eine kleine Nachtmusik*, which the sleeve suggests is complete but which terminates halfway through the first movement. Peter Katin obviously had more control over his piano items, which are very effective, if seldom well placed within the anthology as a whole. Not recommended.

'Classical moods'

(i) Szeryng; (ii) ECO; (iii) Holliger; (iv) Leppard; (v) Concertgebouw Orch., Haitink; (vi) Brendel; (vii) I Musici; (viii) Monte Carlo Orch., Remoortel: (i; ii) VIVALDI: *The Four Seasons: Spring, Op. 8/1.* (ii–iv) HANDEL: *Oboe concerto No. 3 in G minor.* (v) MENDELSSOHN:

A Midsummer's Night's Dream overture, Op. 21. (vi) SCHUBERT: 12 German dances, D.790. Moments musicaux Nos. 1 in C major; 3 and 5 in F minor, D.780. (iii; vii) ALBINONI: Oboe concerto in D minor, Op. 9/2. (i; v) BEETHOVEN: Romance for violin and orchestra No. 2 in F major, Op. 50. SAINT-SAËNS: (i; viii) Introduction and rondo capriccioso, Op. 28. (v) Danse macabre, Op. 40. TCHAIKOVSKY: Romeo and Juliet (fantasy overture).
**(*) Philips 6747 041 (2 discs).

If one wants to create a mood, it is better not to mix media, and Brendel's piano interpolations sound slightly out of place in a concert carefully planned to create a continuing atmosphere. Otherwise this two-disc sampler may be cordially recommended. Among its highlights are the distinguished Holliger performances of the Albinoni and Handel Oboe concertos, and Haitink's beautiful account of the Midsummer Night's Dream overture. Szeryng's contributions too are first-class, and once one has accepted the appearance of the piano (it somehow comes as a surprise even on subsequent playings of the records) Brendel's thoughtful and beautifully recorded Moments musicaux are delightful. Haitink's Romeo and Juliet is a little phlegmatic, but the conception is a spacious one and builds to a broad, satisfying final climax. After this the superbly recorded Danse macabre is a splendid bonne bouche to end the programme.

Volume 2 (with (i) ASMF, Marriner; (ii) Arthur Grumiaux; (iii) ECO, Leppard; (iv) Hajdu; (v) Arrau; (vi) LSO; (vii) Sir Colin Davis; (viii) BBC SO): BACH: (i) Brandenburg concerto No. 3 in G major, BMW 1048. (ii; iii) Violin concerto No. 1 in A minor, BWV 1041. BEETHOVEN: (ii; iv) Minuet in G major. (v) Piano sonata No. 14 in C sharp minor, (Moonlight), Op. 27/2. (ii; iv) DVOŘÁK: Humoresque in G flat major, Op. 101/7. (vi; vii) BERLIOZ: Le Carnaval romain overture, Op. 9. (i) SCHUBERT: Rosamunde, D.787: Ballet music No. 2. MENDELSSOHN: (viii; vii) Hebrides overture, Op. 26. (i) A Midsummer Night's Dream, Op. 61: Scherzo. (v) LISZT: Paraphrase on Verdi's 'Rigoletto', G.434. MOZART: (viii; vii) Die Zauberflöte: overture. (i) March in D major, K.408/2. (viii; vii) NICOLAI: Overture: The Merry Wives of Windsor.
**(*) Philips 6747 199 (2 discs).

Although it fails to coalesce as a concert and there is no consistent prevailing mood, there are excellent performances in this collection. It begins and ends with some stimulating Bach: Marriner's Brandenburg No. 3 is perhaps the best of his whole set; the stylishness of the playing, the point of phrasing, the resilience of rhythm, coupled with first-rate recording, are very satisfying. Grumiaux too is on top form in the Violin concerto, and he is given an attentive accompaniment by Leppard and the ECO. Sir Colin Davis's performances of the four overtures also remain in the memory, the Mozart splendidly strong and alert, the Nicolai vivacious and sparkling. The other ASMF items are good too, and one is struck throughout by the superior recording quality (only the Berlioz is a little below par) and the immaculate pressings. The one great disappointment here is the contribution by Claudio Arrau. His complete performance of the Moonlight sonata is curiously lifeless (not helped by the dry sound balance),

147

and the Liszt *Concert paraphrase* simply does not fit into the rest of the programme at all.

English music

'*The music of England*' (with (i) Philip Jones Brass Ens.; (ii) E C O, Britten; (iii) A S M F, Marriner; (iv) LSO; (v) Collins; (vi) Tear; (vii) Vyvyan; (viii) Ferrier; (ix) Bailey; (x) NSO of London; (xi) Nat. PO, Herrmann; (xii) RPO, Nash; (xiii) LPO, Boult; (xiv) Boston Pops Orch., Fiedler; (xv) Bliss): (i) BLISS: *Antiphonal fanfare for three brass choirs.* (ii) BRITTEN: *Simple symphony.* (iii) BUTTERWORTH: *The Banks of Green Willow.* (iv; v) DELIUS: *On Hearing the First Cuckoo in Spring.* (vi) VAUGHAN WILLIAMS: *Songs of Travel: The vagabond. Linden Lea.* TRAD.: (vii) *Cherry ripe.* (viii) *Blow the wind southerly. The Keel Row.* (ix) WARLOCK: *Sleep.* IRELAND: *Sea fever.* (x; v) Balfour GARDINER: *Shepherd Fennel's dance.* (xi) WALTON: *Richard III: Prelude.* (xii) SULLIVAN: *Henry VIII* (incidental music): *March; Graceful dance.* (xiii) HOLST: *The Perfect Fool: ballet music.* (xiv) VAUGHAN WILLIAMS: *English folksongs suite.* ELGAR: (iii) *Serenade for strings, Op. 20.* (iv; xv) *Pomp and Circumstance march No. 1.*
*** Decca DPA 627/8 [KDPC].

A most attractive anthology. Its highlights, Britten's inimitable performance of his juvenile *Simple symphony*, Marriner's fine recording of Butterworth, and the Holst ballet music from *The Perfect Fool*, have already been listed and praised within our main composer index. But, as can be seen above, the programme has been imaginatively chosen to include, unexpectedly, Balfour Gardiner's attractive *Shepherd Fennel's dance*, and the early and distinguished Collins/ LSO version of Delius's *On Hearing the First Cuckoo in Spring*, where the sound is surprisingly good. The group of songs which comes in the middle of side two is generally successful. Jennifer Vyvyan's *Cherry ripe* sounds too sophisticated, but the two Kathleen Ferrier items are as fresh as the day they were recorded; and Norman Bailey's account of *Sea fever* is beautifully sung. The layout is effective; the sound is almost uniformly excellent; and it was sensible to put the inevitable *Pomp and Circumstance march* at the end. The cassettes match the discs closely in sound quality and are in no way inferior.

Ensemble d'Archets Eugène Ysaÿe, Bobesco

'*Music of Venice*': ALBINONI: *Adagio in G minor* (arr. Giazotto) *for strings and organ. Sonata a cinque in E minor, Op. 5/9.* GEMINIANI: *Concerto grosso* (from Corelli's *Violin sonata in D minor* (*La Follia*), *Op. 5/12*). PACHELBEL: *Canon in D major* (arr. Münchinger). ROSSINI: *String sonata No. 3 in C major.* YSAŸE: *Paganini variations.*
*(*) D G Heliodor 2548 219 [3348 219].

The curiously solemn style of the playing here leaves this programme of essentially Italian music lacking in the Mediterranean warmth and sparkle it needs. The Rossini sonata which opens the concert is entirely without humour, and Pachelbel's famous canon is played very seriously indeed. There is a touch of Gallic elegance in the Albinoni, but the most interesting novelty, the Ysaÿe variations on the famous Paganini theme, is much too deadpan. The recording is warm and full, and it has transferred well to cassette.

'Favourite ballet suites'

(i) LPO; (ii) RPO; (iii) Netherlands Radio PO; (iv) LSO; all cond. Black: (i) DELIBES: Coppélia. Sylvia. (ii) TCHAIKOVSKY: Nutcracker, Op. 71a, (iii) MASSENET: Le Cid. MEYERBEER (arr. Lambert): Les Patineurs. (iv) KHACHATURIAN: Gayaneh.
** Decca DPA 605/6 [KDPC].

The orchestral playing here under Stanley Black is generally first-class and the music-making has plenty of life and colour. The two Delibes suites are especially vivacious, and Gayaneh has a keen edge of brilliance that many will find exciting. These recordings were originally made using Decca's Phase Four techniques, and the Massenet and Meyerbeer suites are self-consciously brilliant as a result. The one real drawback to this set is the recording of the Nutcracker suite, where the very forward balance of the woodwind sounds artificial and the vividness of the sound is accompanied by an extremely limited dynamic range. The cassette transfers are well managed and match the discs closely.

' Favourite orchestral music'

Volume 1 (with (i) London Proms SO, Mackerras; (ii) LSO; (iii) Fjeldstad; (iv) Suisse Rom. Orch., Ansermet; (v) Maag; (vi) Stuttgart CO, Münchinger; (vii) Alwyn): (i) SIBELIUS: Finlandia, Op. 26. (ii; iii) GRIEG: Peer Gynt suite No. 1, Op.

46. (iv) RAVEL: Boléro. DEBUSSY: Suite bergamasque: Clair de lune (ii; v) MENDELSSOHN: The Hebrides (Fingal's Cave) overture, Op. 26. (vi) MOZART: Serenade No. 13 in G major (Eine kleine Nachtmusik), K.525. (ii; vii) TCHAIKOVSKY: Capriccio italien, Op. 45. Marche slave, Op. 31.
**(*) Decca DPA 511/1 [KDPC].

A highly successful anthology on disc, though on tape the sound is somewhat variable (the Tchaikovsky items, in particular, lose their refinement at climaxes). But the LP quality is always good and generally excellent, as are the performances. Mackerras's Finlandia is brashly exciting, but Fjeldstad's Peer Gynt suite is distinguished, as is Ansermet's account of Ravel's Boléro. Maag's LSO version of Fingal's Cave is as imaginative and evocative as any available, and Kenneth Alwyn's Tchaikovsky performances show genuine flair. These date from the earliest days of stereo but the recording remains very effective.

Volume 2 (with (i) LSO; (ii) Stokowski; (iii) Black; (iv) LPO; (v) RPO; (vi) Herrmann): (i; ii) WAGNER: Die Walküre: Ride of the Valkyries. DEBUSSY: Prélude à l'après-midi d'un faune. MUSSORGSKY (arr. Stokowski): Night on the Bare Mountain. RAVEL: Daphnis et Chloé: Suite No. 2 (with chorus). BERLIOZ: La Damnation de Faust: Dance of the Sylphs. (i; iii) DVOŘÁK: Slavonic dance No. 1 in C major, Op. 46/1. SMETANA: Má Vlast: Vltava. (iii; iv) CHABRIER: España. (iii; v) SAINT-SAËNS: Danse macabre, Op. 40. (iv; vi) FAURÉ: Pavane, Op. 50. DUKAS: L'Apprenti sorcier (The Sorcerer's Apprentice).

** Decca DPA 519/20 [KDPC].

The excellent is always the enemy of the good, and in this two-LP concert the performances by Stokowski (which are mixed between the two discs) stand out as having far more character and life than the rest. The Debussy and Ravel items are very successful, and the short Berlioz dance makes a delicious encore at the end. *Night on the Bare Mountain* is given in Stokowski's own version (although the notes do not make this clear) and is vividly dramatic. The rest of the music-making is acceptable: Stanley Black keeps the pot boiling very successfully, but Bernard Herrmann's account of *L'Apprenti sorcier* lacks spontaneity and sparkle. The recording on LP is excellent throughout, but the cassette transfers occasionally show a hint of strain at climaxes, although this is not too serious.

'Favourite piano concertos'

(i) Katin; (ii) LSO, Kundell; (iii) NSO (of London); (iv) Colin Davis; (v) LPO; (vi) Gulda, Vienna PO, Andreae: (i; ii) TCHAIKOVSKY: *Concerto No. 1 in B flat minor, Op. 23.* (i; iii; iv) RACHMANINOV: *Concerto No. 2 in C minor, Op. 18.* (i; iv; v) GRIEG: *Concerto in A minor, Op. 16.* (vi) SCHUMANN: *Concerto in A minor, Op. 54.*

* Decca DPA 503/4 [KDPC].

Though all the performances here are perfectly acceptable, and Peter Katin's accounts of the Grieg and Tchaikovsky concertos are excellent, there seems little point in recommending such a compilation when all these works are available separately in superior versions. The recording of the Rachmaninov is lacklustre and bass-heavy, but otherwise the sound is good on both disc and tape.

'Favourite violin concertos'

(i-iii) Ricci, LSO, cond. (i) Gamba; (ii) Sargent; (iii) Fjeldstad: (i) BRUCH: *Violin concerto No. 1 in G minor, Op. 26.* MENDELSSOHN: *Violin concerto in E minor, Op. 64.* (ii) TCHAIKOVSKY: *Violin concerto in D major, Op. 35.* (iii) SIBELIUS: *Violin concerto in D minor, Op. 47.*

**(*) Decca DPA 505/6 [KDPC].

No one should be disappointed in this collection; indeed the performances of the Bruch and Mendelssohn concertos are among the finest in the catalogue, and they are very well recorded on disc and admirably transferred to tape. The performance of the Tchaikovsky concerto is less distinctive but like the vivid reading of the Sibelius it is certainly enjoyable. This anthology in fact provides an excellent representation of a fine artist who was not always at his best in the recording studio.

'Favourite symphonies'

Volume 1 (with Vienna PO, cond. (i) Monteux; (ii) Kubelik; (iii) Münchinger): (i) BEETHOVEN: *Symphony No. 6 in F major (Pastoral), Op. 68.* (ii) DVOŘÁK: *Symphony No. 9 in E minor (From the New World), Op. 95.* (iii) SCHUBERT: *Symphony No. 8 in B minor (Unfinished), D.759.*

* Decca DPA 501/2 [KDPC].

This is an extremely disappointing compilation. The *Pastoral symphony* is well recorded and fully acceptable as a performance, but this was not one of Monteux's more memorable visits to the recording studios and the playing of the Vienna Philharmonic is below their best. Kubelik's *New World* dates from 1958 and was much admired in its original mono pressings as a fresh, warmly lyrical reading, very well recorded. Unfortunately the stereo is not a success; the sound lacks range and is plummy in the bass (it sounds even worse on tape, with a boomy lower register). Münchinger's view of the *Unfinished* is rather dour and unromantically straightforward, although the sound here is good. As a whole this set cannot be recommended.

Volume 2 (with (i) N Philharmonia Orch., Giulini; (ii) Suisse Rom. Orch., Ansermet; (iii) LSO, Josef Krips): (i) MOZART: *Symphony No. 40 in G minor, K.550.* (ii) MENDELSSOHN: *Symphony No. 4 in A major (Italian), Op. 90.* BEETHOVEN: *Symphony No. 5 in C minor, Op. 67.* (iii) SCHUMANN: *Symphony No. 1 in B flat major (Spring), Op. 38.*
*(*) Decca DPA 527/8 [KDPC].

There seems little reason to commend a popular anthology of this kind that includes at its centre the Ansermet performance of Beethoven's *Fifth*, a conscientious but uninspired piece of music-making which cannot be counted among the several recommended versions in the Decca catalogue. The other performances have varying degrees of merit: Giulini's version of the Mozart *G minor Symphony* is beautifully recorded even if the performance – although very well played – is lacking vitality. Krips's Schumann is both lively and sympathetic though somewhat lightweight, and Ansermet is more successful in Mendelssohn's *Italian symphony* than in Beethoven's *Fifth*, even if it could hardly be listed among his finest recordings.

French music

'The music of France' (with (i) Paris Cons. Orch., Martinon; (ii) Vered; (iii) Suisse Rom. Orch., Ansermet; (iv) N Philharmonia Orch., Munch; (v) Crespin; (vi) ROHCGO, Solti; (vii) NSO, Agoult): (i) BERLIOZ: *Le Carnaval romain overture, Op. 9.* (ii) SATIE: *Gymnopédie No. 1.* DEBUSSY: *Suite bergamasque: Clair de lune.* (iii) *Prélude à l'après-midi d'un faune.* DELIBES: *Coppélia: Mazurka.* (i) ADAM: *Giselle, Act 1: Peasant pas de deux.* (iv) BIZET: *Carmen: Act 1: Prelude*; (vi) *Habañera.* GOUNOD: *Sappho: O ma lyre.* (vi) *Faust: ballet music.* (i) SAINT-SAËNS: *Danse macabre, Op. 40.* (iii) DUKAS: *L'Apprenti sorcier.* CHABRIER: *Marche joyeuse.* RAVEL: *Pavane pour une infante défunte. La Valse.* (viii) FAURÉ: *Pavane.*
**(*) Decca DPA 631/2 [KDPC].

An attractively laid-out collection that is more than the sum of its parts. It opens with one of Berlioz's most perfect masterpieces (which familiarity has not robbed of its avant-garde originality) and moves on through Debussy piano music to French ballet and opera. Régine Crespin's languorously beautiful account of the *Sappho* aria is an unexpected but thoroughly enjoyable novelty. Solti's account of the ballet music from *Faust* may lack something in elegance but has irresistible verve. Ansermet's classic versions of *L'Apprenti sorcier* and *La Valse* were well chosen, but it was a pity that Decca did not select Monteux's account of *L'après-midi*. Ansermet (who conducted for Diaghilev) is here rather too balletic in manner, and the orchestral playing lacks something in refinement. But the reading has characteristic vividness of detail. The recorded sound is very good throughout, and the tape transfers are full and lively. On cassette there is a touch of fierceness in the *Coppélia Mazurka*, and some adjustments of bal-

151

ance may be necessary between items. But for the most part the transfers are highly sophisticated.

'Golden classics'

(i) N Philharmonia Orch.; (ii) Giulini; (iii) Vered, cond. Segal; (iv) LPO; (v) de Peyer, cond. Maag; (vi) LSO; (vii) Stuttgart CO, Münchinger; (viii) Israel PO; (ix) Solti; (x) Dorati; (xi) Yepes, Nat. SO, Argenta; (xii) Ricci, cond. Gamba; (xiii) Katchen; (xiv) Kord; (xv) NSO, Agoult; (xvi) Orchestra di Roma, Varviso; (xvii) Bliss: MOZART: (i, ii) *Symphony No. 40 in G minor:* 1st movt. (iii; iv) *Piano concerto No. 21 in C major, K.467: Andante.* (v; vi) *Clarinet concerto in A major, K.622: Adagio.* (vii) ALBINONI: *Adagio in G minor* (arr. Giazotto) *for strings and organ.* (viii; ix) TCHAIKOVSKY: *Serenade for strings in C major, Op. 48: Waltz.* (iv; x) STRAUSS: Johann, Jnr: *An der schönen blauen Donau (Blue Danube) waltz, Op. 314.* (xi) RODRIGO: *Concierto de Aranjuez: Adagio.* (xii; vi) BRUCH: *Violin concerto No. 1 in G minor, Op. 26: Adagio.* (xiii; vi; ix) RACHMANINOV: *Piano concerto No. 2 in C minor, Op. 18: Adagio.* (xii; vi) MENDELSSOHN: *Violin concerto in E minor, Op. 64: Andante.* (i, xiv) SIBELIUS: *Finlandia, Op. 26.* (xv) FAURÉ: *Pavane, Op. 50.* (xvi) MASCAGNI: *Cavalleria Rusticana: Intermezzo.* (vi; xvii) ELGAR: *Pomp and Circumstance march No. 1, Op. 39.*
** Decca DPA 633/4 [KDPC].

There is a profusion of slow movements here, but the mixture blends quite agreeably and the standard of perform-

ance is high. The opening of Sibelius's *Finlandia* as conducted by Kazimierz Kord is rather ponderous, but otherwise there is little to complain of. The recorded sound is generally excellent on disc, a little more variable on cassette, where occasionally there is slightly less refinement.

(Morton) Gould and his Orch.

'Popular classics': BORODIN: *Prince Igor: Polovtsian dances.* DEBUSSY: *Suite bergamasque: Clair de lune. Rêverie.* BOCCHERINI: *Minuet* (from *Op. 13/5*). KREISLER: *Caprice viennoise.* TCHAIKOVSKY: *Symphony No. 5: Andante cantabile* (only). *The Seasons: June (Barcarolle).* STRAUSS, Johann, Jnr (with Josef): *Pizzicato polka.*
**(*) RCA Camden CCV 5014 [c4].

An excellent anthology, entertaining, lively, and vividly recorded. There is style here as well as electricity (the *Polovtsian dances* should disappoint no one, although they are minus the percussion-led opening number). The inclusion of the slow movement from Tchaikovsky's *Fifth Symphony* may seem a drawback (it does not make its fullest effect heard out of context), but it is played with plenty of romantic fervour and seems to fit quite well into the collection. The *Barcarolle* is a most engaging novelty, showing Tchaikovsky as a first-class miniaturist. The *Pizzicato polka* has real panache. The newly remastered tape is bright and (mostly) clear, but has less inner warmth and bloom than the disc, although it responds well to a cut-back of treble.

Hallé Orch., Handford

'Hallé encores': COPLAND: *Fanfare for the Common Man.* KHACHATU-RIAN: *Spartacus: Adagio of Spartacus and Phrygia.* GOUNOD: *Mors et Vita: Judex.* MACCUNN: *Overture: Land of the Mountain and the Flood.* SATIE: *Gymnopédies Nos. 1 and 3* (orch. Debussy). MASSENET: *Thaïs: Meditation.* TRAD: *Suo Gan.* BARBER: *Adagio for strings.*
*** C.f.P. CFP 40320 [TC-CFP].

Maurice Handford and the Hallé offer an exceptionally attractive collection of miscellaneous pieces beautifully recorded. Many of the items have achieved popularity almost by accident through television and the other media (how else would the MacCunn overture have come – so rightly – to notice?), but the sharpness of the contrasts adds to the charm. The Hallé violins sound a little thin in Barber's beautiful *Adagio*, but otherwise the playing is first-rate. What is particularly attractive about this concert is the way the programme is laid out so that each piece follows on naturally after its predecessor. The cassette transfer is of excellent quality, except for a tendency to shrillness in the violins when they are above the stave in *fortissimo*, as in the Khachaturian and Barber items.

Hallé Orch., Loughran

'Viennese overtures': SUPPÉ: *Poet and Peasant.* STRAUSS, Johann, Jnr: *Die Fledermaus.* HEUBERGER: *Der Opernball.* SCHUBERT: *Rosamunde (Die Zauberharfe, D.644).* BEET-HOVEN: *The Creatures of Prometheus, Op. 43.* MOZART: *Le Nozze di Figaro.*
*(*) C.f.P. CFP 40236.

Loughran is best in the classical and early romantic material. *Rosamunde* is plainspun but effective; *Prometheus* is alert and *Le Nozze di Figaro* does not want for lightness and vivacity. None is memorable, but the playing is good and the recording modern. However, the Suppé seriously lacks flair (the opening is flabby); *Die Fledermaus* is too straightlaced by far, and it is only when the charming waltz tune appears that Loughran finds any magic in the engaging *Opera Ball overture.* There is a superb mid-priced LP and cassette by Boskovsky and the VPO called *'Overtures of Old Vienna'* which explores this latter repertoire much more attractively; it offers sparkling playing throughout and recording to match: Decca Jubilee JB 47 [KJBC].

'French music': RAVEL: *Boléro.* DUKAS: *L'Apprenti sorcier (The Sorcerer's Apprentice).* CHABRIER: *España. Marche joyeuse.* BERLIOZ: *La Damnation de Faust: Hungarian march; Dance of the Sylphs; Minuet of the will-o'-the-wisps.*
** C.f.P. CFP 40312 [TC-CFP].

Although lacking something in charisma, these pieces are well played and vividly recorded. Chabrier's *España* has plenty of life, and the pictorial effects of the Dukas symphonic poem are well brought off; these are both reviewed above. Ravel's *Boléro* is built steadily to its climax, but undoubtedly the highlight of the concert is the suite from *The Damnation of Faust,* with each piece very strongly characterized. The tape transfer is generally well managed, although the wide dynamic range has meant that the quiet opening side-drum in *Boléro* is almost inaudible at normal playback level.

'Immortal classics'

Various artists: music by CLARKE; HANDEL; BEETHOVEN; HOOK; MOZART; MENDELSSOHN; GLINKA; LISZT; GOUNOD; RIMSKY-KORSAKOV; DEBUSSY; CHABRIER; WALDTEUFEL; LEHÁR; STRAUSS, Johann; OFFENBACH; WAGNER; PUCCINI; MASSENET; MASCAGNI; SINDING; ELGAR.
** Decca DPA 615/6 [KDPC].

Not everyone will respond to the title, but this anthology of twenty-five favourites is well made and offers a diverse mixture of orchestral, vocal and piano pieces. Opening with Stokowski's ostentatiously romantic conception of the *Trumpet voluntary*, the programme mixes *The Lass from Richmond Hill* and *You Are My Heart's Delight* (Kenneth McKellar) and *Vilja* (Joan Sutherland) with Liszt's *Liebestraum* (Ilana Vered) and Sinding's *Rustle of Spring* (Joseph Cooper). The orchestral items include Chabrier's *España* (Argenta), the Offenbach *Barcarolle* (Solti), *Fingal's Cave* (Ansermet, not Maag), *The Ride of the Valkyries* (Stokowski) and Massenet's *Meditation* from *Thaïs* (with Josef Sakonov as the lushly romantic soloist). The recording on disc is good throughout; the tape transfers are almost always well managed and sometimes excellent.

Jaye Instrumental Consort (of Medieval Instruments), Gerald English (tenor)

Medieval music: *'The song of the ass': Two ductias; English dance; Rege Mentem; Saltarello; Estampies 1–3; Li Maus d'Amer; Lamento di Tristan; C'est la fin; Kalenda Maya; Novus miles sequitur; Moulin de Paris; In seculum artifex; Sol oritur; Vierhundert jar Uff diser Erde; Trotto; Worldes blis; Alta; Ja nun nons pris; Die süss Nachtigall; Pour mon coeur; Estampie royale.*
*** Pye GSGC 14092.

This entertaining concert originally made a pair with a collection of Elizabethan music (now deleted). The problems of scoring have been met with confidence and flair, and the result could not be more enjoyable. The whole programme is lively and diverse, and the contribution of Gerald English is distinguished. Highly recommended.

LPO (various conductors)

'Favourites of the Philharmonic': GRIEG: *Peer Gynt: Morning.* CHABRIER: *España.* LITOLFF: *Concerto symphonique: Scherzo* (with Katin; all cond. Pritchard). FAURÉ: *Pavane* (cond. Handley). BERLIOZ: *Le Carnaval romain overture.* SMETANA: *The Bartered Bride: overture* (cond. Barbier). GLINKA: *Russlan and Ludmilla overture* (cond. Mackerras). WEBER: *Der Freischütz overture.* NICOLAI *The Merry Wives of Windsor overture.* MENDELSSOHN: *A Midsummer Night's Dream: Scherzo* (cond. Lockhart). TCHAIKOVSKY: *Serenade for strings: Waltz* (cond. Del Mar). STRAUSS, Johann, Jnr: *Tritsch-Tratsch polka; An der schönen blauen Donau (The Blue Danube)* (cond. Güschlbauer). STRAUSS, Johann, Snr: *Radetzky march.* VERDI: *Aïda: Triumphal march* (cond. Davison). BEETHOVEN: *Egmont overture* (cond. Andrew Davis).
** M.f.P. 1001 (2 discs) [TC-MFP].

No one can argue with the title: there are many favourite classical 'pops' here, but they do not make a concert, with overtures dotted all over the place and no attempt to create a prevailing mood or set up appropriate contrasts. All the performances are good; some are excellent (Fauré's *Pavane* under Handley, and Lockhart's *Merry Wives overture*, for instance). The recording is bright and clear, and as a sampler of the C.f.P. range this is more than adequate, even though at least two of the discs from which the items are taken are withdrawn from the catalogue as we go to print. It is curious that a C.f.P. collection should be issued instead on the 'popular' M.f.P. label.

LPO, Davison

'*Favourite marches*': STRAUSS, Johann, Snr: *Radetzky march*. BERLIOZ: *Les Troyens: Trojan march. La Damnation de Faust: Hungarian march.* CHABRIER: *Marche joyeuse.* VERDI: *Aïda: Triumphal march.* BEETHOVEN: *The Ruins of Athens: Turkish march.* RIMSKY-KORSAKOV: *Le Coq d'or: March.* TCHAIKOVSKY: *Marche slave, Op. 31.*
** C.f.P. CFP 40254.

The Fairfield Hall in Croydon was aptly chosen for these recordings; the ripely resonant acoustic adds a feeling of spectacle. The orchestral playing is not wanting in life and vigour, and although the selection is hardly adventurous it makes an agreeable entertainment. The French items come off best; the *Aïda march* is played in abbreviated form, and without a chorus it loses much of its operatic flamboyance.

LPO, Mackerras

TCHAIKOVSKY: *1812 overture, Op. 49* (with Welsh Guards Band). GLINKA: *Russlan and Ludmilla: Overture.* WAGNER: *Lohengrin: Prelude to Act 3.* MUSSORGSKY: *Night on the Bare Mountain.*
** C.f.P. CFP 101 [TC-CFP].

Brilliant, alert performances, characteristic of Mackerras's lively style. The cannonade at the end of *1812* is relatively modest but quite effective, and this has meant a successful cassette transfer without distortion. Elsewhere the sound is very brightly lit (on tape and disc alike), and the overall effect is vivid if not especially atmospheric.

LSO, Previn

'*An André Previn showcase*': PROKOFIEV: *Symphony No. 1 in D major (Classical), Op. 25.* SATIE: *Gymnopédie No. 1* (orch. Debussy). MENDELSSOHN: *Ruy Blas overture, Op. 95.* VAUGHAN WILLIAMS: *The Wasps: overture.* RIMSKY-KORSAKOV: *Tsar Saltan: Flight of the bumble bee. Scheherazade: The young prince and the princess.* STRAUSS, Richard: *Der Rosenkavalier: waltzes.*
*(**) RCA Camden CCV 5025 [**(*) c4].

Previn's RCA recording period stretched from the mid-sixties to the early seventies and included a highly distinguished integral recording of the Vaughan Williams symphonies. The playing he achieved with the LSO had consistent freshness and spontaneity of a kind not always so obvious in some of his later HMV records. Moreover the RCA engineers accorded him extremely vivid sound. Both these qualities are only too readily demonstrated by this excellent sampler. It is a very great pity that, when the master tape for this compilation was originally put together, some misguided sound engineer decided to brighten the treble artificially. Thus the violin timbre is unnaturally sharp-edged, and in the Prokofiev symphony (a splendid performance, discussed above) the focus is fizzy too. The sound is not entirely beyond the reach of the controls, and on side two (Vaughan Williams, Rimsky-Korsakov, Strauss) it can be made fully acceptable with a steep top-cut or filter. The performances are absolutely first-rate, and the languorous excerpt from *Scheherazade* lose_ little by being heard out of context. The cassette transfer is excellent, and apart from a degree of shrillness on side one can be made to sound very well with a treble cut. It is cleaner than the LP, and on side two gives excellent results, although the refinement slips a little in the *Der Rosenkavalier Waltzes*.

LSO, Tausky

'*Music you have loved*': VERDI: *La Traviata: Prelude to Act 1.* GRIEG: *Norwegian dance No. 2, Op. 35.* BINGE: *Elizabethan serenade.* MENDELSSOHN: *A Midsummer Night's Dream, Op. 61: Wedding march.* MASSENET: *Thaïs: Meditation* (with John Georgiadis). WALDTEUFEL: *Waltz: Les Patineurs, Op. 183.* MASCAGNI: *Cavalleria Rusticana: Intermezzo.* HUMMEL: *Trumpet concerto in E flat major:* finale. DELIBES: *Sylvia: Pizzicato.* DEBUSSY: *Suite bergamasque: Clair de lune.* TCHAIKOVSKY: *Chant sans paroles, Op. 2/3.* ELGAR: *Salut d'amour.* GOUNOD: *Faust: Waltz.* STRAUSS, Johann, Snr: *Radetzky march, Op. 228.* BACH/WALTON: *The Wise*

Virgins: Sheep may safely graze. WALTON: *Façade: Popular song.* GRANADOS: *Goyescas: Intermezzo.* SIBELIUS: *Valse triste, Op. 44.* GRAINGER: *Handel in the Strand.* WOLF-FERRARI: *I Quattro Rusteghi: Intermezzo.* HANDEL: *Xerxes: Largo.* STRAUSS, Johann, Jnr (with Josef): *Pizzicato polka.* BENJAMIN: *Jamaican rumba.* MOZART: *Horn concerto No. 4 in E flat major, K.495: Rondo.* THOMAS: *Mignon: Entr'acte.* REZNIČEK: *Donna Diana: overture.*
*** Pickwick PDA 036 (2 LPs).

Unlike Pickwick's '*Forty classical masterpieces*' (see above) with its tantalizing snippets, this two-disc set includes complete pieces; there are twenty-six of them, from the same number of composers. The selection has been made with taste and discernment, and the concert is excellently laid out. This is perhaps not surprising, as the recording producer is Peter Gammond, who provides the excellent musical notes for the Pickwick RCA Camden LPs, and for this issue too, of course. The recording was made in St Giles' Church, Cripplegate, and Bob Auger, the engineer in charge, is to be congratulated on the nicely judged reverberation and orchestral bloom. The LSO is on excellent form and Vilem Tausky directs with spirit and style. The orchestra's soloists are featured in the three concertante items. The whole programme is very enjoyable, but the second disc especially so; *Sheep may safely graze*, the excerpt from *Façade*, Sibelius's *Valse triste*, *Handel in the Strand*, and the Wolf-Ferrari and Rezn* items are all especially vivacious. At bargain-basement price and with clean, quiet pressings, this can be cordially recommended.

Monte Carlo Opera Orch., Frémaux

'*French overtures*' from: BIZET: *Carmen (Prelude).* THOMAS: *Mignon.* ADAM: *Si j'étais roi.* BOIELDIEU: *Le Calife de Bagdad. La Dame blanche.* AUBER: *Fra Diavolo.*
** DG Heliodor 2548 260.

Louis Frémaux shows himself thoroughly at home in this repertoire, played with the proper French accent. The music is all attractively scored and felicitous in invention, and if the horn soloist at the beginning of *Mignon* is not especially gracious, that is the only contribution from the wind which is below par, and the string-playing is neat and stylish, notably so in *Si j'étais roi.* The two charming Boieldieu overtures are shaped with warmth and elegance, and *Fra Diavolo* has point and wit. The recording is of good quality and well balanced. (The cassette has been withdrawn.)

NBC SO, Toscanini

'*Dances from famous operas*': PONCHIELLI: *La Gioconda: Dance of the hours.* VERDI: *Aïda: Dance of the Moorish slaves; Ballet music. Otello: Ballet music.* BIZET: *Carmen: Aragonaise.* CATALANI: *Lorelei: Ondine's dance.* ROSSINI: *William Tell: Ballet music.*
** RCA Victrola (m) AT 109.

This is a strange and varied collection, for not all the pieces suit Toscanini equally well; but if you can accept the dry NBC recording it is well worth hearing.

Russian music

'*Concert of Russian favourites*' (with (i) Dresden State Orch., Sanderling; (ii) Monte Carlo Opera Orch., Frémaux; (iii) Leningrad PO, Rozhdestvensky; (iv) Berlin PO; (v) Maazel; (vi) Leitner): BORODIN: (i) *In the Steppes of Central Asia.* (ii) *Prince Igor: Polovtsian dances.* (iii) KHACHATURIAN: *Gayaneh: Sabre dance.* (iv; v) MUSSORGSKY: *Night on the Bare Mountain.* RIMSKY-KORSAKOV: *Capriccio espagnol, Op. 34.* (iv; vi) TCHAIKOVSKY: *Marche slave, Op. 31.*
**(*) DG Heliodor 2548 269 [3348 269].

The highlight of this collection is Maazel's outstanding account of the *Capriccio espagnol*, which like *Night on the Bare Mountain* (also fine, but a little more mannered) comes from an early concert by the Berlin Philharmonic Orchestra, now long deleted (SLPM 138033). This is unquestionably a great performance, with wonderful, relaxed virtuosity from the Berlin orchestra in the *Scena e canto gitano*, after some gorgeous horn and string playing in the earlier variations. The work closes with breathtaking exuberance, yet every note is in its place. The recording has not been spoiled; it retains the colour of the original and shows what good stereo was possible two decades ago. The disc opens with Rozhdestvensky's frenetically exciting *Sabre dance*, which is followed by Leitner's dignified *Marche slave* (another very characterful performance), and only Sanderling's *In the Steppes of Central Asia*, an elusive work on disc, falls a little below the high standard generally maintained through this collection. The *Polovtsian dances*, although without chorus, are successful. The cassette has not the refinement of the disc: the orchestral sound is brilliant but has less warmth and bloom.

Spanish music

'*The music of Spain*' (with (i) LSO; (ii) Argenta; (iii) Rubio; (iv) Nat. SO of Spain; (v) Berganza, Lavilla; (vi) Suisse Rom. Orch., Ansermet; (vii) Robles; (viii) Ricci, LSO, Gamba; (ix) Campoli, Ibbott; (x) Walker): (i, ii) GRANADOS: *Danza española No. 5 (Andaluza)*. (ii–iv) *Goyescas: The maiden and the nightingale*. (v) *Tonadillas: El tra la la y el punteador; El majo timido*. GURIDI: *Como quieres que adivine*. (vi) ALBÉNIZ: *Iberia: El corpus en Sevilla. Navarra* (both orch. Arbós). (vii) *Rumores de la caleta. Torre Bermeja*. SARASATE: (viii) *Carmen fantasy, Op. 25*. (ix) *Zapateado, Op. 23/2*. (vi) TURINA: *Danzas fantásticas*. (x) MUDARRA: *Fantasia*. TARREGA: *Recuerdos de la Alhambra. Lagrima. Alborada*. (vi) FALLA: *El amor brujo: Ritual fire dance; Pantomime. La vida breve: Interlude and Spanish dance. The Three-cornered Hat: 3 Dances*.
**(*) Decca DPA 629/30 [KDPC].

An excellent, essentially lightweight concert of Spanish music. With Argenta or Ansermet in charge of most of the orchestral music there is plenty of vigour and colour, and the vocal interlude featuring Teresa Berganza is distinguished. Ricci's account of the *Carmen fantasy* is stronger on bravura than charm (he is positioned a little too near the microphone), but his virtuosity is breathtaking. Campoli plays *Zapateado* with aplomb, and Timothy Walker's guitar solos are thoroughly musical, if lacking a little in temperament. He is closely but not unnaturally recorded. The sound

throughout is first-class, with little to choose in quality between disc and tape, although the former displays a marginally wider dynamic range in the more spectacular orchestral climaxes.

'These You Have Loved' (from BBC radio programme)

Volume 1 (with (i) Bath Fest. Orch., Menuhin; (ii) Ambrosian Singers, ECO, Mackerras; (iii) Hallé Orch., Barbirolli; (iv) Ogdon; (v) Schwarzkopf; (vi) LSO, Boult; (vii) Rome Opera Chorus, Schippers; (viii) RPO, Beecham; (ix) Callas; (x) Tuckwell, ASMF, Marriner; (xi) RPO, Collingwood; (xii) Corelli; (xiii) Anievas, N Philharmonia Orch., Atzmon): (i) HANDEL: *Concerto grosso in B minor, Op. 6/12:* 2nd movt. *Messiah: Hallelujah*. (iii) GRIEG: *Peer Gynt, Op. 23: Morning*. (iv) CHOPIN: *Fantaisie-impromptu in C sharp minor, Op. 66*. (v) ZELLER: *Der Obersteiger: Sei nicht bös*. (vi) BRAHMS: *Symphony No. 3 in F major, Op. 90:* 3rd movt. (vii) VERDI: *Il Trovatore: Anvil chorus*. (viii) TCHAIKOVSKY: *Eugene Onegin: Waltz*. (ix) BIZET: *Carmen: Habañera*. (x) MOZART: *Horn concerto No. 4 in E flat major, K.495: Rondo*. (xi) ELGAR: *Salut d'amour, Op. 12*. (xii) PUCCINI: *Turandot: Nessun dorma*. (xiii) RACHMANINOV: *Rhapsody on a theme of Paganini, Op. 43:* 18th Variation.
** C.f.P. CFP 40277 [TC-CFP].

This is the first of four selections associated with Richard Baker's famous radio programme. (All four discs (and tapes) are also available in a box-album: CFP 78254 [TC-CFP].) One certainly cannot question the excellence of the performances, as the roster of artists is most distinguished. This first compilation opens well with the fine Menuhin version of the famous Handelian tune that the BBC once used to introduce the mid-morning religious radio programme; and among the highlights must be counted Schwarzkopf's enchantingly fresh-voiced performance of *Sei nicht bös*. However, the order of items is rather arbitrary – like a radio programme without the disc-jockey's comments. Some of the contrasts jar, notably John Ogden's rather hurried *Fantaisie-impromptu* storming in after Sir John Barbirolli and the Hallé Orchestra have played Grieg's *Morning* from *Peer Gynt* so evocatively. Franco Corelli's stirring *Nessun dorma* is unattractively faded out at the end, and the eighteenth variation of Rachmaninov, which follows, is equally clumsily faded in. These two items should be re-edited. The recording is consistently good, and there is very little to choose between disc and tape; the latter is slightly smoother on top, not to its disadvantage.

Volume 2 (with (i) Bath Fest. CO, Menuhin; (ii) Baker; (iii) Moore; (iv) Gieseking; (v) Gedda; (vi) LSO, Boult; (vii) King's College Choir, Cambridge, Willcocks; (viii) Hallé Orch., Barbirolli; (ix) Blanc; (x) N Philharmonia Orch., Frühbeck de Burgos; (xi) Los Angeles, Schwarzkopf): (i) BACH: *Suite No. 3 in D major, B WV 1068: Air*. (ii; iii) VAUGHAN WILLIAMS: *Linden Lea*. (iv) BEETHOVEN: *Piano sonata No. 14 in C sharp minor (Moonlight), Op. 27/2:* 1st movt. (v) LEHÁR: *Das Land des Lächelns: Dein ist mein ganzes Herz (You are my heart's delight)*. (vi) ELGAR: *Variations on an original theme (Enigma), Op. 36: Nimrod*.

(vii) FAURÉ: *Requiem, Op. 48: Agnus Dei*. (viii) SIBELIUS: *Karelia suite, Op. 11: Intermezzo*. (v; ix) BIZET: *Les Pêcheurs de perles: Au fond du temple saint*. (x) PROKO-FIEV: *Symphony No. 1 in D major (Classical), Op. 25:* 3rd movt. (xi; iii) ROSSINI: *Duetto buffo di due gatti*. (viii) STRAUSS, Johann, Jnr: *An der schönen blauen Donau (Blue Danube) waltz, Op. 314*.

** C.f.P. CFP 40294 [TC-CFP].

The highlights here are vocal, and many will be delighted to have the 1967 Festival Hall recording of Rossini's *Cats' duet*, part of a famous 'Homage to Gerald Moore' concert. Otherwise this collection again sounds like a radio selection without narrative, but the performances are of first-class quality. So is the recording, with the tape matching the disc closely, except for a slight slip in refinement in the Lehár item.

Volume 3 (with (i) Pollini; (ii) Baker; (iii) RPO, Beecham; (iv) Gedda; (v) Germani; (vi) CBSO, Frémaux; (vii) Callas; (viii) Bowman, Brett; (ix) Menuhin, Philharmonia Orch., Susskind; (x) LSO, Previn): (i) CHOPIN: *Nocturne in F sharp minor, Op. 15/2*. (ii) ELGAR: *Sea Pictures, Op. 37: Where corals lie*. (iii) BEETHOVEN: *The Ruins of Athens, Op. 113: Turkish march*. (iv) PUCCINI: *La Bohème: Che gelida manina*. (v) BACH: *Toccata and fugue in D minor, BWV 565*. (vi) SATIE: *Gymnopédies Nos. 1 and 3* (orch. Debussy). (vii) DELIBES: *Lakmé: Bell song*. (viii) PURCELL: *Come, ye sons of art: Sound the trumpet*. (ix) BRUCH: *Violin concerto No. 1 in G minor, Op. 26:*

159

Adagio. PROKOFIEV: *Lieutenant Kijé, Op. 80: Troika.*
**(*) C.f.P CFP 40332 [TC-CFP].

As an anthology this is much the most attractive of the first three '*These You Have Loved*' compilations. It opens with Maurizio Pollini's melting performance of Chopin's *Nocturne in F sharp minor*, followed by Janet Baker, in superb partnership with Barbirolli and the LSO, singing the most famous of Elgar's *Sea Pictures*. Side two is especially effective. Opening with Satie, it continues with Callas's memorable version of the *Bell song*, well contrasted with the splendid Purcell duet. Then comes Menuhin's inspired account of the Bruch *Adagio*, and finally Previn and the LSO on top form in Prokofiev's catchy sleigh ride. If side one does not gell quite so satisfactorily it ends with an excellent version of Bach's most famous organ piece, given exceptionally clear and unmuddled sound, equally impressive on tape and on disc. Indeed there is no great difference between the two, except for a slightly brighter treble response at times on the LP.

Volume 4 (with (i) RPO, Beecham; (ii) N Philharmonia Orch., Giulini; (iii) Los Angeles; (iv) Vienna Singverein, Berlin PO, Karajan; (v) Ogdon; (vi) Johann Strauss Orch., Boskovsky; (vii) Fischer-Dieskau, Moore; (viii) City of Birmingham SO, Frémaux; (ix) Franco Corelli; (x) Rothwell, Hallé Orch., Barbirolli; (xi) LSO, the composer): (i) SIBELIUS: *Pelléas et Mélisande: At the castle gate.* (ii) RAVEL: *Pavane pour une infante défunte.* (iii) VERDI: *La Traviata: Ah, fors'è lui . . . Sempre libera.* (iv) MOZART: *Ave verum corpus, K.618.* (v) CHOPIN: *Polonaise No. 3 in A major (Military), Op. 40/1.* (vi) STRAUSS,

Johann, Snr: *Radetzky march.* (vii) SCHUBERT: *Erlkönig.* (viii) CHABRIER: *España.* (ix) LEONCAVALLO: *I Pagliacci: Vesti la giubba.* (x) BACH: *Cantata No. 208: Sheep may safely graze* (arr. Barbirolli). (xi) KHACHATURIAN: *Gayaneh: Sabre dance.*
*** C.f.P. CFP 40337 [TC-CFP].

Finest of all is Volume 4 with the selection well up to standard while the performances cannot be faulted. It is good to have the vocal items, and many will welcome the inclusion of the famous Sibelius signature tune of the TV programme *The Stars by Night.* Taken as a whole this makes an excellent entertainment, with individual pieces nicely contrasted. The sound is first-class on both disc and tape.

Tone poems

'*Great tone poems*' (with (i) N Philharmonia Orch., Kord; (ii) RPO; (iii) Henry Lewis; (iv) Kingsway SO, Camarata; (v) LPO, Herrmann; (vi) LSO; (vii) Black; (viii) Stokowski): (i) SIBELIUS: *Finlandia, Op. 26. Legends: The Swan of Tuonela, Op. 22/2.* (ii; iii) STRAUSS, Richard: *Till Eulenspiegels lustige Streiche, Op. 28.* (iv) BORODIN (arr. Camarata): *In the Steppes of Central Asia.* (v) DUKAS: *L'Apprenti sorcier (The Sorcerer's Apprentice)* (vi; vii) SMETANA: *Mà Vlast: Vltava.* (ii; vii) SAINT-SAËNS: *Danse macabre, Op. 40.* (vi; viii) DEBUSSY: *Prélude à l'après-midi d'un faune.* MUSSORGSKY (arr. Stokowski): *Night on the Bare Mountain.*
*(*) Decca DPA 601/2 [KDPC].

An impressive anthology that is apparently good value for money; but there are a few drawbacks. The performances, apart from the Stokowski, and to a lesser extent Henry Lewis's *Till Eulenspiegel*, are good but not outstanding. *In the Steppes of Central Asia* is enjoyably eloquent, but is heard in a slightly abbreviated arrangement. Herrmann's *Sorcerer's Apprentice* too is disappointingly phlegmatic. The sound is generally of high quality on disc but less reliable on cassette, where the high-level transfer causes the refinement to slip in *The Sorcerer's Apprentice, Vltava* and the powerful Stokowski arrangement of *Night on the Bare Mountain*.

Warsaw Nat. PO, Semkow

'*España*': CHABRIER: *España*. RIMSKY-KORSAKOV: *Capriccio espagnol, Op. 34.* RAVEL: *Rapsodie espagnole.* FALLA: *El amor brujo: Pantomime; Dance and Ritual fire dance.*

*** D G Heliodor 2548 029 [3348 029].

An extraordinarily successful collection which amounts to more than the sum of its parts. Chabrier's *España* (reviewed above) is full of zest; Rimsky's *Capriccio* offers rather measured basic tempi, but the orchestral playing is alert and sympathetic (the horns are gorgeously rich) and there is excellent detail. The Ravel *Rapsodie* is memorably sensuous, with richly spun melodic lines, and the three excerpts from *El amor brujo* only serve to whet the appetite for more. On disc the recording is splendid, full, atmospheric, with flashing percussion and plenty of warmth and depth. It is quite admirably transferred to tape, the treble fractionally too bright, perhaps, but with clean transients, full body and a natural atmospheric resonance. Highly recommended.

Instrumental Recitals

Berman, Lazar (piano)

'A concert programme': SCHU-MANN: *Piano sonata No. 2 in G minor, Op. 22. Fantasiestücke, Op. 12, Nos. 3, Warum?; 4, Grillen.* LISZT: Concert paraphrases of Schubert: *Die Winterreise* (excerpts): *Der Leiermann; Tausch-ung. Die junge Nonne. Ave Maria. Der Erlkoenig. Die schöne Müllerin* (excerpt): *Wohin?. Harmonies poétiques et religieuses: Funérailles. Hungarian rhapsody No. 9.* SCRIA-BIN: *Études, Op. 42, Nos. 1–8. Fantasia, Op. 28.* RAVEL: *Jeux d'eau. Gaspard de la nuit: Ondine.* RACH-MANINOV: *6 Moments musicaux, Op. 16.* CHOPIN: *Étude in B minor, Op. 25/10.* DEBUSSY: *Étude No. 6 (Book 1).* PARTSHALADZE: *Piano concerto in A major, Op. 12* (with Moscow RO, Svetlanov).
*(**) Murray Hill (m) 943492 (4 discs).

Many of these performances derive from 78s, and that may well prove an obstacle to all but the most fervent Berman admirer. In many instances the quality of the playing is such that sonic limitations seem of small account; the Scriabin studies are particularly sensitive, and the variety of keyboard colour that Berman has at his command can be felt in spite of the dimmish sound. In the Liszt he is in excellent form, showing himself a thorough musician who makes

the most of the brilliance but never indulges in flamboyant display. In the Rachmaninov there is some wow, and the pianos used in these records are not always in tip-top condition. In the Schumann sonata the transfer plays a full semitone flat and the sound is thin and papery. The last record introduces the Soviet composer Mareb Partshaladze, whose piano concerto is neoromantic and derivative, pleasing but unmemorable. This compilation is for Berman admirers and collectors of rare material; the sound quality will not bother strongly motivated collectors as much as it will the non-specialist.

Byzantine, Julian (guitar)

VILLA-LOBOS: *Preludes Nos. 1–5. Chôro typico.* PONCE: *Campo.* MAZA: *Homenaje a la guiterra.* LAURO: *Danza negra. Suite vene-zolana: Valse. Valse No. 3.*
**(*) C.f.P. 40209 [TC-CFP].

A pleasing recital, offering thoughtful and thoroughly musical playing, although there is not perhaps the distinction and individuality of Julian Bream or John Williams in the attractive Villa-Lobos *Preludes*. The recording is attractively live and immediate; one needs to set the volume back or the guitar sounds larger than life. The cassette transfer is of immaculate quality, matching the disc closely.

Horowitz, Vladimir (piano)

'Twentieth-century masterpieces': SCRIABIN: Piano sonata No. 9 in F major (Black Mass), Op. 68. Preludes: in D major, Op. 11/5; in G sharp minor, Op. 22/1. Études: in B flat minor, Op. 8/7; in C sharp minor, Op. 42/5. BARBER: Piano sonata, Op. 26. PROKOFIEV: Piano sonata No. 7 in B flat major, Op. 83.
**(*) RCA Victrola (m) VH 014.

A stunning recital in every way. The Black Mass sonata of Scriabin is played with demonic intensity and altogether dazzling virtuosity: it is unlikely ever to be surpassed. Barber's Piano sonata is a thrilling performance too, the technical difficulties inspiring Horowitz to the greatest brilliance. Both these performances were recorded in the early 1950s; the Prokofiev dates from 1945, not long after the work was written. The shallow recording may well have prompted the unfavourable response from Prokofiev himself (according to his son Oleg, he preferred Richter); and in the finale the sheer virtuosity and rhythmic drive might strike some listeners as too much of a good thing. The sound in the Prokofiev calls for much tolerance, but the playing throughout is in a class of its own.

'Instruments of the orchestra'

Violin; viola; violoncello; double bass; piccolo; flute; oboe; cor anglais; clarinets; bass clarinet; bassoon; contra-bassoon; horn; trumpet; trombone; bass trombone; tuba; timpani; percussion; harp. Introduced by Sir Adrian Boult, featuring members of the LPO.
** C.f.P. CFP 40074.

Sir Adrian seems excessively sober here, and his direct approach (very reserved and didactic) is clearly intended for educational use. The recording is accurate and the playing accomplished, but the presentation is rather clinical, and the sensuality and excitement that many orchestral instruments can create, even on their own, seldom come over. Also the use of piano accompaniments in the few solos (the Mozart Horn rondo, for instance) is not satisfactory in a disc of this nature. Surely Classics for Pleasure could have used some illustrative examples of orchestral texture too. Still, within its limitations of range, this is well done, and the recording quality is certainly exact.

Katin, Peter (piano)

'Fifty classical piano favourites' by: BEETHOVEN; HAYDN; SCHUBERT; GRIEG; BRAHMS; ALBÉNIZ; SCHUMANN; GRANADOS; ELGAR; TCHAIKOVSKY; MOSZKOWSKI; CHOPIN; MENDELSSOHN; RUBINSTEIN; SAINT-SAËNS; DAQUIN; DEBUSSY; DVOŘÁK; CZIBULKA; IBERT; MOMPOU; WILSON; HELLER; RICHARDS; HANDEL; ASCHER; MacDOWELL; ENGELMANN; MASSENET; GRÜTZMACHER; LIADOV; MERKEL; KOPYLOV.
**(*) Pickwick 50 DA 322 (2 discs).

If you need to put fifty items on to four LP sides, some sacrifices have to be made, even if each side plays for about half an hour. Yet a surprising number of these pieces are heard either complete or, in the case of a song melody, with one stanza included. Where abbreviations are made (as in the two Schubert Impromptus) each excerpt is sensibly edited, and one hopes it may tempt listeners to move on to a disc which offers all the Impromptus without cuts. The range of the programme is extraordinarily wide, with many novelties. The second disc is especially attractive, including delectable morceaux like Ibert's *Little White Donkey*, Mompou's *Les Jeunes Filles au jardin*, Daquin's *Le Coucou*, and Merkel's *Butterfly*. Of course the recital is essentially lightweight, but the music is played with unfailing sensitivity. No fewer than seven Chopin items are included, and Katin is completely at home in this repertoire; other favourites include Mendelssohn's *Spring song*, MacDowell's *To a Wild Rose*, and five Grieg miniatures. The recording is first-class, full and well balanced, with minimum loss of focus towards the ends of the longer sides. This compilation is not designed for sophisticated collectors, but it would make an excellent present for someone whose experience of the piano repertoire is comparatively undeveloped. The pressings are good, if not absolutely silent; our copy has an unattractive 'scrape' at the beginning of side four.

London Virtuosi (including James Galway)

'*Serenade for flute*': BEETHOVEN: *Serenade in D major for flute, violin and viola, Op. 25*. BACH: *Flute sonata in E major* (for flute and continuo), *BWV 1035*. TELEMANN: *Trio sonata in E minor for flute, oboe and continuo*.
*** C.f.P. CFP 40318 [TC-CFP].

Since these recordings were made for Abbey Records in 1973 James Galway has become a star, and another member of the London Virtuosi, John Georgiadis (then the leader of the LSO), has taken up a successful solo career. It was a bright idea of C.f.P. to make a recital out of these performances. Beethoven's *Serenade* is the best-known work of the three. The light and charming combi-

nation of flute, violin and viola inspired the youthful composer to write in an unexpectedly carefree and undemanding way. The sequence of tuneful, unpretentious movements reminds one of Mozart's occasional music, and this engaging performance is well projected by a bright, clean recording. The balance is a trifle close, but the sound is otherwise excellent. The other two works are hardly less attractive, and the playing in the Telemann, slightly more expressive than the Bach, achieves a distinction of style. On tape the sound quality has marginally less life and range at the top; otherwise the cassette transfer is first-class.

Organ music

'*Favourite organ music*' (with (i) Karl Richter, organ of Victoria Hall, Geneva; (ii) Preston, Westminster Abbey or King's College Chapel, Cambridge; (iii) Richter, cond. and organ of St Mark's, Munich, with CO; (iv) Nicholas, Norwich Cathedral): BACH: (i) *Toccata and fugue in D minor, BWV 565. Fantasia and fugue in G minor, BWV 542.* (ii) *Chorale prelude: Wachet auf, BWV 645.* HANDEL: (iii) *Organ concertos; in B flat major, Op. 4/2; in D minor, Op. 7/4.* (iv) *Water music: Air. Xerxes: Largo.* CLARKE: *Trumpet voluntary.* DAVIES: *Solemn melody.* BOËLLMANN: *Suite gothique: Toccata.* KARG-ELERT: *Chorale improvisation: Nun danket alle Gott.* (ii) PURCELL: *Trumpet tune.* FRANCK: *Pièce héroïque.* WAGNER: *Tannhäuser: Pilgrims' chorus.* WIDOR: *Symphony No. 5 in F minor, Op. 42/1: Toccata.*
**(*) Decca DPA 523/4 [KDPC].

It is difficult to fault the selection

here, which balances French and German solo repertoire with a couple of Handel concertos and some effective transcriptions. The first disc is outstanding in every way; the music here is played either by Simon Preston at Westminster or by Michael Nicholas at Norwich. The standard of performance is very high indeed and the recording is spectacular, highlights being the famous Widor *Toccata* and the flamboyant Boëllmann *Suite gothique*. Karl Richter's approach to Bach and Handel is conscientious rather than displaying any special flair. Of the Handel concertos Op. 7/4 is more successful than Op. 4/2. The recording remains good on disc but the tape transfers are less successful, and there is a lack of refinement in the Bach items.

Parker-Smith, Jane (organ)

BACH: *Toccata and fugue in D minor, BWV 565. Cantata No. 147: Jesu, joy of man's desiring.* BACH–GOUNOD: *Ave Maria.* MENDELSSOHN: *A Midsummer Night's Dream, Op. 61: Wedding march.* WIDOR: *Organ symphony No. 5 in F minor, Op. 42/1: Toccata. Organ symphony No. 8 in B major, Op. 42/4:* finale. BOËLLMANN: *Prière à Notre-Dame.* REGER: *Benedictus.*
*** C.f.P. CFP 40324.

Jane Parker-Smith is a brilliant young organist who had already made a reputation while she was still a student at the Royal College of Music. In this début recital, which she recorded in 1973, she demonstrates an easy bravura and a strong grasp of musical essentials. The famous Bach *Toccata and fugue* is exciting and spontaneous, but not more so than the Widor *Toccata*. This is one of the most exuberant versions on disc, notable for its lively use of the pedals, which are given a generous (and easily

reproduced) bass response here. The *Wedding march* too has plenty of life, and Miss Parker-Smith shows a contrasting restraint in her approach to *Jesu, joy of man's desiring* and the Bach Gounod *Ave Maria*, which are tastefully registered. An excellent recital on all counts, showing real star quality.

Piano music

'Favourite piano music' (with (i) Katchen; (ii) Gulda; (iii) Kempff; (iv) Katin): (i) BACH: *Cantata No. 147: Jesu, joy of man's desiring* (arr. Hess). MOZART: *Piano sonata No. 15 in C major, K.545:* 1st movt. BEETHOVEN: *Piano sonata No. 8 in C minor (Pathétique), Op. 13:* 2nd movt. (ii) *Piano sonata No. 14 in C sharp minor (Moonlight), Op. 27/2.* (iii) *Für Elise.* (i) MENDELSSOHN: *On wings of song* (arr. Liszt). BRAHMS: *Hungarian dance No. 5 in F sharp minor. Intermezzo in E flat major, Op. 117/1.* (iv) *Rhapsody in G minor, Op. 79/2.* (i) CHOPIN: *Polonaise in A flat major, Op. 61.* (iii) *Impromptu No. 1 in A flat major, Op. 29. Ballade No. 3 in A flat major, Op. 47. Piano sonata No. 2 in B flat minor (Funeral march), Op. 35;* 3rd movt. *Fantaisie-impromptu in C sharp minor, Op. 66.* (iv) *Waltzes: in D flat major, Op. 64/1, in C sharp minor, Op. 64/2.* (ii) DEBUSSY: *Suite bergamasque: Clair de lune.* (iv) LISZT: *Liebestraum No. 3, G.541. Consolation No. 3, G.172.* SCHUMANN: *Romance, Op. 28/2.*
** Decca DPA 509/10 [KDPC].

The differing styles of the participants and the changing recording acoustic prevent this compilation from gelling into a recital; but taken in groups the performances are undoubtedly rewarding. They show consistent musical sensitivity, and there are moments of distinction, especially from Katchen (one thinks particularly of his Mendelssohn and Brahms). Kempff's Chopin is wayward though always illuminating; his recording, however, is a little lacking in fullness and bloom. Katin is characteristically fresh and direct, with clear sound to match. The cassettes are well managed and rival the discs closely in quality.

Richter, Sviatoslav (piano)

BACH: *The Well-tempered Clavier. Book 1, Nos. 1, 4, 5, 6 and 8.* SCHUBERT: *Allegretto in C minor, D.915. Ländler in A major, D.336/1.* SCHUMANN: *Abegg variations, Op. 1.* RACHMANINOV: *Prelude in G sharp minor, Op. 32/12.* PROKOFIEV: *Visions fugitives, Op. 22, Nos. 3, 6, 9.*

*** DG Heliodor 2548 286 [3348 286].

This is a live recital, dating from 1962, and although the audience betrays its presence with the usual coughs and rustles, it is not too distracting. The quality of sound is good, a little dry but completely acceptable. The recording successfully encompasses the wide dynamic range of Richter's Bach playing. His style is coolly expressive, thoughtful, and makes no concessions to the harpsichord: this is Bach on the piano and no mistake about it. The effect is undoubtedly refreshing. The rest of the programme is repertoire in which Richter is thoroughly at home, and the playing is masterly: here the piano timbre seems marginally less rich. An excellent bargain, both on disc and on tape (which is successfully transferred at a high level).

Williams, John (guitar)

Guitar recital 1: ALBÉNIZ: *La torre bermeja.* PONCE: *3 Mexican popular songs.* VILLA-LOBOS: *Étude No. 1 in E minor.* CRESPO: *Nortena.* DUARTE: *Variations on a Catalan folk song, Op. 25.* SOR: *Variations on a theme of Mozart, Op. 9.* SEGOVIA: *Oración study in E major. Estudio. Humorada.* TANSMAN: *Barcarolle.* GRANADOS: *La maja de Goya.* LAURO: *Valse criollo.*
Guitar recital 2: BACH: (Unaccompanied) *Violoncello suites Nos. 1 in G major, BWV 1007; 3 in C major, BWV 1009.* SCARLATTI, D.: *Sonata in E minor, L.352.* SCARLATTI, A.: *Gavotte.*

**(*) Decca DPA 579/80 [KDPC].

This collection dates from 1959 and was originally issued on the Delysé label. When Decca took over the catalogue the material was remastered and rearranged into this double-recital format, with the classical items (Bach and Scarlatti) in one group and the other devoted to the mainly Latin material. John Williams's playing shows complete technical assurance, and his keenly intelligent mind provides concentration even in the trifles (he is nowhere more beguiling than in the little Tansman *Barcarolle*). There is undoubtedly a lack of temperament in the Spanish repertoire, but the playing is never dull; the control of colour and dynamic keeps the music alive. The Bach suites, arranged by John Duarte, are transcribed into keys suitable to the guitar: No. 1 is transposed up a fifth to D and No. 3 down a third to A minor. They are played soberly and conscientiously, and some listeners may seek more flair; yet the thoughtfulness of the music-making, with its conscious use of light and shade, is certainly impressive. The recording is of high quality; it does not sound in the least dated, and if the volume is carefully set both disc and tape give a remarkable illusion of the presence of the soloist, with the guitar recorded in the right scale.

Zaradin, John (guitar)

WEISS: *Ballette*. FRESCOBALDI (arr. Segovia): *Air and variations*. LAURO: *Valse criollo*. ALBÉNIZ (arr. Tarrega): *Granada*. MALATS:

Spanish serenade. RODRIGO: *Concierto de Aranjuez*.

** C.f.P. CFP 40012 [TC-CFP].

Classics for Pleasure had the excellent idea of coupling their recording of the Rodrigo *Concierto de Aranjuez* (reviewed above) with a recital by the soloist. His playing has plenty of character, and there are some attractive miniatures here. The recording is good on disc, and the cassette transfer is well managed, faithful and with bloom as well as clarity.

Vocal Recitals and Choral Collections

Burrows, Stuart (tenor)

'*Songs for you*' (with (i) Constable or John, piano; (ii) Ambrosian Singers, Morris; Martin Neary, organ): (i) TOSELLI: *Serenata.* GLOVER: *Rose of Tralee.* WILLIAMS: *My little Welsh home.* SANDERSON: *Until.* BOUGHTON: *The Immortal Hour: Faery song.* CLAY: *I'll sing thee songs of Araby.* JACOBS-BOND: *A perfect day.* WOODFORDE-FINDEN: *Kashmiri song.* LESLIE: *Annabelle Lee.* D'HARDELOT: *Because.* RASBACH: *Trees.* MARSHALL: *I hear you calling me.* PURCELL, E.: *Passing by.* HAYDN WOOD: *Roses of Picardy.* MURRAY: *I'll walk beside you.* BRAHE: *Bless this house.* (ii) SULLIVAN: *The lost chord.* GOUNOD: *O divine Redeemer.* PARRY: *Jesu, lover of my soul.* NEGRO SPIRITUALS: *Steal away; Jericho.* DVOŘÁK (arr. Ditson): *Goin' home.* MALOTTE: *The Lord's Prayer.* ADAMS: *The holy city.* TCHAIKOVSKY: *The crown of roses.* LIDDLE: *How lovely are Thy dwellings.* SCHUBERT: *Ave Maria.* MONK: *Abide with me.*
(*) Decca DPA 607/8 [KDPC].

Stuart Burrows's headily beautiful tenor and fresh open manner could hardly be more apt for this collection of popular songs and ballads. His is a voice which takes naturally to being recorded, and the results can be warmly recommended to anyone tempted by the selection. Some may wish that the singing was more strongly characterized, but much of this repertoire responds to a lyrical presentation. This collection consists of three recitals from different sources. The second record concentrates on sacred music, with a backing by the Ambrosian Singers; it is very well recorded. The two recitals on the first disc have different accompanists. Side one (John Constable accompanying) comes from the Oiseau-Lyre catalogue and is beautifully recorded. Side two (with Eurfryn John), like the sacred music, originated on the Delysé label and is a stereo transcription of mono, with a degree of edginess on the voice at times. This is perhaps slightly more obvious on the cassette than the disc, but otherwise there is not a great deal of difference between them.

Ferrier, Kathleen (contralto)

'*Anthology*': MAHLER: *Das Lied von der Erde* (with Patzak, Vienna PO, Walter). BRAHMS: *Alto rhapsody, Op. 53* (with LPO and Chorus, Krauss). *4 Serious songs, Op. 121* (with Newmark, piano). *2 Songs with viola, Op. 91.* Lieder by BRAHMS, SCHUBERT, SCHUMANN (including *Frauenliebe und Leben, Op. 42*), WOLF. Arias from BACH: *St Matthew Passion; St. John Passion*; HANDEL: *Judas Maccabaeus;*

Messiah; Samson; Rodelinda; Ata-lanta; Admeto; GLUCK: *Orfeo (What is life?)*; MENDELSSOHN: *Elijah.* English folksongs and songs by QUILTER, PURCELL, STANFORD, PARRY, VAUGHAN WILLIAMS, WAR-LOCK. Arrangements by BRITTEN and HUGHES (with Newmark, Stone or Spurr, piano).
*** Decca (m) AFK 1–7 (NB. AFK 4 is stereo).

This set gathers together nearly all that Kathleen Ferrier recorded for Decca. (Among the omissions are the *Rückert Lieder*, which were originally used for a filler for the three-sided version – here condensed to two – of *Das Lied von der Erde*.) Each of these seven records is treasurable for the way the personality of a great singer comes over with the immediacy of live contact. The set includes the famous coupling of Bach and Handel arias for which Sir Adrian Boult and the LPO re-recorded the accompaniments in stereo with such skill that the new orchestral sound masked the old. The folksongs are especially valuable, for Kathleen sang them totally without artifice, with a natural warmth and great humanity. The effect is often breathtakingly beautiful, especially to ears coming to these performances for the first time. Elsewhere there are technical and stylistic points to criticize (the sound sometimes calls for a degree of tolerance), but the set as a whole reinforces Ferrier's claims as one of the most magnetic musical personalities of her time, whose impact was the more remarkable because her career was so relatively brief. A selection that is comparable, though not identical (it includes the *Rückert Lieder*, omitted on disc), is available on cassette: K 160 K 54.

Holm, Renate (soprano), **Werner Krenn** (tenor)

'*Wine, women and song*' (with Vienna Volksoper Orch., Paulik): arias from: STRAUSS, Johann, Jnr: *Der Zigeunerbaron; Eine Nacht in Venedig.* MILLÖCKER: *Der Bettelstudent.* SUPPÉ: *Boccaccio.* LEHÁR: *The Merry Widow; The Land of Smiles; Schön ist die Welt; Paganini; Der Zarewitsch; Der Graf von Luxemburg; The Circus Princess.* DOSTAL: *Clivia; Die ungarische Hochzeit.* KÜNNEKE: *Cousin from Nowhere.* KATTNIGG: *Bel Ami; Maidens from the Rhine.* ZERNIK: *Chi sa?* (song).
*** Decca DPA 595/6 [KDPC].

Renate Holm and Werner Krenn make an excellent partnership in this repertoire; their voices have plenty of individual character yet blend well together. Much of the singing is warmly beautiful, and it is sometimes vivacious; but the programme was chosen to include rather too much lyrical music of a similar style. This was originally issued on Decca's top-priced LP label, and it is a pity that the recording budget was not extended to include a chorus and feature more contrasting lively numbers. Even so, this is a valuable and comprehensive selection, splendidly recorded on disc and tape alike.

King's College Choir, Cambridge, Willcocks

'*Festival of King's*': ALLEGRI: *Miserere* (with Goodman). PALESTRINA: *Stabat Mater.* GIBBONS: *This is the record of John.* BYRD: *Mass in 4 parts.* CROFT: *Burial service.* TALLIS: *O nata lux. Videte miraculum.* VIVALDI: *Magnificat.* BACH: Motet:

169

Jesu, priceless treasure, BWV 227. St John Passion: Rest calm; Lord Jesu, thy dear angel send. BLOW: *God spake sometime in visions.* PURCELL: *Hear my prayer, O Lord.* HANDEL: *The King shall rejoice. Chandos anthem: The Lord is my light.* VAUGHAN WILLIAMS: *Fantasia on Christmas carols* (with Hervey Allen). HOLST: *Lullay my liking.* ORDE: *Adam lay y-bounden.* TRAD.: *Coventry Carol* (arr. Shaw). HOWELLS: *Collegium regale: Te Deum; Jubilate.*
*** Argo D 148 D 4 (4 discs) [K 148 K 43].

An admirable collection of vintage King's recordings under Sir David Willcocks. The choice and layout are imaginative, and the often inspirational quality of the singing is matched by its polish. The Allegri *Miserere*, with its miraculously cool treble solo from Roy Goodman, makes a splendid opening; other highlights include the Vivaldi *Magnificat* and the comparatively little-known Handel *Chandos anthem*. The delightfully spontaneous Vaughan Williams *Carol fantasia* is equally welcome, as is the surprise inclusion of the beautiful Croft setting of the *Funeral service*, and of course the other carols. The recording is consistently excellent, the tapes almost matching the discs in refinement. The only fault of balance is in *This is the record of John*, which is unrealistically forward. This causes minor transfer problems on cassette; but the tape layout (on six sides, as against eight on LP) has the advantage that the Handel anthem is complete on one side.

Opera

'*Favourite opera*': solos, duets and choruses from: MOZART: *Le Nozze di Figaro* (inc. *Overture*); *Don Giovanni.* GLUCK: *Orfeo.* ROSSINI: *Il Barbiere di Siviglia.* DONIZETTI: *L'Elisir d'amore; Lucia di Lammermoor* (including *Sextet*). VERDI: *Nabucco; Rigoletto* (including *Quartet*); *Aïda.* BIZET: *Carmen.* SAINT-SAËNS: *Samson et Dalila.* MASCAGNI: *Cavalleria Rusticana* (including *Intermezzo*). LEONCAVALLO: *I Pagliacci.* PUCCINI: *La Bohème; Gianni Schicchi; Madama Butterfly; Turandot.*
** Decca DPA 507/8 [KDPC].

This is a sound collection; the order has been sensibly arranged so that items follow on naturally. After an attractively Mozartian start, the Donizetti, Verdi and Puccini selections are excellently chosen. Artists include Lisa della Casa and Cesare Siepi (Mozart), Teresa Berganza (Gluck), di Stefano, Sutherland (Donizetti and Verdi), Resnik (Saint-Saëns), Tebaldi and Bergonzi (Puccini). The sound is consistently good on disc, and the tape transfers are well managed (the *Barber* and *Carmen* excerpts lack a degree of sparkle in the orchestra, but these are isolated instances).

'*Opera gala*': arias from: LEONCAVALLO: *I Pagliacci.* VERDI: *La Traviata; Rigoletto; Aïda; Il Trovatore.* ROSSINI: *Il Barbiere di Siviglia.* GOUNOD: *Faust.* PUCCINI: *Turandot.* BIZET: *Carmen.*
** DG Heliodor 2548 272 [3348 272].

An acceptable collection at bargain price but hardly a 'gala'! It opens well with a distinguished account of the *Prologue* from *Pagliacci* by Giuseppe Taddei, and there is a vibrant *Celeste Aïda* from Carlo Bergonzi, followed by a strong but slightly stiff *Stride la vampa* from Fiorenza Cossotto. Teresa Berganza's *Una voce poco fa* is reliable, but a little too positive: heard away from the complete set it lacks a feeling of capriciousness. Then comes the other highlight, Montserrat Caballé's sparkling version of the *King of Thule* and *Jewel song* from *Faust*. After this Antonietta Stella sounds rather shrill during *In questa reggia*, and Grace Bumbry's closing *Habañera* is rather deadpan. The recording is good on both disc and tape.

Opera choruses

'*Famous opera choruses*' from: WEBER: *Der Freischütz*. WAGNER: *Der fliegende Holländer; Tannhäuser; Lohengrin*. VERDI: *Il Trovatore; La Traviata*. BERLIOZ: *La Damnation de Faust*. BEETHOVEN: *Fidelio*.
** DG Heliodor 2548 212 [3348 212].

There are some excellent performances here, notably the vivacious Weber *Huntsmen's chorus*, sung by the Bavarian Radio Chorus under Jochum. The Wagner items are by the Bayreuth Festival Chorus under Wilhelm Pitz; the Verdi excerpts come from La Scala complete sets. One of the highlights is the *Prisoners' chorus* from *Fidelio*, strongly and movingly sung under Fricsay. The recording is excellent on disc, more variable on cassette: here the *Soldiers' chorus* from Markevitch's complete set of *La Damnation de Faust* is transferred at a higher level than the rest of the items on side two and brings coarseness into the tape sound picture.

'*Favourite opera choruses*' from: VERDI: *Il Trovatore; I Lombardi; Nabucco; Aïda; Otello; Macbeth*. LEONCAVALLO: *I Pagliacci*. PUCCINI: *Madama Butterfly*. WAGNER: *Der fliegende Holländer; Tannhäuser*. GOUNOD: *Faust*. BIZET: *Carmen*. TCHAIKOVSKY: *Eugene*

Onegin. BORODIN: *Prince Igor*. MUSSORGSKY: *Boris Godunov*.
**(*) Decca DPA 525/6 [KDPC].

One wonders about the attractions of a pair of discs filled with opera choruses. But some of the excerpts (for example, those from *Otello, The Flying Dutchman* and *Boris Godunov*) are quite long, and on disc the sound is excellent. Other items come from complete sets (including the early stereo *Il Trovatore*, where the *Anvil chorus* has a poorly focused lower range). There is no doubt about the excellence of the performances generally, and the *Coronation scene* from *Boris Godunov*, with Joseph Rouleau as Boris, comes off very well. The tape transfers have inevitably suffered from the almost insuperable problems which arise when the balance and amplitude of the sound vary from piece to piece, and there are patches of congestion, notably in the spectacular choral scene from Act 1 of *Otello* (Erede) and *The Flying Dutchman* recording under Dorati.

Operatic duets

'*Favourite operatic duets*' from ROSSINI: *Semiramide*. VERDI: *Il Trovatore; La Traviata; Don Carlos; La Forza del destino*. PUCCINI: *Tosca; Madama Butterfly; La Bohème*. BIZET: *Les Pêcheurs de perles; Carmen*. BERLIOZ: *Béatrice et Bénédict*.
**(*) Decca DPA 517/8 [KDPC].

The Sutherland/Horne Act 1 duet from *Semiramide* is a classic by any standards, and there are other interesting inclusions here too: the Bergonzi/Fischer-Dieskau duet from Act 2 of *Don Carlos* (superbly exciting) and by contrast the lovely *Nocturne* from *Béatrice et Bénédict* (April Cantelo and Helen Watts). Perhaps most interesting of all, however, is the successful transfer of an early Decca mono recording of *Au fond du temple saint*, stirringly sung by Libero de Luca and Jean Borthayre. The rest of the programme includes oft-used Decca items by familiar artists such as Tebaldi and Bergonzi. The closing scene of *Carmen* (Resnik and del Monaco) is undoubtedly vibrant, and with generally excellent recording throughout (sometimes a little dated in the string timbre) this is an entertaining if variable selection. The tape transfers are generally successful, although occasionally the sound has not quite the range and sparkle of the discs.

Royal Opera House, Covent Garden, Chorus and Orch., Gardelli

'*Famous opera choruses*': VERDI: *Aïda: March scene. Nabucco:* *Chorus of Hebrew slaves. Il Trovatore: Anvil chorus.* MASCAGNI: *Cavalleria Rusticana: Easter hymn.* **(*) HMV 45 r.p.m. HMV 7.

These performances are taken from a particularly successful LP collection. They are vivid and polished, perhaps a little studio-bound in atmosphere but with splendid inner detail, fully revealed by the quality of these transfers, which match a strikingly natural clarity at lower levels with brilliantly expansive climaxes. There is consistent evidence of Gardelli's care in rehearsal, not least the finely controlled crescendo in the *Chorus of Hebrew slaves* from *Nabucco*. Pauline Tinsley is the good if not opulent soloist in the *Easter hymn* from *Cavalleria Rusticana*.